COUNTRY HOUSES OF DORSET

BINGHAM'S MELCOMBE
The oriel bay of the hall from the courtyard.

COUNTRY HOUSES
OF DORSET

BY
ARTHUR OSWALD

COUNTRY LIFE LIMITED
LONDON

First published in 1935
by Country Life Limited
Tavistock Street, London, W.C.2
Printed and bound in England
by Hazell Watson & Viney Ltd
Aylesbury & Slough
© *Country Life 1935 & 1959*

Second, revised and enlarged, edition 1959

Contents

Preface

Country Houses of Dorset, which was published twenty-four years ago, has long been out of print, and second-hand copies are not easily obtainable. In response to enquiries about a re-issue this second edition has been produced, and the opportunity has been taken to revise and make some expansions of the original book as well as to correct mistakes and bring accounts of the houses up to date. The high printing and publishing costs ruling to-day have precluded any substantial increase in the number of houses described, but accounts of four more have been added, three of them in chapter IV, which covers the century and a half between 1650 and 1800. In the Preface to the first edition it was remarked that the book made no claim to be exhaustive and that it would not have been difficult to double the number of houses described in it, but I believe that on the whole my original selection was fairly representative.

It may be as well to repeat here what I said about the plan of this book. 'While each house is described separately, I have thought it best for purposes of comparison to adopt a more or less chronological arrangement, though for obvious reasons this method could not be rigidly adhered to. Many houses blend the work of different periods; the original building has often undergone alterations, sometimes of a drastic nature; comparatively few houses have retained unimpaired the form in which they were built. Considerable latitude has therefore been necessary. The broad division established here is that between the traditional manor house—a type which abounds in Dorset—and the Classic house, the introduction of which dates from the middle of the seventeenth century.'

The Introduction, which was intended to give a broad survey of a number of different subjects, architectural and historical, that a study of the country houses of Dorset presents, has been considerably extended in the light of new information and further research. I have added a good deal to what I wrote about the Jacobean mason-architect, William Arnold, who, though a Somerset man, worked also in Dorset, and the section on the eighteenth-century architects of Blandford has been enlarged. 'Travellers and Visitors in Dorset' is an addition which gives a rapid cinematographic impression of Dorset houses viewed through different eyes over a period of nearly three centuries. The minor introductions to the two long chapters I and IV have both been expanded, and that to chapter IV gives some new information about later Georgian architects responsible for work in Dorset.

To revise, after an interval of nearly a quarter of a century, a book written in the exuberance of youth is a matter of some delicacy and even tenderness for the author. Making an entirely fresh start, he would certainly write something different, but would the result be better or worse? I have contented myself with minor revisions of most of the descriptions and have only re-written extensively the accounts of those houses—Wolfeton, Milton Abbey and Sherborne Castle, for instance—about which I have collected further facts or revised my ideas. A defect of the original book that remains is the inadequate number of plans, but Dorset is now being systematically surveyed by the Royal Commission on Historical Monuments, in whose volumes plans of all the more important houses are or will be given. To have provided plans of all or most of the houses described here would have added very substantially to the costs of production.

Since 1935 there have been many changes in Dorset as everywhere else in England. So far as its country houses are concerned, however, it has suffered less from a second war and its after effects than might have been supposed. When one compares Dorset with some other counties—Yorkshire, Norfolk and Suffolk, for instance—where so many houses have been demolished, the casualties seem remarkably light. The most tragic loss is Tyneham, victim of the War Department. Up to the time of writing no other house among those described has gone, but the fates of Duntish Court (or Castle Hill) and of the old manor house at Kingston Maurward are in doubt. Langton House, near Blandford, to which a brief reference was made in the first edition, has been pulled down. As it was one of the few country houses designed by C. R. Cockerell, it is much to be regretted that no adequate record of it was made. Four more houses—Milton Abbey, Hanford, Crichel and Motcombe—have joined the ranks of Canford and Bryanston and become schools, though Crichel, it is understood, is soon to return to private occupation. Chantmarle is now a training centre for police officers, Kingston Maurward an agricultural college and Parnham a home for old people. Wolfeton, Chettle and Merly have been divided into flats. These are changes characteristic of the times and much to be welcomed where the alternative is demolition or dereliction. At the same time it is good to be able to point to such a high proportion of the county's country houses still in private occupation. Several of the parks, however, are in a sorry state.

It has not been possible to revisit all the houses described in this book, but every effort has been made to record new facts and changes of ownership, some of which have occurred since these pages went to be printed. For the most part the photographs are those of the first edition, but the number has been increased, and advantage has been taken of the accounts of Dorset houses that have appeared in *Country Life* since 1935 to substitute more recent photographs of some. In these days it is seldom possible for gardens to be as beautifully kept as they were before the last war, so that old photographs of exteriors are sometimes preferable. The photographs of Lulworth Castle are a record of that house before the fire of 1929.

I have to thank many for their help and co-operation both over the original book and this second edition, the owners first of all; and I have been especially indebted to the late Mr Ralph Bond, formerly of Tyneham, and to Lady Pinney, of Racedown, whose death occurred only this year. To Mr Howard Colvin I owe some new information about eighteenth-century architects and builders who worked in Dorset, and his *Dictionary of English Architects, 1660-1840* has been of much assistance. Mr A. R. Dufty answered questions about Sherborne Castle and Wolfeton, and he kindly read a draft of my revised account of William Arnold in the Introduction. Acknowledgements in footnotes are made to others who have given help on particular points or allowed me to use unpublished material. As was indicated in the Preface to the first edition, about a third of the houses described here have been the subjects of articles in *Country Life*. To their authors, the late H. Avray Tipping and Mr Christopher Hussey especially, I remain indebted. In preparing this second edition I have made much use of the first volume of the Royal Commission's *Inventory of Historical Monuments in Dorset* covering the western third of the county. My accounts of houses in that region have been checked and in some instances revised in the light of the descriptions given in that work, although I have not always followed the conclusions reached.

The majority of the photographs were taken either for articles on houses that have appeared in *Country Life* or especially for this book. The copyright of these is owned by *Country Life*. Simon Basil's plan of Sherborne Castle as it was before the Digby additions (pl. 150) is from a collection of early maps, plans and drawings at Hatfield and is reproduced by kind permission of the Marquess of Salisbury. The plan of Cranborne Manor House (pl. 149), probably drawn by William Arnold, is also at Hatfield. It is reproduced here from *English Homes*, Period III, vol. ii, p. 354. The architect's original elevation of Kingston Lacy (pl. 151) is in the possession of Mr Ralph Bankes, who kindly allowed it to be photographed for the first edition of this book. Plates 8, 81, 109, 122, 176, 202, 204, 206 are all from photographs taken for the Royal Commission on Historical Monuments (England) and are reproduced by permission; the Crown Copyright is reserved. The photographs of plates 117 and 150, reproduced by permission of the Ministry of Works, are also Crown Copyright. In addition, the following acknowledgements are made or repeated: to Mr Charles E. Brown (pl. 28), National Buildings Record (pl. 29), Miss M. E. Wood (pl. 30), the late Dr Dru Drury (pl. 36 and 37), Mr Leslie D. Frisby (pl. 114), Messrs Raphael Tuck (pl. 116), Mr W. Carpenter-Jacobs (pl. 134), Mr Michael

Pinney (pl. 205), Messrs S. Thomas and Sons of Weymouth (pl. 203). Plates 22, 33, 35, 110, 111 and 207 are from photographs by the author. The drawing of the hiding-place at Trent Manor by Sidney Heath (p. 105) was made originally for *Some Dorset Manor Houses* and appears in this book by his permission.

My last debt, which was also the first, is to my uncle and aunt, the late Dr and Mrs Horace Smith. It was through them that I first became interested in the manor houses of Dorset, and their home was my headquarters at intervals for some eighteen months while the material for this book was being collected.

June, 1959   ARTHUR OSWALD

Alphabetical List of Houses

DESCRIBED AND ILLUSTRATED

ADDITIONAL ILLUSTRATIONS

Introduction

MORE than most of our counties, Dorset is a unity, with limits fairly well defined geographically, except along parts of its northern boundary. There, it is true, distinctions are blurred. Cranborne Chase is shared with Wiltshire, the Blackmore Vale merges insensibly into Somerset, while, away to the west, in the Vale of Marshwood, one might almost be in Devon. Nevertheless, the feeling of unity persists, in spite of the variety of scenery—rolling upland, much of it in the form of open chalk downs; wooded combes; pastoral valleys with lush meadows by the streams; and tracts of moorland and heath, more particularly in the east. The coast, for the most part still unviolated, is equally varied, with its alternation of chalk and limestone, cliffs and level beach (whether the sands of Studland or the shingle of Chesil Bank). But these contrasts, which are characteristic of Dorset, never seem harsh or sudden. The transitions are gentle, like the southern air. It is as if there had been a conscious moulding and shaping and planing away of sharp outlines and rough edges.

The knowledge that Dorset is almost entirely an agricultural county contributes to the feeling of unity. Apart from three or four seaside resorts, it is a county of villages and market towns, a country of pre-industrial fabric. In recent years large areas have been appropriated to military training, and it will not be long before there is an atomic research station on Winfrith Heath; nevertheless, one is still vividly aware of the old pattern reproducing an economy which had its architectural expression in the market town and the cluster of cottages grouped about church and manor house. The decay of the manorial system and the building of 'gentlemen's seats' in the eighteenth century often meant the destruction of the old manor houses; but in Dorset, remote from the centres of fashion, innovation was gradual and the homes of former generations were preserved in larger numbers than in most parts of England, often as farmhouses, when they did not continue in the occupation of the family, as many did. Even after Weymouth and Lyme had become fashionable watering-places, Dorset as a whole was slow to change, as we know from Thomas Hardy's novels. Whatever may be the reason, it can claim an unusually large number of manor houses of Stuart, Tudor and even mediaeval days. Many have gone; some are mere fragments; others have been rescued from dereliction in the last fifty years. But when allowance has been made for all the casualties, it is remarkable how many remain. A factor that must have been responsible for the preservation of not a few is the fine building stone used in their construction, although in some instances it offered too tempting a quarry.

The manor houses of Dorset are among the elements that go to make up our mental image of the county, along with the camps and earthworks of its heights, its cliffs and coves, its unhurried rivers and fickle winterbornes, the names of its villages, the speech of its countrymen. The characteristic setting is in the shelter of trees and under the protection of a hill. It is in the valleys, as the author of *The Survey of Dorset* puts it, 'for the most parte the Gentlemens Houses are seated, for avoideing those sharpe Blasts which this Southerne Parte is subject to'. He was referring more especially to the southern region of Dorset, but the same might be said of most of the county. William Barnes, in a sentimentalised picture, suggests the deep seclusion of the Dorset manor house.

> An' woaks ageän wi' bossy stems,
> An' elems wi' their mossy stems,
> Do rise to screen the leafy wall
> An' stwonen ruf ov Ivy Hall.

Times and tastes have changed, and there is unlikely to be a mantling of ivy to-day, but almost always there are great trees, like old retainers, near at hand.

In this book the longest chapter is the one devoted to the manor houses, for they are typical of Dorset. Castles were comparatively few, and only two of them—Corfe and Sherborne Old Castle—were outstanding for their strength or grandeur. Only one mediaeval castle of Dorset is still inhabited—under a roof of thatch; but Woodsford really falls within the category of fortified manor house. As a result of the early use of building stone for domestic work, there are several thirteenth- and fourteenth-century survivals, and still more of the fifteenth century. The early Tudor houses share characteristics with their contemporaries in Somerset, as do some of those of Elizabethan and Jacobean times. Cranborne Manor House, Sherborne and Lulworth Castles—the last now, unhappily, a gaunt shell—form an exceptionally interesting trio as the hunting lodges of Elizabethan statesmen and courtiers. 'Great houses' are few in number; there is nothing to compare in size and magnificence with Knole, Hatfield or Blenheim; but Forde Abbey, Melbury, Milton Abbey, Crichel, St Giles's House and Kingston Lacy are all built on the aristocratic scale and all of them achieve architectural distinction in their different ways. The eighteenth century saw one gigantic Classic building rise in Dorset—Vanbrugh's ill-fated Eastbury. But it left its legacy in the interesting group of houses emanating from a local school of architect-builders at Blandford, who are discussed in a later section. Georgian country houses are commoner in the east than in the west of the county, which being more remote was less accessible to change. The work of this period is a study of its own and presents many engaging features. But when all has been surveyed, it is to the old manor houses that one returns most often in retrospect, to Bingham's Melcombe and Athelhampton, Chantmarle and Mapperton, Purse Caundle and Sandford Orcas, each with a lovely name to match its charm.

MEDIAEVAL DORSET

Although no pronounced geographical features now mark the transition to Wiltshire and Somerset, Dorset was once a comparatively isolated and self-contained shire. Thomas Hardy, by reviving the ancient name of Wessex, created the impression that Dorset was the heart of the West Saxon kingdom, whereas it was comparatively late—not until the beginning of the eighth century—that it came to be included, and then the capital and seat of the new bishopric was established at Sherborne on the northern boundary. Much of the northern border was shielded by waste and forest, represented in mediaeval days by Cranborne Chase, Gillingham Forest and the White Hart Forest in the Vale of Blackmore; to the east and southeast there were the great heaths and the swamps surrounding Poole Harbour; to the west was the river Axe, and southward the sea. So for a long period Dorset was a backward county like Sussex. Moreover, it suffered repeatedly from Danish inroads. Nevertheless, the Saxons, mingling with the older Celtic stock, found the river valleys fair and fertile. When one looks, first at the vast hill-top camps and numberless barrows that stud the downs, and then at the strings of villages, each with its church and manor house, that thread the courses of the streams, it is curious to think with what different eyes two different peoples viewed the same country. The process of colonising the valleys may have continued into late Saxon and even Norman times. It would be difficult otherwise to explain the number of villages with the same name—Tarrants, Tollers, Cernes, Piddles and Winterbornes—and only a suffix, often of the owning lord, to differentiate one from its neighbour. These hamlets and villages are strung so closely along the streams that often there is less than a mile between them, and not infrequently one finds that others, which once were there, have gone, leaving scarcely a trace behind.

In spite of a mild climate and fertile valleys, Dorset in the Middle Ages was less prosperous than many other counties. Wages were low, at any rate before the Black Death, and what became the county's staple product, the wool of its sheep, was not of great repute until the end of the mediaeval period. Although cloth-making was carried on in Sherborne when Leland visited Dorset, there was no great clothing industry to compare with those of other regions. The maritime trade enjoyed by

Bridport, Melcombe Regis and Poole must not be forgotten, but in relation to the county as a whole this was local in its effects. 'The golden fleece' was what eventually brought wealth to Dorset landowners. It was not, however, until after the middle of the fifteenth century that sheep-farming developed on a notable scale to earn the eulogies that we find paid to the Dorset flocks by Leland and Camden and, in later days, by Defoe. The fact that so many of the parish churches were enlarged or rebuilt in the fifteenth and early sixteenth centuries is further confirmation of a growing prosperity at that time.

The economic change was accompanied by changes in the social structure, and in particular by the rise of a mercantile class; and probably, as elsewhere in England, the monasteries, which in Dorset held a large proportion of the manors, had come to adopt the practice of letting them out on lease instead of farming them themselves, so that more opportunities presented themselves to the enterprising. Many of the old families seem to have participated in the sheep-farming boom. Sir Roger Newburgh of East Lulworth, who died in 1515 holding nine manors and other lands, bequeathed to his executors 800 ewes at Ashton, 400 ewes and 600 wethers at Waterston, 400 ewes in West Burton, 700 ewes in East Lulworth and 1,000 ewes in Southcombe.[1] Similarly, the wills[2] of Sir John Trenchard of Wolfeton, who died in 1495, and of his son, Sir Thomas, who died in 1550, show how much of their wealth was on the backs of their sheep. The Trenchards, though new to the county, had married into an old Dorset family, and at Wolfeton they built one of the great Tudor houses. Among the new men who appeared on the scene was John Williams, the Dorchester merchant, who in 1513 acquired Herringston, where his descendants still continue, and, a few years later, Tyneham for a younger son. The John Samways who obtained Toller Fratrum at the Dissolution was also a Dorchester merchant. The abbeys themselves must have profited by the increase in sheep-farming. Abbot Middleton's hall at Milton, the porch-tower at Cerne, and Abbot Chard's splendid additions to Forde, all quite new at the Dissolution, may have been built largely 'out of wool'. The suppression of the monasteries brought far-reaching changes. Men whose fathers or grandfathers had been in their employ took part in the scramble for lands. The Mellors of Winterborne Came are said to have been descendants of the miller of Abbotsbury Abbey. It was at this time that the great estates of the men who assisted in the downfall of the abbeys—Sir John Tregonwell of Milton, Sir Giles Strangways of Melbury and Sir John Horsey of Clifton Maybank—came into existence or were greatly extended.

The splendid early Tudor houses of these men and others like them have under-

[1] Hutchins, *History and Antiquities of Dorset* (3rd ed.), i, 369.
[2] P.C.C. 27 Vox and 20 Coode.

2. FORDE ABBEY

Thomas Chard's porch-tower on the south side of his
great hall, dated 1528.

1. CERNE ABBEY

The porch-tower of the destroyed great hall built by
Abbot Thomas Sam (1497–1509).

3 and 4. (*Left*) ATHELHAMPTON, the west wing, and (*right*) SANDFORD ORCAS, the porch. The similarity of the carved details points to nearness in date (*circa* 1530–50) and to common authorship. Note the lozenge-shaped panels.

gone such varying fortunes, not only in Dorset but all over the country, that it is difficult to make comparisons. But if we take three other great sheep-raising counties—Gloucestershire, Wiltshire and Somerset—some interesting facts may be noted. In the Cotswolds it is the Elizabethan and Jacobean houses that predominate; in Wiltshire and Somerset we find a remarkable number of fifteenth-century survivals. Dorset, on the other hand, is notable for its early Tudor buildings, and although there is much interesting work of Elizabethan and early Stuart days, it cannot compare in abundance with Cotswold building of the same time. It would be rash to draw conclusions from these facts, since old houses may owe their preservation to so many different factors, but it would appear that during the first half of the sixteenth century there was a great deal of exceptionally fine domestic building going on in Dorset, for which Wiltshire and the Cotswolds afford no parallel and which, though overlapping into Somerset, is found there chiefly on the south-east border.

BUILDING MATERIALS

We are on safer ground when we come to consider the materials used in Dorset houses. And here a brief geographical survey may be useful. The backbone of the county is the chalk upland, which comes in from Wiltshire, near Melbury Down on Cranborne Chase, and runs south-westwards across the county to the plateau above Beaminster. This ridge is usually known as the Dorset Heights, whose northern escarpment looks over the rich clays of the Vale of Blackmore. West of Beaminster the chalk throws out a spur that culminates in Pilsdon Pen overlooking the Marshwood Vale, another region of clay. But more important is the ridge that runs south-eastward past Weymouth and Lulworth, into the Isle of Purbeck, where it forms the narrow range of Purbeck Hills ending in Ballard Down and Old Harry Rocks. Between this long spur and the central block of the Dorset Heights lies the basin of the Frome, the eastern half of which is covered by the sands of the Great Heath around Wareham and Poole Harbour. Chalk, clay and sand account for three-quarters of the surface area of Dorset. But we have so far ignored the oolite, which is the source of the county's unrivalled building stone. This great system of limestone, which goes up through west Wiltshire and Gloucestershire and right across the Midlands into Lincolnshire and Yorkshire, may be said to begin in Dorset, where, however, it outcrops spasmodically and in widely separate areas. In the north the lower and middle series are found on the Somerset border. Just outside the county, west of Yeovil, the lower oolite yields the shelly limestone found at Ham Hill, of which so many Dorset houses are built; the Coral Rag of the middle oolite was quarried around Marnhull and Sturminster Newton. The two series reappear

C.H.D.—3

south of the chalk between Bridport and Weymouth, and some of the beds have been quarried here and there both for building stone and for slates. The upper oolite, which yields the finest stone of all, only occurs on the two 'islands'—Portland and Purbeck—and in a narrow stretch under the line of the downs between Portisham and Poxwell. The highest beds of all yield the Purbeck marble.

The manor houses of Dorset divide their allegiance between the golden Ham Hill stone of the north and the ashen-grey limestones of Purbeck and Portland. Ham Hill was used for most of the houses in the north-west and centre—e.g. Sherborne Castle, Melbury, Forde Abbey, Chantmarle, Clifton Maybank, Sandford Orcas, and the porch-tower at Cerne Abbas. To the other group belong Lulworth Castle, Creech Grange, Tyneham, Herringston, Kingston Maurward, Poxwell and Warmwell. Sometimes the two are found together, as at Wynford Eagle, or Ham Hill is reserved for dressings and carved work, as at Athelhampton and Bingham's Melcombe. Portland stone itself was not much used until the eighteenth century, after Inigo Jones and Wren had discovered its fine qualities for London buildings. Although it had been employed locally from very early times—the Rufus Castle is built of the island stone—and was exported as far as Exeter soon after 1300, it is chiefly from Purbeck and quarries around Portisham that the grey stone manor houses of south Dorset are built. Among eighteenth-century houses faced with Portland stone, Came House, Kingston Maurward and Kingston Russell may be mentioned. The Portland quarries, however, since the time of Charles I have been almost wholly devoted to export, just as at an earlier period were the marble quarries of Purbeck. But the marble industry was in decline by the time the houses we have to deal with were built. Its great period of activity was the thirteenth century. One might expect to find it, however, used for decorative work, since it continued to be employed for tombs and grave-stones in churches until Elizabethan days; but there are no carved chimney-pieces of Purbeck marble to compare with the admirable examples worked in Bethersden marble that are found in Kent.

In early days there was, no doubt, timber building in Dorset, particularly in the wooded north. But, except for some houses in Sherborne, there is very little timber-frame construction to be seen in the county, the humbler dwellings being built of cob. There are, on the other hand, as we should expect in a county so largely consisting of chalk, a number of examples of houses in which flintwork was used. Masonry composed of alternating courses of flint and stone is found at Melcombe Horsey, Winterborne Clenston and in the old wing at Chantmarle. The tradition survived into the eighteenth century, and can be admired in the fine walling of the Georgian churches at Charlton Marshall and Wimborne St Giles.

Brick does not appear in Dorset much before the seventeenth century, and then

5 and 6. (*Left*) BINGHAM'S MELCOMBE, detail of the upper part of the hall bay, and (*right*) detail of carving on the porch from CLIFTON MAYBANK removed to Montacute in 1786. The handling of the Renaissance motives and the technique of the carving suggest that the same individual worked on both houses. Date, about the middle of the 16th century.

8. WOLFETON HOUSE

Renaissance doorway of stone at the head of the main staircase. Possibly by the French carver, Allen Maynard, who worked at Longleat.

7. MONTACUTE, SOMERSET

The centre of the east front. The porch, dated 1601, has stylistic affinities with William Arnold's work at Cranborne Manor House.

spreads from the sandy regions of the east. Wichampton, near Crichel, has brickwork of the time of Henry VIII, but this is an early and almost isolated example. Edmondsham, in the same district, is dated 1589. But it is only after 1600 that the fashion begins to grow. Bloxworth (1608), the south front of Waterston and the little gatehouse at Poxwell (1634) are all built of brick. The most beautiful example of this time is the manor house at Anderson, finished in 1622, where every third course is one of dark purple bricks, much enriching the texture of the walls. After the Restoration the use of brick was greatly extended. Kingston Lacy, as originally built, had walls of unfaced brick; Dewlish, Spettisbury, Chettle, Merly and Frome St Quintin are eighteenth-century examples, to which Kingston Maurward (1720) and Whatcombe (1750) might originally have been added. The best examples of Georgian brickwork, however, are to be found in Blandford. The whole town had to be rebuilt after the fire of 1731. This necessity provided the stimulus for a brickwork tradition of great virtuosity. Whole house fronts are found faced with burnt headers, giving a kind of metallic sheen, and much use is made of colour contrasts and panelled effects. After George III's accession the tradition received a check as the fashionable dislike for red brick penetrated to the provinces. When Sir William Chambers designed Castle Hill (now Duntish Court), he faced his brick walls with stucco, and Humphry Sturt in enlarging Crichel adopted the same expedient. 'Brick, Mr Pitt, brick,' is said to have been George III's laconic comment when he visited Kingston Maurward—a remark which its owner took so much to heart that, when next the King paid him a visit, the whole house had been refaced in Portland stone.

The traditional roof material of Dorset houses is the local stone slate, a heavier form of slate than that quarried in the Cotswolds, though less massive than the Horsham slab of Sussex. Many of the old manor houses still preserve their stone-slated roofs, the true and perfect covering for these old stone buildings. Where tiles have been substituted, not infrequently three or four courses of stone slates have been left above the eaves with very pleasant effect. The lovely mossed and lichened roof of Woolbridge Manor House is an example; Bloxworth and Poxwell are others. Thatch, the benediction of Dorset cottages, has occasionally spread to manor houses that have come to humbler status. Two beautiful instances of this are Hammoon and Woodsford Castle; the thatched roof of the second has been estimated to cover 3,300 square feet.

REGIONAL CHARACTERISTICS

Early Tudor Work. Dorset houses, both in the sixteenth century and again in the eighteenth century, show a number of regional characteristics, some of which will be considered here along with the names of local masons and architects that have been preserved. The early Tudor domestic work of Dorset and the neighbouring parts of Somerset has a markedly individual character. The famous quarries at Ham or Hamdon Hill formed the centre of the region, with Sherborne, Yeovil and Crewkerne as the principal towns. The church towers of Somerset, many of them built of Ham Hill stone, had provided the local masons with their chief field of activity in the fifteenth century. But during the reign of Henry VIII church building declined in intensity, and it stopped altogether at the Reformation. The enrichment of a new class of men, as a result of the economic changes already noted, brought about a great increase in the number and size of fine houses, and a fresh stimulus to building came from the Dissolution of the monasteries. It is evident that the local schools of masons were saved from unemployment and possible extinction by the new demand. Abbot Chard's additions to Forde Abbey (pl. 2) and the porch-tower at Cerne Abbey (pl. 1) show the form that the late Gothic style took when applied to domestic buildings. In the finest work such as this there is great beauty and delicacy in the treatment of mouldings, the Ham Hill stone lending itself to refinement of detail. The most distinctive feature of the early Tudor houses is the use of octagonal shafts at the angles. These are usually of fluted section and are carried up to support an heraldic finial or sometimes a pinnacle with an ogee cap. Athelhampton (pl. 3), Mapperton (pl. 76), Little Toller (pl. 71), Bingham's Mel-combe (Frontispiece) and Clifton Maybank (pl. 65) all show this characteristic treatment; at Sandford Orcas (pl. 4) and Melbury (pl. 132) it occurs without the heraldic finial; it was retained at Creech Grange when the front of that house was rebuilt in the nineteenth century (pl. 82), and there are evidences of it at Ham-moon (pl. 70). The origin of this feature appears to have been the octagonal buttress, which occurs in some of the later church towers, e.g. at Cerne Abbas. In the examples dating from the middle of the sixteenth century, e.g. the oriel bay at Bingham's Melcombe (Fronistpiece), the circumference of the shaft is greatly diminished and the buttress origin forgotten. By 1560 the use seems to have been discarded. It was not confined to the West of England, as it may be seen at Hampton Court, Hengrave Hall (Suffolk) and in brick at East Barsham (Norfolk), but in Dorset and Somerset it acquired an almost stereotyped character. The upper portion, which supports the heraldic beast, is usually twisted, like contemporary chimneystacks, examples of which survive at Mapperton (pl. 76) and in restored form at Little Toller Farm, Toller Fratrum (pl. 71). Barrington Court, the great Somerset house of this time, is the exemplar of all the early Tudor houses that have been mentioned, and shows us what Mapperton would have looked like if the full E plan had been adopted and how splendid Clifton Maybank must once have been.

The Clifton Maybank façade, which was added as a screen to the west front of Montacute in 1786, represents the summit of the achievement of the early sixteenth century. Not only is the treatment exceedingly rich and the carving of unusual delicacy, but the Renaissance influence, which is first seen (*circa* 1525) in Chard's work at Forde Abbey (pl. 122), also makes its appearance. A comparison of the heraldic panel over the doorway at Montacute (pl. 6) with the one on the oriel bay at Bingham's Melcombe (pl. 5), or the achievement of arms which once adorned the gatehouse at Athelhampton (pl. 56), leaves no doubt that all three were the work of the same group of carvers if not of the same man. The evidence of initials and heraldry points to the years 1540–60 for their execution. Very similar motives are to be seen on the canopied monument in Sherborne Abbey to the two Sir John Horseys, father and son, who died respectively in 1546 and 1564; here, however, the workmanship is much coarser. The Renaissance influence appears in other details. For instance, the angle shafts of the bay at Bingham's Melcombe (Frontispiece), on the porch at Sandford Orcas (pl. 4), and on the west wing at Athelhampton (pl 3), show a curious attempt to reproduce the volutes of an Ionic capital. Sandford Orcas and the Athelhampton wing possess so many points of likeness that a common source is again to be inferred. The hall at Athelhampton (pl. 54), on the other hand, is probably fifty years earlier than the wing and shows a close resemblance in the treatment of its windows to the hall of Milton Abbey (pl. 121), the date of which, 1498, is carved in the interior. An interesting example of this early Tudor work, though it actually dates from the time of Queen Elizabeth, is the south end of the old house of the headmaster of Sherborne School. This was formed out of the eastern chapels of the Abbey in 1560. In a frame flanked by twisted columns is a finely carved achievement of the arms of Edward VI. Below are six coats of arms, including those of the Bishop of Salisbury and the Horseys of Clifton Maybank, and, underneath them, eighteen sets of initials of Governors of the school at the time.

It is now coming to be realised that in the first phase of Renaissance influence in England, which extended from Henry VIII's reign until the early years of Elizabeth's, the inspiration seldom came direct from Italy. The Classic motives, which then appeared in carving and painting and which to-day can best be studied in church monuments, were propagated by artists and craftsmen imported chiefly from northern France, which affords the closest contemporary analogies. The same is true of the more advanced architecture between 1545 and 1570: the buildings exerting most influence were French. The carver or group of carvers responsible for the heraldic panels of Clifton Maybank, Bingham's Melcombe and Athelhampton is more likely to have been French than Italian, although the hand of an

Englishman who had been in close contact with these men is perhaps to be detected in the coarser work of the Horsey monument. Allen Maynard, a native of France, who was granted letters of denization in 1566, is one of the few foreign carvers of the time whose names are known. Mr Mark Girouard, who has traced his career from 1563 to 1585, has revealed him as a sculptor and designer working for Sir John Thynne at Longleat and identifiable by idiosyncrasies of style elsewhere in Wiltshire and in the adjoining counties.[1] He has attributed to Maynard the doorway at the head of the staircase at Wolfeton (pl. 8), a pedimented composition of an unusually pure Italian type. Mr Girouard has suggested that there may have been a group of French carvers, active in and around Winchester in the 1550s, to which Maynard belonged. He is a late instance of the French wave of fashion. By the 1580s the winds were blowing strongly from the Low Countries, and Renaissance ornament assumed the wild and distorted forms that had been developed in Flanders, Holland and Germany. Dorset, however, was fortunate in escaping the full force of this onslaught.

Elizabethan and Jacobean Work. Externally the impression produced by the Dorset houses built during this period is one of general simplification in the design. There is less carved detail; the angle shafts disappear; flat tops take the place of the arched heads seen in the lights of early Tudor windows. There is an early instance of this last change at Sandford Orcas (pl. 68). On the other hand, the arch-headed light persists in the windows at Lulworth Castle (pl. 141) and as late as 1612 at Chantmarle (pl. 101). Classic features were slow to make their appearance. Where they do occur, chiefly in doorways or chimney-pieces, they are coarse and crude essays derived from the Flemish and Dutch pattern-books which were widely circulated at the time. Quite as often, however, the old form of flattened Tudor arch with the ogee moulding persists both for doorway and fireplace. Where these Elizabethan and Jacobean houses show a great advance is in their planning and in the symmetry of their elevations. An idiosyncrasy of some West of England houses of the time is the placing of chimney-stacks over gables, regardless of the difficulty involved in carrying up the flues. Wraxall (pl. 106), Hanford (pl 98), Bloxworth (pl. 108), Upcerne (pl. 109) and Purse Caundle (pl. 44) show this curious idea. At Wolfeton and at the old house at Kingston Maurward the masons used a special refinement in treating the windows: the mouldings both of mullions and jambs are given little bases as though they were Gothic arch mouldings.

These and other details go far to show that Gothic traditions died hard in the West of England. In the building of Chantmarle, where several of these archaisms

[1] 'New Light on Longleat' in *Country Life*, Vol. cxx, p. 594 (September 20, 1956).

10. WAYFORD MANOR, SOMERSET

The porch shows such close analogies with the one at Cranborne that it may reasonably be attributed to Arnold.

9. CRANBORNE MANOR HOUSE

The south porch, added by Robert Cecil, Earl of Salisbury, about 1610. William Arnold was the master mason.

11 and 12. Carved stone chimney-pieces from the same workshop: (*left*) in the great chamber at MONTACUTE, SOMERSET (*circa* 1600) and (*right*) at WAYFORD MANOR, SOMERSET (dated 1602). Compare also plates 13 and 14.

occur, we are fortunate in knowing the names of the architect and craftsmen who were employed.[1] The house, dated 1612, is built of stone from Ham Hill, and the two chief masons, Joseph and Daniel Rowe, came from that neighbourhood; they 'took the building of the walls to taskwork at 20d. a perch for the first story and 2s. a perch for the upper stories.' The architect, or 'surveyor,' as he is described, was one Gabriel Moore, 'born about Chinnock in Somersetshire.' The three Chinnock villages lie two or three miles to the south of Ham Hill. Moore received a pound a month with keep 'for his paines only' in directing and surveying the building, the design of which Sir John Strode, the owner, claimed to have made himself. It is very regrettable that the chapel with its 'fretted' ceiling has been destroyed. The plasterer who fashioned it was another Somerset man, one Eaton of Stogursey. The joiner, on the other hand, came from Salisbury.

It has already been remarked that during this period Classic features occur most often in doorways and chimney-pieces. In west Dorset and the adjoining part of Somerset there is a group of chimney-pieces and church monuments, dateable between 1590 and 1610, which can be clearly recognised as emanating from the same source. Some of the chimney-pieces are carved in stone, but in many instances plaster has been used for overmantels, the designs of which closely resemble those of the carved examples. Montacute, which was built by Sir Edward Phelips in the last years of the sixteenth century, has several of these chimney-pieces, one of which bears the date 1599. There are two at Wolfeton, one in stone (pl. 14), the other in plaster (pl. 15), and there is another at Herringston; both these houses are near Dorchester. Two plaster overmantels, formerly at Melplash Court between Beaminster and Bridport, are now at Mapperton; one of these is dated 1604 (pl. 18). There is another example in stone, dated 1602, at Wayford Manor, near Crewkerne, just outside the Dorset boundary (pl. 12). Others occur at Stockton House, in the Wylye Valley, near Salisbury (pl. 13). In Devon there are dated examples at Holcombe Rogus (1591) and at Walronds, Cullompton (1605), both near the Somerset border; also one, dating from 1599, as far away as Weare Giffard, near Bideford.[2]

There are several characteristics by which these chimney-pieces can be identified as deriving from a common source. The most obvious is the use of a large cartouche for the overmantel surrounded by elaborate strapwork, with scrolls curling forward, as though cut in card; the central panel is filled with heraldry or a relief of some al-

[1] Hutchins (3rd ed.), iv, 6.

[2] Stockton House is illustrated in *Country Life*, vol. xviii, p. 558 (October 21, 1905). For Holcombe Rogus and Walronds, Cullompton, see letter from Cecil French, *Country Life*, vol. cxviii, p. 1386 (December 8, 1955); for Weare Giffard, *English Homes*, Period II, vol. i (Figs. 365 and 368) and *Country Life*, vol. xxxvii, p. 16 (January 2, 1915).

legorical or mythological subject. Swags of fruit and flowers often accompany the cartouche, and it is sometimes flanked by rather clumsy scrolls with figures in relief perched on them. The designs have been taken from engravings in Flemish and Dutch pattern-books current at the time, but the execution is coarse and crude, and often comic in the rendering of figure subjects. From the proximity of Montacute to the Ham Hill quarries it would be tempting to locate a single workshop in that region. This, however, would not account for the examples in plaster. The likelier explanation is that the designs were provided by one master mason, who made use of some Flemish or Dutch pattern-book[1] in his possession, and that they were interpreted by mason-carvers and plasterers in his employ as best they could. This hypothesis would not rule out the possibility that the master mason had a workshop somewhere in south-east Somerset where chimney-pieces in stone and church monuments were turned out. In addition to the examples noted there are two rather later plaster overmantels at Dunster, in north Somerset, which are closely related to the group under consideration. One, dated 1620, is in the Castle; the other is in the Luttrell Arms Hotel. There is also a whole series in the Court House at East Quantockshead, another Luttrell home, not far from Dunster.[2] These seem to have been done at intervals between 1614 and 1629, the dates which appear on two of them. Marshwood, also a Luttrell house, rebuilt by George Luttrell, contains yet another.

One of the Montacute chimney-pieces (pl. 11), that in Edward Phelips' great chamber, is a two-tiered composition which compares closely with examples at Wayford Manor (pl. 12), at Wolfeton (pl. 14), and in the drawing-room at Stockton House (pl. 13). These are all in stone. The lower section of the Montacute chimney-piece is flanked by pairs of Corinthian columns, the overmantel by shell-headed niches. The overmantel panel has a cartouche with coarse strapwork in high relief, and in the middle there is a reclining lady; it is set in a frame carved with egg-and-tongue ornament, very large in scale. A curious feature, recurring in the examples at Wolfeton, Herringston and Stockton, is the insertion, in the lower section above the fireplace opening, of the bottom half of a second cartouche ornamented with strapwork. At Wolfeton the place of the niches is taken by two more pairs of columns, and the reclining lady in the middle of the cartouche, evidently Charity, has two companions, with the emblems of Faith and Hope, in the frieze of the entablature. These three Virtues, two seated and one reclining, also occur on the chimney-piece in the great chamber at Herringston. Two similar little figures leaning on their

---

[1] The designs of the cartouches and strapwork may have been derived from Abraham Bruyn or Vredeman de Vries.

[2] The Dunster chimney-pieces are illustrated in Sir H. C. Maxwell Lyte's *History of Dunster* (1909), opposite p. 333. For those at East Quantockshead, see *Country Life*, vol. xxxi, pp. 171–3 (February 3, 1912).

13 and 14. Chimney-pieces at STOCKTON HOUSE, WILTSHIRE and (right) at WOLFETON HOUSE, near Dorchester. The superimposed pairs of columns, the rectangular panel framing a large cartouche and the lower portion of a second cartouche filling the space above the fire-place opening are features of both.

24]

15 and 16. Plaster overmantels at WOLFETON HOUSE (*left*) and MONTACUTE, Somerset (*right*), showing close analogies (*circa* 1600).

elbows are to be seen on the Kymer monument in West Chelborough church, north-east of Beaminster;[1] as they occur in association with the large-scale egg-and-tongue motive and with strapwork ornament, it is clear that the monument comes from the same source as the chimney-pieces. In the Green Drawing-room at Sherborne Castle (pl. 146) there is another large chimney-piece with two tiers of paired columns and a heraldic cartouche in the middle of the overmantel, but in this later example, dating from after the Digby purchase of the castle, the analogies are less close and the work is more accomplished.

A second type of chimney-piece, which had a wide distribution, is represented by the large plaster overmantel of 1604 now in the hall at Mapperton but originally at Melplash (pl. 18). This has an elaborate achievement of arms framed in a panel, which is flanked by large-scale scrolls and strapwork, bunches of fruit and a pair of figures seated on the scrolls. There is a very close parallel to it in the overmantel in the great hall at Weare Giffard, north Devon, where coeval plasterwork on the end wall is dated 1599. The one at Walronds, Cullompton, dated 1605, is of similar character. In a somewhat simplified fashion the design also occurs at Montacute, in the chimney-piece in the Garden Chamber (pl. 17), where a kneeling figure of King David takes the place of heraldry in the panel. In all these examples, except the one at Weare Giffard, there is a frieze below the overmantel ornamented with the Tudor rose—a feature that occurs in other chimney-pieces. A smaller type of plaster overmantel has the panel flanked by caryatid figures. One of this kind in the inner drawing-room at Wolfeton (pl. 15) is matched very closely by an example at Montacute (pl. 16). They are of almost identical design, but at Wolfeton there is a naively rendered relief of the Judgment of Paris in the cartouche, taking the place of the heraldic shield of the Montacute panel. The overmantels at Dunster and East Quantockshead combine elements of all three types.

Crude as the carving or modelling is, these chimney-pieces are interesting in showing how provincial masons and plasterers tried to grapple with the new and alien forms imposed on them and what strange distortions and odd conjunctions of Classic ornament resulted from their attempts. Further investigation would doubtless add other examples to those noted. From their distribution it would seem that the centre of gravity lay somewhere in south-east Somerset near the Dorset border, and it is highly probable that they should be connected with a master mason known to have been working in that region.

The Arnolds of Somerset. When the building of Wadham College, Oxford, was begun in 1610, there were difficulties about obtaining local masons owing to a dispute

---

[1] Royal Commission on Historical Monuments, *Dorset*, vol. i, pl. 87.

between the University and the city building guild. The home of Nicholas Wadham, the founder of the college, was in Somerset, at Merifield, near Ilminster. After
his death, in October, 1609, the responsibility for carrying out his wishes fell on his
widow, Dorothy, as executrix, and on the overseers of the will, who acted with
great promptitude. To avoid delay, Dorothy Wadham decided to employ masons
from her own part of the country. The building accounts[1] show that 29 men were
sent from Somerset to Oxford in April, 1610. At their head was WILLIAM ARNOLD,
who, as chief mason, was paid at the rate of £1 a week, later on reduced to 10s.
when he ceased to give regular attendance. Some recently discovered letters prove
that it was on Dorothy Wadham's insistence that Arnold was engaged.[2] Writing
(February 10, 1610) to her half-brother, Lord Petre, who was one of the overseers
of her husband's will, she pressed him to 'ymploye one Arnold in the work, who is
an honest man, a perfectt workman, and my neere neighboure, and soe can yeld
me contynewall contentmentt in the same.' She went on to say that Arnold had
been 'commended' to her by her 'good frend and lovinge neighboure Sr Edward
Phelipps,' and so she had 'faithfullie promysed hem the work.' This recommenda-
tion from Sir Edward Phelips raises a strong presumption that he had employed
Arnold on the building of Montacute House. When other facts are taken into consideration, the presumption becomes a virtual certainty.

William Arnold was duly engaged to 'be imployed in the provysyon of tymber
& stones for Wadham Colledge as also for drawyng of a plott & for the byldyng of
yt.' A letter to Lord Petre from Sir Edward Hext[3], another of the overseers (March
19, 1610), describes how Arnold's 'plott' had been seen and approved by the King,
the Archbishop, the Lord Chancellor and the Lord Treasurer. The Lord Treasurer
(Robert Cecil) was at the same time making use of Arnold's services himself, and the
two were closeted together 'every day a whole houre in private.' A later passage
in the letter reveals that their conferences were about the alterations to Cranborne
Manor House which Arnold was undertaking. 'Within these too dayes my Lord

---

[1] Extracts from the accounts are given in T. G. Jackson, *Wadham College, Oxford* (1893).

[2] Correspondence among the Petre archives at Ingatestone Hall, now deposited by Lord Petre in the
Essex Record Office (D/DP. Q 13/3/7, 8, 11). For permission to quote from these letters I am indebted to
Miss Nancy Briggs, who kindly sent me copies of her transcripts, and to the Essex County Archivist, Mr
F. G. Emmison. (See 'The Foundation of Wadham College, Oxford', by Nancy Briggs, in *Oxoniensia*, vol.
xxi, p. 61.) The account of the Arnolds given here is revised and expanded from an article by the author,
'Montacute Revised: Sir Edward Phelips and his Architect,' in *Country Life*, vol. cxviii, p. 1020 (November 3,
1955).

[3] Sir Edward Hext, who died in 1624, built a church at Low Ham, near Langport, Somerset, which has
been described as 'one of the most perfect examples in England of the late persistence of the Gothic tradition'. It is reasonable to suppose that he employed William Arnold as his architect.

17. MONTACUTE, SOMERSET

Plaster overmantel in the garden chamber (*circa* 1600).

18. MAPPERTON, near Beaminster

Plaster overmantel, dated 1604, formerly at Melplash Court. Compare plate 17.

19. CHETTLE HOUSE

A brick house with Baroque characteristics attributed to Thomas Archer (*circa* 1710–15).

20. MARLOW PLACE, BUCKINGHAMSHIRE

The pilasters at the angles have the same peculiar capitals that occur at Chettle and there are other analogies between the two houses.

Threasorer sendes him to Cranborne about his workes there. . . . If I had not tyed him fast to this businesse we shold hardly keepe him; he ys so wonnderfully sought being in deede the absolutest & honestest workeman in Ingland.' Cecil had purchased the old hunting lodge at Cranborne about the time when Edward Phelips was completing the building of Montacute. Between 1608 and his death in 1612 he remodelled the mediaeval house, making additions at the east and west ends, refenestrating the whole building and adding the charming Classic porches or loggias on the north and south fronts (pl. 139 and 9). The mediaeval tower at the south-west corner was heightened and balanced by a new one; on the north side a balustraded terrace was formed. The accounts preserved at Hatfield[1] record a payment in December, 1609, of £5 to William Arnold for 'drawing a plott for Cranborne house,' and the following November 'Arnold the freemason' was paid £40 'in part of £250 agreed upon to build a tarryce & a kitchen.' William Arnold's 'plott,' we may be reasonably sure, is the plan, preserved at Hatfield, showing the two porches, the terrace ('tarris'), the new kitchen and the other proposed additions (pl. 149). In the surviving accounts there do not seem to be specific reference to the two porches, but Arnold's responsibility for them can hardly be in doubt.

The south porch at Cranborne shows very close analogies with the porch of Wayford Manor[2] (pl. 9 and 10). The triplet of arches, with accented voussoirs and rose ornaments between them, is common to both; so is the miniature entablature incorporating a triglyph frieze. Inside both porches there are shell-headed niches. If these porches are compared with the east front of Montacute and its porch (pl. 7), several features are found to recur: the miniature entablature with triglyph frieze (the lowest of three that run across the front at Montacute), the shell-headed niches (which at Montacute are set in pairs in the main wall of the front on either side of the porch), and the roundels, really hemispheres hollowed out of the wall, which occur at Cranborne and Montacute and are not confined to the porch but appear elsewhere on their fronts. The close resemblance between the chimney-piece (dated 1602) at Wayford and the one in the great chamber at Montacute has already been noted. Wayford Manor supplies a secure stylistic link between Montacute on the one hand and Cranborne Manor House on the other. It can be confidently accepted as one of William Arnold's works.

The building accounts of Wadham College, Oxford, and Cranborne Manor House do not disclose the parish from which Arnold came, but by 1617 he was

---

[1] Extracts from the building accounts are given in articles on Cranborne Manor House by Christopher Hussey in *Country Life*, vol. lv, p. 914 (January 7, 1914), and by H. A. Tipping in *English Homes*, Period III, vol. ii, p. 360.

[2] Described and illustrated in *Country Life*, vol. lxxvi, p. 336 (September 29, 1934).

living at Charlton Musgrove, near Wincanton, as appears from Chancery proceedings instituted against him by George Luttrell, of Dunster Castle, for whom he had been working.[1] In October, 1617, Luttrell entered into an agreement with William Arnold, 'of Charlton Musgrove, gentleman' concerning 'a house or parcell of building to be sett up and built within the Castle of Dunster.' Arnold was to supply a 'plot' and an 'upright' (i.e. plan and elevation) of the projected building and to oversee the work until the roof was on. He was to receive £40 in instalments, his travelling expenses and a beneficial lease of lands in the north-west part of Dunster. Luttrell found him an unsatisfactory architect, and within two years brought an action against him, stating that the original plans had been altered in execution and that work estimated to cost £462 was likely to amount to £1,200. Mention, however, is made of Arnold's 'great experience in architecture,' which, taken together with Sir Edward Hext's tribute, gives us a firm idea of his importance. His work at Dunster comprised the remodelling of the south range of the castle, which he gave a new front facing the courtyard. It was much altered by Salvin in 1869, but an engraving of 1800, reproduced by Sir H. C. Maxwell Lyte in his *History of Dunster* (p. 365), shows what it was like. As at Cranborne, Arnold effected a successful recasting of a mediaeval building.

It is clear that Arnold was not merely a mason contractor. For Wadham College, Cranborne and Dunster there is definite evidence of his making designs. He followed in the footsteps of the mediaeval architects who were master masons trained at the bench. The fact that he can be associated both with Montacute and with Dunster, where there are chimney-pieces with the stylistic idiosyncrasies which we have considered, makes it probable that he was also concerned with some of the other houses in which these chimney-pieces are found.[2] In Dorset his handiwork is to be suspected at Wolfeton and Melplash; perhaps also at Warmwell (pl. 97) and West Stafford House, where shell-headed niches and arcaded porches occur; and it is possible that the carved frontispiece at Waterston (1586) was an early work. At Lulworth Castle (pl. 141) there is a balustraded terrace comparable with the one at Cranborne Manor House, and there are the same lion-mask spouts as those to be seen on the north loggia at Cranborne, also the shell-headed niches. Whether Arnold designed this sophisticated Elizabethan pile is debatable, but he may be assumed to have undertaken masonry contracts for parts of it, if not for the whole. There is also the possibility that he was concerned with the building of Sherborne

[1] Sir H. C. Maxwell Lyte, *op. cit.*, p. 366.

[2] It is worth remarking that among the Devon houses previously mentioned Walronds, Cullompton, was owned by a branch of the Petre family, relations of Dorothy Wadham. The plaster overmantel dated 1605 displays the Petre coat of arms.

Castle. An architect as much in demand as the passage quoted from Hext's letter implies would not have been able to give detailed supervision to all the work he undertook, and it may be assumed that much of the decoration—carving, plaster-work and woodwork—was carried out independently by the craftsmen employed.

The shell-headed niches to be seen at Lulworth, Cranborne, Wayford and Monta-cute are found elsewhere in England and became part of the mason's stock-in-trade of Renaissance ornament, but they seem to have been particularly favourite features in Dorset, Somerset and Wiltshire. The shell sometimes has the flutings radiating upwards, sometimes downwards. Occasionally, as at Montacute and Lulworth, the niches harboured statues, but usually they appear to have been purely orna-mental. Though worked into chimney-pieces at Montacute, Wayford and Stockton, they most often occur flanking the entrance or contrived in the inner walls of a porch, where they served as seats. Besides being found at Lulworth and Cranborne, they also occur in Dorset at Waterston (1586), Hanford House, Poxwell, Warmwell, Chantmarle, Mapperton and Sherborne Castle.

Other members of the Arnold family were masons. In the Wadham building accounts the names of EDMUND (or EDWARD) ARNOLD and THOMAS ARNOLD appear; the former deputised for William Arnold in his absence. Among the records of Sherborne School there is a payment to GODFREY ARNOLD, who in 1614 carved the statue of Edward VI that is still to be seen in the schoolhouse dining-hall.[1] The parish register of Charlton Musgrove contains no record of William Arnold's baptism or marriage, but the following entry probably refers to him:

1636/7. William Arnold alias Gouerson was buryed: Mar. 12.
Later that year, on October 26, there is the burial of 'Godfrey Arnold alias Gouer-son.' The reason for this alternative surname can only be surmised. Whereas up to 1619 there are many Gouersons (or Goversons) recorded and only two Arnolds, after 1640 there are numerous Arnolds and only one Gouerson, but between those years one finds sometimes one name, sometimes the other and sometimes the two together with the *alias*. William Gouerson (presumably William Arnold) was churchwarden in 1600, 1601 and 1622, Godfrey Gouerson in 1619. Between 1595 and 1612 four daughters of William Gouerson were baptised, but no son. An *Edmund* Gouerson, son of John, was baptised June 9, 1594, and between 1628 and 1644 several children of *Edward* Gouerson (or Edward Arnold) were christened. Edward Arnold was churchwarden in 1645 and 1646, also (if the same person) in 1668, and was buried November 13, 1678.

A possible explanation of the *alias* might be that William and Godfrey, if they were brothers, came to adopt their mother's surname in preference to their own.

[1] W. B. Wildman, *A Short History of Sherborne* (4th ed., 1930), p. 69.

If she was an Arnold she may have been of gentle birth, like John Arnold, Dorothy Wadham's steward and executor, who was entitled to bear arms.[1] This John Arnold may indeed have been a relation or connection of the architect. But, to complicate matters still further, the Charlton Musgrove register, under November 4, 1590, records the burial of Arnold Gouerson.[2] Twenty-six years later a man who seems to have borne the same name appears in the accounts for Oatlands Palace in Surrey, when works were carried out there for Anne of Denmark, James I's queen: he received a payment for 'his extraordinary pains' but it is not stated what these were.[3] It was probably the same individual who in 1621 supplied large quantities of freestone to Sir Roger Townshend for the building of Raynham Hall, Norfolk.[4] His name, as it appears in the Raynham accounts, is said to be Arnold Governorson. The entries imply that he had a quarry at Ketton in Rutland, whence the stone was sent to King's Lynn. A man with such a name was almost certainly a member of the family that had settled at Charlton Musgrove, but it would be rash without further evidence to assume that he was William Gouerson *alias* Arnold.

The Blandford Architects. During the eighteenth century the most important centre of building activity was at Blandford, where we meet with a family of architects and masons even more numerous than the Arnolds. 'A pretty neate Country town,' Celia Fiennes called it about 1680; 'a handsome well built Town, chiefly famous for making the finest Bonelace in England' is Defoe's description nearly half a century later. Both these comments were made before the disastrous fire of 1731; but Blandford seems to have thriven on fires, for three previous ones are recorded in 1579, 1677 and 1713. The 1731 conflagration was far worse, however, than any of its predecessors. In a few hours it 'not only reduced the Church, but almost the whole Town, to Ashes,' even involving the two villages of Bryanston and Blandford St Mary across the river. The work of rebuilding fell largely to two men, JOHN and WILLIAM BASTARD,[5] sons of Thomas Bastard,[5] who is described on a monument which they erected in the church as 'eminent for his Skill in Architecture.' The father died about 1720, having built up a considerable business, for in 'A List of Sufferers'

---

[1] T. G. Jackson, *op. cit.*, p. 30.

[2] The building accounts for Longleat show that Arnold Gouerson, a joiner, was working there from 1555 to 1559. I am grateful to Mr Mark Girouard for this information. He has suggested to me that Gouerson may have been an Anglicised version of a foreign surname.

[3] James Lees-Milne, *The Age of Inigo Jones* (1953), p. 65. The name is given as Arnold Gonerson, but perhaps has been mis-read.

[4] *Country Life*, vol. lviii, p. 748 (November 14, 1925).

[5] A pedigree of the Bastard family is given in Hutchins, *op. cit.*, iii, 523.

21. THE FORMER RED LION INN, BLANDFORD

Pilasters with the characteristic capital having inward-turning volutes adopted by the Blandford architects. Capitals of this kind, used by Borromini, occur in the work of Thomas Archer.

22. SPETTISBURY HOUSE

Pilaster with a capital similar to those in
plate 21 (*circa* 1735). The house has been
demolished.

23. RANSTON

Capitals of columns at the head of the
staircase (1758). A late instance of the use
of this type of capital.

24 and 25. Portraits of the Blandford architects, John and William Bastard (1687–1770 and 1689–1766). William Bastard (*right*) holds a model of a church steeple, probably the rejected design intended for Blandford church.

drawn up after the fire,[1] the losses of the firm of 'Bastard & Co' are estimated at £3,709 10s. 4d., the largest individual sum incurred in the whole town. Altogether there were six sons of Thomas Bastard, senior. The eldest, also a Thomas (1686–1731), died within a few weeks of the fire, perhaps from the epidemic of small-pox that was raging at the time. On his monument he is described as 'joiner and architect.' (His elder son, John, afterwards set up in London as a 'mason and architect,' dying in 1778.) Next come John (1687–1770) and William (1689–1766). An inscription, added to their father's monument after their deaths, tells us that they were 'educated in the same Art, rebuilt this Church, the Town Hall, with several other Publick & Private Edifices.' The fourth son, Samuel, became a ship-modeller in the royal dockyard at Gosport. The fifth, Benjamin (1698–1772), set up at Sherborne.[2] Joseph, the youngest son, described as 'builder and surveyor,' migrated to Basingstoke. This gives us eight members of the family associated with building of some kind or another, and to them should be added two more in the third generation, both Thomases, who later on seem to have been partners in the Blandford firm.[3]

John and William are the two chief names to be reckoned with, though the father, Thomas, must have been responsible for much work in and about Blandford in his time. He probably designed, among other buildings, the charming Classic church at Charlton Marshall (1713) and the rectory at Spettisbury (1716), which was re-fronted towards the end of the century. John Bastard was six times Bailiff of Blandford, his brother, William, twice. They are both described as 'joiners' in their wills; and in two deeds, dated 1740 and 1750, John is styled 'cabinet-maker.' But although joinery and furniture were an important part of their business (see p. 37), they were, like other eighteenth-century joiners, also architects and builders. John seems to have been the better draughtsman and was probably more of an architect than his brother, if we may judge by their portraits, which hang in the Town Hall, for John is shown holding compasses, whereas William points to a model of a steeple—the rejected steeple intended for Blandford church (pl. 24 and 25). The brothers were sufficiently proud of the Town Hall to have their name carved on it: 'BASTARD ARCHITECT 1734.' Of the 'Private Edifices' which they claimed to have built, one

---

[1] Printed in a pamphlet published for the Corporation of Blandford in 1931 to commemorate the bi-centenary of the fire.

[2] In 1745 he was paid £5 for erecting the dial on the south gable of the old headmaster's house, which now once again forms part of the abbey (Wildman, *op. cit.*, p. 73). He was the architect of the fine house in Sherborne now occupied by Lord Digby's School.

[3] Thomas 'the younger' (1724–91), younger son of the Thomas who died in 1731, and Thomas 'the elder' (1720–71), son of Samuel of Gosport. For further information about the Bastards see H. M. Colvin, 'The Bastards of Blandford,' in the *Archaeological Journal*, vol. civ (1948) and the chapter on Blandford in *Old Towns Revisited* (ed. A. Oswald, 1952).

was, no doubt, the former Greyhound Inn, now the National Provincial Bank, on the south side of the market place. The parish rate books show that the Bastard brothers were proprietors of the inn for some years after the fire. The old Greyhound is distinguished by its pediment and four pilasters. Two other façades on the same side of the market place are also adorned with a pediment and pilasters: one was the former Red Lion Inn (pl. 21), the other (said to have been an inn called the Grape) was, as to its eastern half, traditionally the Bastards' own house before it became the headquarters of the local Literary Institution. The pilasters on these two fronts are notable for their unorthodox Corinthian capitals, which have volutes that turn inward instead of outward, to give a distinctive, if not very pleasing, effect. Capitals of the same type occur elsewhere in Dorset. They were to be seen on the front of Spettisbury House (1735), which has been destroyed since the photograph for pl. 22 was taken; and they occur on the south front of Came House (1754) and at Ranston (1758), adorning columns on the landing of the main staircase (pl. 23).

This form of capital, which it would be tempting to call the Bastard capital if it were confined to the Blandford region, is found occasionally in other parts of England, particularly in the work of Nathaniel Ireson of Wincanton and Francis Smith of Warwick.[1] Its origin can be traced to the Roman Baroque architect, Borromini, whose designs were so abhorrent to Lord Burlington and his followers. They seem, however, to have been studied with attention by THOMAS ARCHER when he visited Italy as a young man, for most of the eccentricities that characterise his work are derived from Borromini and other Italian Baroque architects of the *seicento*. Mr Geoffrey Webb first pointed out the marked resemblance between Chettle, the Chafins' early Georgian mansion on Cranborne Chase, and Marlow Place, Buckinghamshire, built about 1720 for John Wallop, later Earl of Portsmouth (pl. 19 and 20).[2] The house at Marlow displays the Borromini capital and also a second peculiar form of capital which recurs at Chettle and which seems to have been inspired by details used by Carlo Maderna. There are other points of likeness between the two buildings, sufficient to justify their attribution to the same designer. Mr Webb's suggestion that their architect was Thomas Archer is now generally accepted. Chettle used to be ascribed to Sir John Vanbrugh, but probably only on account of its

[1] Ireson used this type of capital at Crowcombe Court, Somerset (1734), and for an unexecuted design for the north front of Corsham Court, Wiltshire (1747). It occurs (*circa* 1726) in the interiors of Davenport House, Shropshire, and Ombersley Court, Worcestershire, two houses known to have been built by Smith, and also in the entrance hall at Mawley Hall, Shropshire (*circa* 1730), which has been attributed to Smith.

[2] *Country Life*, vol. lxiv, p. 466 (October 6, 1928). According to Sheahan (*History of Buckinghamshire* (1862), p. 898), Marlow Place was built 'for George II, when Prince of Wales.' See H. M. Colvin, 'The Architectural History of Marlow and its Neighbourhood,' in *Records of Buckinghamshire*, vol. xv (1947).

proximity to the vast mansion which Vanbrugh designed for Bubb Dodington at Eastbury.

The fact that Archer rather than Vanbrugh was the important influence on the Blandford architects is significant. It is known that Francis Smith and his elder brother, William, were employed at St Philip's, Birmingham, and at Heythrop Hall, two of Archer's most important works, so that the appearance of certain Baroque idiosyncrasies in their own work is easily explained. And it is reasonable to suppose that the Bastards may similarly have come into contact with Archer by acting as the builders at Chettle. In 1715 Archer purchased an estate at Hale, near Fordingbridge, which, though in Hampshire, is only 15 miles from Chettle. There he built himself a country house, at which he seems to have spent much of his time, especially in his later years. One can imagine him taking an interest in the rebuilding of Blandford after the fire, and perhaps offering advice. In 1723 he bought Leeson, a farm at Langton Matravers, near Swanage, possibly for the sake of the Purbeck stone obtainable in that area. Mr Howard Colvin has suggested that Archer may have been the architect of Kingston Maurward, built 1717–20 by George Pitt of Stratfieldsaye.[1] The engraving in the first edition of Hutchins' *Dorset* (1774) shows a brick house with Baroque characteristics, but most of these distinctive features disappeared when the building was cased in Portland stone in 1794 (pl. 175).

At least two other master builders besides the Bastards are known to have done work in Blandford and its neighbourhood after the fire. NATHANIEL IRESON of Wincanton (1686–1769) has already been mentioned. He was a native of Warwickshire and a man of many parts: architect, sculptor, builder, brick-maker, plasterer, skilled potter, quarry-owner and also money-lender.[2] From 1720 to 1722 he was building Stourhead for Henry Hoare to Colin Campbell's designs and whilst engaged on that work settled at Stourton. In 1726 he moved to Wincanton, where he built Ireson House and lived for the rest of his life. His practice as an architect and builder was chiefly in east Somerset and south Wiltshire, but it seems to have overlapped into the Bastards' country, for, according to the notes about him collected by the historian of Wincanton, George Sweetman, he was in 1741 'busy' with the building of Blandford church. The new church had been opened at Easter, 1739, so that this statement, if accurate, is likely to refer to the completion of the tower by the wooden cupola in place of the steeple which the Bastards had designed.

[1] *Archaeological Journal*, vol. civ, p. 188, n. 41. See also Marcus Whiffen, *Thomas Archer* (1950). The possibility that John James was the architect should, however, be considered (see pp. 37 and 154).

[2] H. St George Gray, 'Nathaniel Ireson of Wincanton: Master-Builder,' *Proceedings of Somerset Archaeological and Natural History Society*, vol. lxxxvii (1941), pp. 81–4.

Ireson, as we have noted above, used the Borromini capital on two of his designs, and as his elevations at Crowcombe Court show the influence of Archer in other ways, he may be presumed to have been familiar with Archer's work, though whether the contact dated back to his Warwickshire days or came about after he had established himself at Wincanton there is no means of deciding. He may have been responsible for other work at Blandford, where the front of Coupar House shows features that recall his design for the entrance front of Crowcombe Court. On the east and west fronts at Crowcombe he used pilasters with the Borromini capital like those on the south side of the market place at Blandford. The date of Ireson's contract for building Crowcombe Court was July 6, 1734, just three years after the fire at Blandford, where re-building by that time was in full swing.

Another rival, or collaborator, of the Bastards—we do not know which—was FRANCIS CARTWRIGHT of Bryanston (1695–1758). Bryanston and Blandford St Mary are villages that adjoin one another. In his will Cartwright describes himself as 'of Bryanstone,' but mentions his newly erected house in Blandford St Mary.[1] His monument, a wall tablet, in Blandford St Mary church, has, carved below the inscription, an architect's set-square, dividers and rule, with a scroll on which is incised a 'drawing' of a Palladian house. Comparison with a photograph suggests that the design is intended for the north front of Came House, near Dorchester, built in 1754. As Cartwright died in 1758, this will have been among his last works, and evidently the one in which he took most pride. Earlier, he had worked at Creech Grange, where accounts dealing with the alterations to that house carried out by Denis Bond between 1738 and 1741 show that 'Mr Cartwright' was the mason or builder responsible. Mr Colvin has found that the churchwardens of Blandford paid him £20 14s. 4d. in 1742–3 for unspecified work which, were there not the statement about Ireson's activities, one would be inclined to suppose referred to the cupola on the tower. In the subscription for the new bells opened in November, 1749, 'Cartwright Fra: & Men' contributed £5 1s. Described as 'Carver' in his will, Cartwright may have been a mason by training; he mentions all his 'stock of Stone Marble Timber and Boards,' and it may be significant that the two houses with which he can be associated are of stone, not brick. There was a prominent family of London masons of the name of Cartwright to which he is likely to have belonged.[2] A considerable part of his business was probably that of the monumental mason. In 1728 Sir Justinian Isham, 4th baronet, of Lamport Hall, North-

---

[1] P.C.C. 211 Hutton. Extracts from the will are given by Mr Colvin, *Archaeological Journal*, vol. civ, p. 187, n. 31.

[2] Some facts about them are given by D. Knoop and G. P. Jones in *The London Mason in the Seventeenth Century*, p. 38. See also the index of the Wren Society volumes.

amptonshire, paid a 'Mr Cartwright' £35 6s. for a monument to his daughter, Susannah (1696–1726) in the north transept of Bath Abbey,[1] but this might have been one of the London Cartwrights. The Borromini capital which occurs on the south front of Came House seems to link Cartwright, like Ireson, with Archer, but he could have acquired this feature third-hand from the Bastards.

It may have been in consequence of the fire that Cartwright came to settle near Blandford. Certainly the town would have provided work for more than one firm. And the building of Eastbury, a few miles away, was a long-drawn-out business on which local masons and craftsmen were doubtless employed. The knowledge that, besides the Bastards, Cartwright and Ireson have both to be reckoned with makes it difficult, in the absence of documentary evidence, to put forward attributions for individual buildings in the Blandford region. A number of mannerisms, in addition to the Borromini capital, appear in the work of the Blandford school during the period covered by George II's reign. At Chettle the great cornice is furnished with projecting brackets, almost anticipating a favourite Regency motive, and these also occurred on the front of Spettisbury House and appear, in somewhat modified form, on the tower of Blandford church. Apron pieces below the sills of windows were commonly used by Vanbrugh and Archer in their elevations, and they are to be seen on the fronts of houses in and around Blandford. But it would be a mistake to exaggerate the influence of Archer on the local builders, who in the main followed the accepted Palladian style, though using their own tricks of detail. A central window in a composition is not infrequently adorned with enriched scrolls on either side of the jambs, and chimney-pieces are often treated in the same manner.[2] The plasterwork is of a pretty, rather feminine character, and when the vogue for Rococo set in, it obviously appealed to the Bastards. There is an individual treatment for finishing off the balustrade of a staircase. The usual arrangement adopted by joiners in the first half of the eighteenth century was to let the handrail curl round at the bottom on a cluster of balusters encircling the newel post. The Blandford method was to allow the balustrade to stop abruptly with a stout post and to end the handrail in a scroll shaped like a clenched fist (pl. 26). The latest instance of this treatment that has been noticed is at Crichel, where Humphry Sturt's staircase, erected after 1765, follows the local manner, perhaps because some older work was incorporated in it. By this time the Blandford builders had adopted the new fashion of using ironwork for balustrades. Staircases of this later type occur at Stepleton (pl. 201), Moreton, Ranston (pl. 187), Whatcombe and Came.

[1] Lamport MSS (Isham Diaries 'K'). I am indebted to Sir Gyles Isham, Bt., for this reference.
[2] A bedroom chimney-piece of this type which was destroyed in the fire at Lulworth Castle (pl. 27) is known from Edward Weld's accounts to have been supplied by 'Mr Bastard' (1756).

Among eighteenth-century houses in the east of Dorset the following may be noted as showing characteristics of 'the Blandford School.'

SPETTISBURY HOUSE. Brick. Built, according to Hutchins, about 1735 and enlarged between 1762 and 1777. In 1800 it became a convent. The greater part of the house was pulled down in 1927, but the front remained standing in a ruined state for some years afterwards.

CRICHEL. Brick, subsequently coated in stucco. The house was rebuilt by Sir William Napier after the fire of 1742 and embodied in Humphry Sturt's mansion (*circa* 1765–75).

STEPLETON HOUSE. Stone. Alterations were made to the exterior and interior *circa* 1740 by Thomas Fownes, who probably also built the stables. The wings, dated 1758, were added by Julines Beckford. Their similarity to the stable block at Came House warrants an attribution of these additions to Francis Cartwright.

MORETON HOUSE. Portland stone. Built in 1744 by James Frampton. The hipped roof and eaves cornice are old-fashioned for the date.

WHATCOMBE HOUSE. Brick, subsequently coated in stucco. Built in 1750 by Edmund Morton Pleydell. Altered and enlarged in 1802.

MERLY HOUSE. Brick. Built between 1752 and 1756 by Ralph Willett, who claimed to have designed the house himself. One of the Bastards or Cartwright may have been the builder.

RANSTON. Brick, coated in stucco. The west front and staircase (1758) added to an older house. Thomas Ryves, the owner, is said to have made the design for the front.

To these, perhaps, should be added the west front of SMEDMORE, built about 1761, and the eighteenth-century additions to EDMONDSHAM.

The Bastards of Blandford were responsible for at least one of the eighteenth-century buildings at POOLE. The fine house, in Market Street, built for Sir Peter Thompson in 1746–49, shows marked Blandford characteristics both within and without.[1] It is built of red brick and has Sir Peter's coat of arms, crest and motto over the entrance; the interior retains its original staircase of mahogany, several chimney-pieces and enriched ceilings. Sir Peter Thompson (1698–1770) was a rich merchant in the Hamburg trade, a Fellow of the Royal Society and a Fellow of the Society of Antiquaries. A letter to him from John Bastard has been preserved, and it is clear from this that the house had been built (and, no doubt, designed) by him.[2]

[1] Hutchins (3rd ed.), i. 67, and John Sydenham, *History of Poole* (1839), p. 447.

[2] A transcript of this letter was kindly sent to me by Mr A. F. V. Johnstone, of Poole. A letter-book of Sir Peter Thompson, in private ownership, contains five later memoranda concerning the Bastards; three are of John Bastard and two of Thomas Bastard; the dates range from 1761 to 1764. I am grateful to Mr E. F. J. Mathews for informing me about this letter-book and to Mr Johnstone for particulars of the memoranda.

When it was written (July 6, 1752), Bastard's account was still outstanding, and its settlement was requested. Literary composition was not the architect's forte, but he was unabashed by obstacles of spelling and grammar, and after a long and not very lucid explanation of 'ye maner of mesuring naked flooring' pride in his handiwork would not be denied: 'you nor nobodey Else can say but yours is dun strong and well have had time to Prove it—the house stands bleak, and much Exposed. and I think ther never was a house beter defended against storms nor more care taken in Rooffing, and Lead work. I never saw nor hard of a drop that came in aney whare.' Some finishing touches still remained to be done: the writer had not yet had time 'to Inrich ye cornishes of ye 3 Rooms now painted, in ye maner they was dun before'. The concluding paragraph is particularly interesting. It reveals that the Bastards had been on friendly terms with John James, of Greenwich, and that they had entertained him at Blandford. Reverting, apparently, to the subject of 'naked flooring' Bastard remarked: 'as to this mehood [method?] I now use . . . was shown me ferst by Mr John James of Greenwich[1], & he was alow'd to be as good a Carpenter as aney in his time, & he was Ooften at ower house.' After having been used for many years as Municipal Offices, Sir Peter Thompson's house is now occupied by the Poole School of Art.

In conclusion, some evidence may be given that throws light on the Bastards' activities as interior decorators and suppliers of furniture. In 1732–33 John Bastard provided woodwork and furniture for HAZLEGROVE HOUSE at Queen Camel, Somerset. It included handsome carved oak wainscoting for the 'best parlour,' picture frames, a set of walnut chairs, a walnut frame for a marble table-top, and a bedroom chimney-piece.[2] Carew Hervey Mildmay was the client. Edward Weld's accounts show the Bastards working in a similar capacity at LULWORTH CASTLE between 1740 and 1756.[3] In 1740 'Mr Bastard' was paid his bill for work in the hall (£207 16s. 1d.), in 1741 for the 'New Parlour' (£88 17s. 6d.), in 1745

[1] St George's, Hanover Square, is James's best-known building. He was trained as a carpenter. In 1724 he built for himself a country house called Warbrooks at Eversley in Hampshire. He is not known to have done any work in Dorset, but John Bastard's statement that he was often at their house arouses speculation. Did he undertake carpentry contracts at Eastbury or Chettle? Or was he the architect of Kingston Maurward? James died in 1746.

[2] The account, dated July 23, 1733, and receipted by John Bastard, was printed in *Country Life*, vol. lxvii (Jan. 18, 1930), p. 99. According to Phelps, the historian of Somerset, the new part of Hazlegrove House was 'built of hewn free-stone after a design of a Venetian architect in 1730 but is only a portion of the original plan.' The fine carved wainscoting formerly in the parlour was illustrated in *Country Life*, vol. lxv (May 18, 1929), p. lxix.

[3] For the extracts taken from these accounts in the possession of Colonel J. W. Weld I am indebted to Mr H. M. Colvin.

'about ye Chappel' in the north-west tower (£139 13s. 0d.). In 1756 he fitted up a bedroom and the 'Green Moreen Tower'; the 'Marble Chimney & Carving' in the latter cost £15 11s. Furniture supplied included 'a Mohogany Table' (1740), 'a Library Bureau of 6 foot by 3 of Walnut tree & a Cloaths Press ditto' (1756), a Bedstead with 'Pillars, Casters, Rods, Topping' (1756), also curtains and chairs. Among the drawings in Colonel Weld's possession are two for the wall treatment of the drawing-room at Lulworth Castle; both are endorsed John Bastard. In execution the design was modified, but the room, which was known as the old drawing-room, remained with John Bastard's chimney-piece and panelling un-altered until the fire of 1929.

TRAVELLERS AND VISITORS IN DORSET

Descriptions of houses in diaries and travel journals are often fruitful and entertaining sources of information, though they can be tantalising by their silence on questions they might have answered for us. JOHN LELAND, the father of English topography, makes mention of a few Dorset houses in his famous *Itinerary*,[1] which some time between 1534 and 1542 took him to Sherborne and also on a west-to-east journey from Devon by way of Lyme, Bridport, Beaminster, Melbury, Weymouth and Wareham to Wimborne and Poole, and then out of the county over Cranborne Chase. He saw Clifton Maybank in the days of the Horseys and Thornhill, where dwelt 'Master Thornehul an auncient gentilman'; he mentions Woodsford Castle and the goodly manor place of the Newburghs at East Lulworth 'hard by the paroch chirch.' At Melbury 'Mr Strangeguayse' had lately done much building, 'avauncing the inner part of the house with a loftie and fresch tower.' That hexagonal lantern tower still dominates the building.

There is an interval of nearly a century before we have another record of a journey through Dorset. In September, 1635, LIEUTENANT HAMMOND, 'of the Military Company in Norwich', rode through the county, going from east to west.[2] Coming from Salisbury, he went by way of Wimborne and Wareham into Pur-beck, then to Lulworth Castle, where he received generous entertainment; thence riding along the coast he visited Weymouth and Portland, and so to Dorchester, Bridport and Lyme Regis on his way to Exeter. He gives a description of Corfe Castle, then 'all in very good repayre', though, unfortunately, his account is all too brief. Lulworth Castle, where he was presented to the Earl of Suffolk 'as he came

[1] *The Itinerary of John Leland* (ed. L. Toulmin Smith, 1910). See especially vol. i, pp. 152–5, 244–58, 304–5; iv, pp. 73, 106–10; v, pp. 107–11.

[2] *A Breife Description of a Journey made into the Westerne Counties* (ed. L. G. Wickham Legg, 1936), Royal Historical Society, Camden Miscellany, vol. xvi, pp. 68–73.

from hunting with a great French Monseur', is described at greater length. He found it 'stately and loftie, and newly built of Freestone and other durable white stone, such as the Island of Purbecke affords Plenty off, and in a 4, square veriformity, with 4. great and lofty, high round Towers at the corners'. The dining chamber, 'very stately, large and rich, with a faire Cloth of State', had opening from it a 'neat withdrawing Roome' in one of the towers. He penetrated to 'the brave archt Cellers for Wine and Beere' and went up onto the leads, from which 'through a daintie glade, you may see within 2. Mile thereoff, the Ships sayling on the Maine'.

CELIA FIENNES came half a century later. The first of her tours[1] described in her diaries took her on a round of visits to relations' houses in Dorset about the year 1685. She stayed at Merly, near Wimborne, at Quar, in the Isle of Purbeck, at Piddletrenthide, at two houses in the region of Bridport and Lyme, and, on the way back, with her cousin, Thomas Erle, at Charborough. There are no long accounts of houses such as appear in the later diaries, but her description of Charborough, then a comparatively 'new built house,' enables one to visualise it before the eighteenth-century and later alterations.

Less lively but more informative are the observations of DR RICHARD POCOCKE,[2] who in the course of his tours of England traversed Dorset in September, 1750, and again, by a different route, in October, 1754. This untiring and insatiable traveller, who later became Bishop of Ossory, was Archdeacon of Dublin at the time when he made his 'journeys into England'. Antiquities were his main interest, not only cathedrals, abbeys and churches, but also Roman and prehistoric remains: in Dorset he visited and described the Cerne Giant and the vast ramparts of Maiden Castle. Natural history and geology of a kind likewise engaged his attention, but he was also a connoisseur, eager to view great houses, their gardens and parks, and the 'improvements' made by their owners. On his first tour he passed Kingston Lacy on his way to Poole, where he took note of Sir Peter Thompson's new house; having tramped about the ruins of Corfe Castle and investigated the Purbeck quarries, he stayed at Mr Trenchard's house at Lytchet Matravers, from which he went to inspect Mr Drax's improvements at Charborough and to ·look at Wareham. There he was taken round the town by Mr Hutchins: 'He is compiling an History of Dorsetshire.' On his ride to Weymouth he saw Lulworth Castle, 'said to be the design of Inigo Jones, but erroneously.' He likewise noted and rejected the still more absurd attribution to Inigo Jones of the Jacobean portion of Wolfeton when he visited it in 1754.

---

[1] *The Journeys of Celia Fiennes* (ed. Christopher Morris, 1947), pp. 10–15.

[2] *The Travels through England of Dr. Richard Pococke* (ed. J. J. Cartwright, 1888–9), Camden Society New Series, vols. 42 and 44. For the descriptions of Dorset, see vol. i, pp. 84–98, and vol. ii, pp. 136–50.

In the account of his second tour he gives long descriptions of St Giles's House and Eastbury. That of Eastbury is particularly interesting as a record of what the gigantic house was like when it and its owner were in their hey-day. He greatly admired the plantations at Bryanston, 'famous for one of the most beautiful terraces in the world.' At Milton Abbey he inspected both the church and the house, which Lord Milton had begun to case all round 'in a beautiful modern taste.' He saw Wolfeton before its mutilation, noting that the screen of the old hall was finely carved 'and the Kings of England, small and and at full length' were round the wainscot in it and that there were 'a great number of arms in painted glass all over the house.' On the ramparts of Maiden Castle his eye was caught by 'Came, Mr Daymore's new house which is now building,' no doubt standing out very white in the landscape away to the east. We need not follow him to Sherborne, where, before going on into Somerset, he has much to say about the abbey but gives only a sentence to the 'good old house call'd the lodge, belonging to Lord Digby, who is improving the place.'

It was in the capacity of a captain of dragoons in the South Hampshire Regiment that EDWARD GIBBON, the historian, visited Dorset. The threat of a French invasion during the Seven Years' War had spurred him and his father to volunteer for the militia. 'Condemned during two years and a half to a wandering life of military servitude,' Gibbon found himself spending several months at Blandford in the summer of 1760 and again in 1762. He liked the town and wrote with appreciation of the hospitality shown by the gentlemen of the county, 'particularly Messrs Porteman, Pleydwell, Bower, Sturt, Brain, Jennings, Drax and Trenchard.'[1] Among the neighbouring houses which he visited were Stepleton ('Julines Beckford's place, unmeaning, expensive and unfinished'), Ranston ('Mr Reeve's small but laid out and finished with the most refined taste and elegance'), Milborne ('an old venerable structure . . . park prettily laid out'), Crichel, St Giles's House, Horton and Bryanston. He thought St Giles 'excessively large but very irregular.' The party did not go inside: 'His Lordship came out to ask us in, but the invitation was so faint that we declined it.' Like Dr Pococke, he admired the winding river and the grotto. He was frequently entertained by Mr Portman at Bryanston. 'His place (on which and the House his father laid out £25,000) is delightfull. His cliff is the side of a hill about a mile long laid out with great taste, cut out into a thousand walks, planted with great variety, and a river running at the bottom. The house is large and well fitted up, but inconvenient and ill-furnished.' It was soon to be rebuilt by Wyatt.

In July, 1762, just after Gibbon had said farewell to Blandford, HORACE

[1] *Gibbon's Journal*, ed. D. M. Low (1929). See especially pp. 12, 48–56, 67–79.

26. STAIRCASE AT
COUPAR HOUSE,
BLANDFORD
The scroll finishing off
the handrail is charac-
teristic of early Georgian
joinery in the Blandford
region.

27. LULWORTH
CASTLE. Chimney-
piece with characteristic
detail supplied by 'Mr
Bastard' in 1756.
Destroyed in the fire of
1929.

28. CORFE CASTLE

Originally a royal castle, it was the home of the Bankes family at the time of the Civil War.

WALPOLE visited Dorset. His accounts of the two houses which he saw—Sherborne Castle and Melbury—are interesting chiefly for his notes on the pictures.[1] JOHN BYNG, twenty years later, had not the time to make one of his leisurely tours. He rode down to join Mrs B. and the ladies for ten days at Weymouth and could not potter on the way, and when he left, having enjoyed himself more than he would admit, he did not go off the route he took through Dorchester and Blandford and over the Downs to Salisbury. He remarked, however, at Bryanston 'the new-built house and grounds of Mr Portman, which are not yet finish'd,' noted that 'the great edifice' at Eastbury was being pulled down, and liked the look of Chettle—'a seemingly good hunting seat of Mr Chafin's, which must be well placed for fox or hare hunting.'[2]

FANNY BURNEY in August, 1789, accompanied Queen Charlotte on a visit to Lulworth Castle. She was much impressed by Mr Weld's Roman Catholic chapel.[3] While staying at Weymouth, GEORGE III made many excursions to the seats of the nobility and gentry in the neighbourhood, including, besides Lulworth Castle, where he stayed, Poxwell, Came House, Sherborne Castle and Milton Abbey. In 1804 Lionel Damer, as Colonel of the Dorset Volunteers, entertained the King at Came after His Majesty had inspected the regiment in Fordington Field outside Dorchester. When Wolfeton was visited by George III it lost a remarkable sixteenth-century table, which stood in the bay window in the gallery. The King seems to have admired it, and it was therefore presented to him; it is said to have been installed in the royal dairy at Frogmore. It was a marble table, octagonal in shape, supported by four carved lions in wood, probably resembling the octagonal tables in Sir William Sharington's tower at Lacock Abbey. The King's remarks sometimes disconcerted his hosts. It has been mentioned how Morton Pitt of Kingston Maurward took so deeply to heart the royal criticism that his house was of brick that he had it completely cased in Portland stone. When staying at Milton Abbey the King, impressed by a portrait of the sporting parson, William Chafin, owner of Chettle, insisted on seeing the original so that he could assure himself that it was a good likeness. This he was able to do, to the considerable embarrassment of the squarson when presented to him.

DORSET FAMILIES

Although Dorset has been more fortunate than most counties in preserving old ties and traditions, many of the families that figure most often in this book have

---

[1] *The Walpole Society*, vol. xvi, pp. 46–8.

[2] *The Torrington Diaries: the Tours Through England and Wales of the Hon. John Byng* (ed. C. Bruyn Andrews, 1934), vol. i, pp. 104–5.

[3] *The Diary and Letters of Madame D'Arblay* (ed. Austin Dobson, 1905), vol. iv, pp. 307–8.

C.H.D.—6

now disappeared. Claviles, Strodes, Martyns, Trenchards, Horseys, Tregonwells, Turbervilles are all names of the past. Perhaps the most remarkable instance of an unbroken descent was that of the Binghams at Bingham's Melcombe, which only came to an end in 1895; from early in the thirteenth century, or for nearly seven hundred years, the property had passed in continuous ownership from father to son. Probably the longest unbroken descent in the male line is now that of Herringston, which has been in the Williams family since 1513. There are still a few instances of estates that have never, as far back as records go, changed hands by sale. This applies to Charborough and to the manor house at Winterborne Clenston. From the William de Winterborne who held it in the time of Henry III Clenston has passed hereditarily through the Heryngs, de la Lyndes, Mortons and Pleydells to its present owner, Mrs Pleydell-Railston. Hardly less remarkable is the case of Smedmore. There is also the interesting record of the Duke of Bedford's farm at Berwick, near Swyre, which has belonged to the Russells for over five hundred years and was theirs long before the family became famous. Other examples of family ownerships going back three or four centuries are those of St Giles's House, Melbury, Cranborne Manor House, Kingston Lacy, Lulworth Castle, Sherborne Castle and Crichel. It may be noted how many families in the eighteenth century owed their fortunes to estates in the West Indies—Julines and Peter Beckford at Stepleton, Henry Drax of Charborough, the Pinneys of Bettiscombe and Racedown, Ralph Willett, who built Merly, and John Newton, who enlarged Spettisbury House.

DORSET ARTISTS

Dorset cannot rival Devon or East Anglia as a 'nursery' of famous painters, but it can claim to have given birth to Sir James Thornhill and Alfred Stevens, as well as to two less-known artists, Giles Hussey and Thomas Beach. THORNHILL (1675–1734) came of a very old Dorset family, taking its name from Thornhill, near Stalbridge, which the painter towards the latter part of his career was able to re-purchase. He was born at Weymouth, or rather Melcombe Regis, his mother being a Sydenham of Wynford Eagle. In Dorset there are examples of his work at Charborough Park and the fine house in Sherborne known as Lord Digby's School, where the staircase halls were painted by him; in St Mary's Church, Weymouth, there is a 'Last Supper' which he painted for the altar-piece; there was also a ceiling by him at Eastbury. The publication by the Walpole Society of the Vertue notebooks has revealed some of Thornhill's activities as an architect; he is said to have designed the alterations which he made to Thornhill House (pl. 134), and he drew a design for the Town Hall at Blandford after the fire. His daughter, Jane, married

Hogarth, who had been his pupil, and in whose house at Chiswick Thornhill's widow died. ALFRED STEVENS (1818–75) was a native of Blandford. His father, a decorator and painter, was employed on the early Victorian alterations at Chettle House. Probably the young Alfred Stevens assisted him; it is known that he modelled the reliefs over the doorways in the staircase hall. He owed his education to Samuel Best, the parson of Blandford St Mary, who made it possible for him to go to Italy during the most impressionable years of his life. GILES HUSSEY (1710–88), painter, mystic and mathematician, was born at Nash Court, Marnhull, where his family, who were Catholics, had long been seated. He was a beautiful draughtsman, but was led away into developing an abstruse theory, which he claimed had been mysteriously revealed to him, basing the principles of beauty on the musical scale of harmonies. There were several of his portrait drawings at Lulworth Castle. Later in life he succeeded to the Marnhull estate, but eventually moved to Devon, where he ended his life as a recluse.   Milton Abbas was the birthplace of THOMAS BEACH (1738–1806), who through Damer's influence became a pupil of Reynolds. Much of his life was spent at Bath, but there are a number of his portraits in Dorset houses. In the library at Came House there used to hang a series of portraits painted by him of the eleven officers who commanded the Dorset Volunteers during the Napoleonic Wars. An interesting monograph on Beach by his great-great-grand niece, Miss Elise Beach, was published in 1934.

THE COUNTY HISTORIANS

This introduction can fittingly close with a note on the authors of the two county histories. The delightful *Survey of Dorset* was first published in 1732, but it was written a century earlier—between 1625 and 1634. The manuscript had no title-page, and it was assumed that the author was John Coker of Mappowder from a remark made by the writer in the account of Mappowder, 'it befits me not, being a member of the house, to speak of it.' It has been conclusively proved, however, that the *Survey* was not written by Coker, but by his brother-in-law, THOMAS GERARD of Trent, the father of Anne Wyndham, who a few years later gave shelter in her house to the fugitive Charles II.[1] Thomas Gerard was born in 1593, studied at Gloucester Hall, Oxford, and at the age of twenty-five married Anne Coker. He was very proud of his wife's family and caused the Coker pedigree to be painted on the walls of Trent church, balancing his own. Gerard was an enthusiastic herald and antiquary, a great admirer of Camden and a friend of William

[1] See *Somerset and Dorset Notes and Queries*, vol. v, article 83, and *Proceedings of the Dorset Field Club*, vol. xxxv (1914), p. 55.

Burton, the Leicestershire historian. Besides his *Survey of Dorset* he left a similar but unfinished work on Somerset, to which county Trent at that time belonged. This, *The Particular Description of Somerset*,[1] contains two or three references to the author's Dorset Survey, and is composed in the same style and on the same geographical plan of following the rivers from their sources. Gerard's early death in 1634 prevented him from publishing either book. The *Survey* is charmingly written with many personal touches. It is pleasant to come across references to 'faire newe houses,' like Anderson and Poxwell, 'latelie built'; the Tudor houses he describes as 'built in our fathers' days.'

Hutchins' monumental *History* was first published in two folio volumes in 1774. It was the fruit of forty years' research. Its author, JOHN HUTCHINS, was persuaded to embark on the work by Jacob Bancks while he was curate at Milton Abbas. In 1729 Bancks procured him the living of Swyre. From 1733 to 1744 he was also rector of Bingham's Melcombe, and from 1744 until his death, of Holy Trinity, Wareham. When his rectory at Wareham was burnt to the ground in the fire of 1762, the gallant Mrs Hutchins risked her life to rescue her husband's papers. Hutchins died in the year before his great work was published.

[1] Printed by the *Somerset Record Society*, vol. xv.

CHAPTER ONE

The Manor Houses of Dorset (up to 1650)

THE meaning that we give the term 'manor house' to-day is far removed from its original significance. We think of an old, time-worn building, picturesquely mullioned and gabled, with walls weathered by the rain and patinated with lichen. It would be useless to try to brush off this veil of romantic suggestion which clothes the words so well, and if in the heading of this chapter they are not intended in quite so picturesque a sense, they are used with a definite antithesis to the 'gentleman's residence' or 'seat' of Georgian days. In a county like Dorset, where the traditions of the local builders were slow to recognise changes in architectural fashion, there are no abrupt ends or beginnings. From the earliest mediaeval houses of which fragments remain up to those of the reign of Charles I there is a continuous progression, and it would be hopeless to try to divide them off into periods. But the Civil War does provide a break. After the Restoration the Classic influence on our architecture, which was so long in affecting the remoter parts of England, makes the full weight of its momentum felt for the first time. The Elizabethan and Jacobean houses are essentially Gothic in their design, Classic features (often crude and clumsy enough) being confined to a few ornamental details. Although many features of the old manorial system continued long after the Commonwealth, the term 'manor house' can conveniently be made to cover the traditional English 'mansion house' of lord or squire before the days when gables gave way to cornices, mullions to sashes, and the proximity of the village church was abandoned for the 'prospect' afforded by some neighbouring 'eminence.'

Norman castle building is represented in Dorset only by the magnificent ruins of Corfe (pl. 28), the scantier remains at Sherborne and the tower of the 'Rufus' castle at Portland. Dorchester, Wareham, Marshwood, and Sturminster Newton all once had castles, of which some grass-covered banks and a few fragments of masonry are the most that survives. Of the four Henry VIII blockhouses at Abbotsbury, Portland, Sandesfoot and Brownsea Island there are more substantial remains. But the only mediaeval castle that falls within the scope of this book is one whose fangs have been drawn so thoroughly that it is not easy to recognise it as a castle at all. Woodsford, however, was never so much a castle as a fortified manor house, built at a time when security was no longer the all-important consideration it once had been. The licence for its crenellation was granted by Edward III in 1337. In the same year similar licences were issued to Walter Heryng to fortify his houses at Langton Herring and Winterborne (Herringston), and in 1371 to Sir John de Chideock. The manor house at Chideock had a fine tower, which has been destroyed since Buck depicted it two hundred years ago.

Woodsford, in the arrangement of the living-rooms, raised up on vaulted basements, has parallels in Cranborne Manor House (p. 123) and the very interesting remains of Owermoigne Court.[1] At Owermoigne, which was a moated house, the surviving west range has the hall and solar raised above an undercroft in the same manner. The hall is well lighted by beautifully fashioned windows (pl. 30) which remain in an excellent state of preservation. They are of two trefoil-headed lights with a pierced quatrefoil under the arch; internally, the arch opening is carried on slender shafts with moulded capitals and bases, and the window seats remain with their stone rests on either side, though now hidden owing to the raising of the floor level. The details of these windows and of other surviving features point to a date about 1270. The owners of the manor at that period were the le Moignes, who held it from the time of Henry I to that of Henry VI.

These windows at Owermoigne may be compared with the less highly finished examples at Barnston, near Corfe Castle, dating from about 1280 (pl. 37). Though altered in Tudor days, Barnston is a remarkably well-preserved example of a manor house of the time of Edward I. In Purbeck there are two other houses which go back to the thirteenth century. Godlingston, which has been restored in recent years, has an early pointed doorway with trefoil head that gave entrance to the hall, and at its south end there is a semicircular tower with walls of great thickness (pl. 29). At Scoles, corrupted from Scoviles, a farmhouse near Corfe Castle, there is an ancient outbuilding that has a double-lancet window; in its west wall there is a series of rectangular recesses, the purpose of which has never been satisfactorily explained.[2]

Woodsford, Cranborne and Owermoigne are examples of the more compact type of mediaeval house, having defensive elements about them in the raising of the living-rooms to first-floor level above a basement used for storage. More often the early manor house consisted of a loosely-knit group of buildings, the most important of which was the great hall where the manorial court was held. Derived from the Saxon barn-like dwelling and notable for its high-pitched timber roof, the hall was the nucleus of the mediaeval homestead with the adjacent buildings sub-

---

[1] Also 'King John's House' at Tollard Royal, just over the Dorset border on Cranborne Chase.

[2] Detailed descriptions of Owermoigne Court, Barnston, Godlingston and Scoles are given in *Thirteenth-Century Domestic Architecture in England*, by Margaret E. Wood, published as a supplement to the *Archaeological Journal*, vol. cv (1950).

ordinate to it. In course of time, they came to be more closely organised, especially in regions where stone was the building material, being ranged round two or more sides of a court. None of the Dorset houses illustrated now shows the full courtyard plan, though Herringston, Athelhampton and Wolfeton were formerly quadrangular. Where the buildings of a mediaeval house did not extend round all four sides, there would have been a walled enclosure with a gate or gatehouse, as at Bingham's Melcombe, on the side opposite the principal range. This latter contained the hall, entered at one end by a screens passage, off which opened the doors leading to buttery, pantry and kitchen. The opposite end, where the family dined on a raised dais, was in later days lighted by a bay window or oriel. Beyond this end of the hall would be the parlour and solar, usually in a block set at right angles, and other rooms the number of which would depend on the size of the owner's family or the depth of his purse. The normal arrangement is well illustrated by Athelhampton.

There are several mediaeval halls surviving in Dorset, although some of them, like those at Barnston, Clenston and Fiddleford, are disguised by the later insertion of floors. One of the earliest was the fourteenth-century hall at Tyneham, standing at the back of the Elizabethan house. Only portions of its open timber roof remained, but enough was left to show that it was of an unusual type with the arched braces that support the principals carved with cusps. At Scaplen's Court, an old house in Poole, there is a fifteenth-century hall, now roofless, thought to have been used as the mediaeval Guildhall. The following are later examples, including the Tudor halls at Milton and Forde. The hall at Forde Abbey was originally longer.

Purse Caundle.	c. 1460–80.	Edward IV.	26 ft. × 20 ft.
Athelhampton.	c. 1495–1500.	Henry VII.	38 ft. × $21\frac{1}{2}$ ft.
Milton Abbey.	1498.	Henry VII.	$53\frac{1}{2}$ ft. × $26\frac{1}{2}$ ft.
Forde Abbey.	1528.	Henry VIII.	$54\frac{1}{2}$ ft. × 28 ft.

Other mediaeval remains include Corscombe Court and the manor house at Toller Whelme in the same parish, the late fifteenth-century porch at Childhay (pl. 33), the early range containing a chapel at the back of Chantmarle, a richly carved early Tudor doorway at Thornhill, the remains of the older manor house at Clifton Maybank, the Manor House and Court House at Poyntington and 'John of Gaunt's' kitchen at Canford with its huge chimney-breasts (pl. 34). The last is probably of fifteenth-century date, and the legend that associates it with Gaunt cannot be substantiated; in Hutchins' time there were much more extensive remains of what must have been one of the most important mediaeval houses in Dorset. At Cerne Abbas, besides the early Tudor porch-tower, built about 1500 as part of the abbot's hall, there is also a fifteenth-century building, which may have been the guesthouse. On its upper floor there is a hall and a chamber beyond, but its most interesting feature is the beautiful oriel window projecting from the north wall (pl. 31). A fifteenth-century fireplace, which was formerly in this building, is now in the adjoining Abbey Farm, which was built after the Dissolution from stone from the abbey buildings. On the fireplace are the initials of John Vanne, abbot of Cerne from 1458 to 1470.

Compared with their predecessors, the houses of the Tudor period show a closer co-ordination of the various parts. The hall no longer rises the full height of the house. With the substitution of fireplaces and chimneys for the open hearth it became possible to place rooms over the hall, and so Parnham and Sandford Orcas were planned in contrast to Athelhampton and Purse Caundle. The porch now comes to be knit into the composition and gradually assumes the dominant part in the whole design. From the fifteenth-century porch at Childhay to the Jacobean examples at Chantmarle and Anderson, with Athelhampton, Parnham and Kingston Maurward as the intermediate stages, one can trace a century and a half of progressive evolution towards the ideal of perfect symmetry. It was in this attainment of unity and balance in the plans and elevations of their houses that the Elizabethan and Jacobean builders showed an advance on their predecessors; this, and not the introduction of Classic ornament, which they used with clumsy unfamiliarity, was their real achievement. It is pleasant to see how they rang the changes on three, four and five gables, with or without projections, including or excluding the porch; Tyneham, Edmondsham, the old Crichel, Kingston Maurward, Chantmarle, Anderson, Hanford, Wraxall and Wynford Eagle, between them show how varied the tunes could be within the chosen mode. The plan of the house, meanwhile, has shrunk from the enclosed quadrangle to the E or H, and finally to the rectangular block. This last form was attained when it came to be realised that every room need not be lighted from both sides and that it was possible to cover wider buildings with less steep and lighter roofs. Anderson may be taken to represent the latest development in this chapter, and it is interesting to contrast with it Hanford, a contemporary house, which was built on what was by then the archaic quadrangular plan.

Barnston (2 miles W. of Corfe Castle). The farmhouses in the Isle of Purbeck would make an interesting study in themselves, for several of their number go back to mediaeval times. By far the best preserved and probably the oldest of them is the little manor house at Barnston, lying on the north side of the road from Knowle to Steeple. The south front of this beautiful stone building shows windows of Tudor date. It is necessary to walk round to the back to find undeniable evidence that the

29. GODLINGSTON

A thirteenth-century manor house near Swanage.

30. OWERMOIGNE COURT

A mediaeval house with hall at first-floor level. The windows suggest a date about 1270.

31. CERNE ABBEY

Fifteenth-century oriel in one of the surviving domestic
buildings of the Abbey.

32. PURSE CAUNDLE

Late fifteenth-century oriel of the solar or great chamber of
the manor house.

34. CANFORD MANOR

Massive chimney-breasts in the mediaeval range popularly known as 'John of Gaunt's kitchen'.

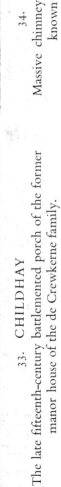

33. CHILDHAY

The late fifteenth-century battlemented porch of the former manor house of the de Crewkerne family.

35, 36 and 37. BARNSTON, a late thirteenth-century manor house in the Isle of Purbeck. (*Left*) The sixteenth-century bay on the south front; (*middle*) the north gable; (*right*) window in the north wall (*circa* 1280).

house is at least as old as the time of Edward I. The clue to its date is furnished by the early form of window in the north wall of its cross-gable, consisting of twin lancets with a pierced quatrefoil above them (pl. 36). Another double-lancet window, recently unblocked, can be seen in the wall of the wing to the right. The three shallow buttresses supporting the wall of the gable end are of the kind found in 'Early English' work. Taken together, the three features point to a date about 1280.

The house consists of three portions—a hall to the east, the double-storey cross-range in the centre and a two-storey wing projecting westward. Originally the hall went up the full height of the building and probably had an open hearth in its centre. In the sixteenth century a flat ceiling with massive beams of oak, finely moulded, was inserted to give a second storey above; at the same time a fireplace

BARNSTON
Ground-floor Plan. A, Parlour with solar above; B, Hall.

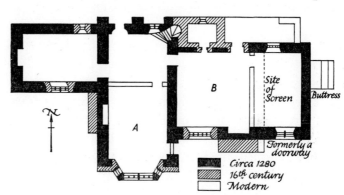

was formed in the south wall. The hall is now partitioned into two rooms, but a little to the east of the modern division there may be seen in the transverse beam the marks of the screen which formerly stood at this end, separating the hall from the passage by which it was entered. The original entrance, now altered to form a window, was near the east end of the south wall. Alterations in Tudor days were also made to the cross-range containing the solar. The south wall was faced with ashlar and given a two-storey bay window (pl. 35) of a similar kind to those at Creech Grange and Parnham. The chimney-breast against the west wall seems to have been added at the same time. But, fortunately, the north gable wall was left untouched, though some disturbance was caused in the north-east corner by a stone staircase, either added or altered to provide access to the new floor above the hall. How the first-floor rooms were originally reached it is difficult to say: perhaps by ladders internally. The north window lighting the solar is in almost perfect preservation (pl. 37), retaining not only its stone seat and sills, but the original hooks on which were hung the wood shutters before the days of glass. Even the stone sockets for the bars fastening the shutters remain projecting from the central mullion.

Barnston derives the first part of its name from the Saxon thegn, Bern, who held it in the Confessor's time. At the Conquest it was among the five Dorset manors held by Walter de Clavile, whose descendants were again to own it in the fifteenth century. The builder of the house was one of the Estoke family, who held it until the reign of Henry VI, when it came by marriage to John Clavell of Leeson in the parish of Langton Matravers. Through his wife, Joan Wyot, he also acquired Smedmore (p. 162), but Barnston was in those days the more important house and it continued to be the Clavells' home until the time of James I. It was sold by Sir William Clavell in 1623 after he had moved to Smedmore. Since 1852 it has belonged to the Bonds of Creech Grange.

Woodsford Castle (4 miles E. of Dorchester). At a first glance there is little suggestion of a castle about this long, rambling house, with its creeper-covered walls and immense roof of thatch, standing above the River Frome. What one sees is a beautiful old farmhouse, larger than most farmhouses, it is true, and important enough to have been a manor place, but giving little indication of its original character. A walk round the building discloses unexpected features: a square tower with arrow-slits in it, a round turret with a loophole, a machicolation jutting out from the wall, proving that this was once a place of strength. Woodsford, however, was not a castle in the usual sense of the word, but, rather, a fortified house, built in the reign of Edward III. The Belets, who were the Norman and early Plantagenet lords of the manor, probably made little defensive use of the site, the only importance of which was its proximity to the ford across the river. Towards the end of the thirteenth century the name of de Whitfield appears in connection with the place, and in 1337 William de Whitefeld was given licence to crenellate his manor house of 'Wyrdesford,' as Woodsford was then spelt. It has usually been assumed that the castle was built by Sir Guy de Bryan, to whom Sir John Whitfield granted the manor in 1368. But the entry in the Patent Rolls indicates that it was begun, if not completed, thirty years earlier; moreover, the date agrees perfectly with the architectural features that remain. The fame attaching to Guy de Bryan for the distinguished part he played in the French Wars makes it tempting to attribute the building of the castle to him; but with his great estates in Devon and Wales he would hardly have spent much time here, and in 1389 he enfeoffed Robert Fitzpaine in 'Werdesford Belet' and his other Dorset manors.

The building, a long narrow range running north and south, has a square tower at its north-east angle. There were two other towers on its eastern face, one in the centre and one at the south-east angle, traces of them remaining in the broken wall surface and blocked doorways. The west side of the house (pl. 38) must be imagined

38. WOODSFORD CASTLE. Licence to crenellate his manor house of 'Wyrdesford' was granted to William de Whitefeld in 1337. The immense expanse of thatched roof has disguised the fact that Woodsford was once a fortified house.

39 and 40. WOODSFORD CASTLE

(*Above*) Looking along the west side from the south; (*below*) the north end and stair
turret at the north-west angle of the hall.

as looking into a court, enclosed with walls and probably having towers at the outer angles. A fortified gatehouse would have spanned the approach from the road. There were, no doubt, other buildings, possibly of timber, within the walled enclosure, but the part which survives must always have been the main building. As at Cranborne, the dwelling-rooms were placed at first-floor level. On the ground floor there is a series of chambers with vaulted roofs of segmental form, one of which has an enormous fireplace arch and is still used as the kitchen. The modern entrance is up a straight flight of stairs in the northern section of the west wall, a considerable length of which has been rebuilt. Farther south on this side an original newel stair-case remains, enclosed in a projecting turret with stone roof and rounded end. A line of corbels between the kitchen doorway and the turret suggests that there was a covered walk outside this section of the wall.

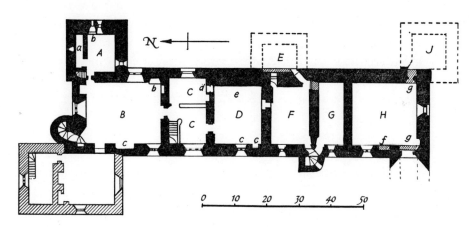

WOODSFORD CASTLE

Plan of rooms at first-floor level. A, North-east tower; B, Hall; CC, Chapel; D, Solar (Kitchen below); E, Site of intermediate tower; F, 'Guard Room'; G, Ante-chamber; H, South hall; J, Site of south-east tower. a, Garderobe; bb, Lavabos with drains; cc, Modern fireplaces; d, Piscina; e, Chimney-breast of kitchen; f, Ancient fireplace; gg, Blocked doorways.

Beginning at the north end, the first room of the upper floor was the hall, lighted by square-headed windows in its north and east walls. The mullion and transom of the north window have been restored, but the moulded jambs and label and the traceried head are original. At the north-west corner of the room a doorway gives access to a newel stair in the round turret which projects from the north wall (pl. 40); originally this will have led up to the parapet walk, the level of which is prob-ably indicated by the large corbel standing out from the wall face. Near the south-east corner of the room there is a recess with a long shallow basin and drain. The first-floor room in the north-east tower is entered by a doorway in the east wall. Here are two splayed windows with cusped heads and in the east wall another lavabo with segmental head and moulded sill in almost perfect preservation. On the north side of the tower, divided by a parti-wall, there is a garderobe and shoot; west of this, another newel stair in the thickness of the wall leads to an upper floor. The towers must have risen some distance above the parapet level of the main build-ing, the walls of which were raised when it received its roof of thatch. To the south of the 'King's Hall' was the chapel. It was lighted by an east window of considerable size, now blocked up, and has in its south wall a fourteenth-century piscina with cusped ogee head, shelf and drain. The adjoining room, called the 'Queen's Room,' is over the kitchen. The room beyond gave access to the tower projecting from the east front and is known as the 'Guard Chamber'; at its south-west corner is the stair turret already mentioned. Beyond again is another, narrow room, but the remaining southern portion of the range has been much altered and has lost its original floor levels. Here in the west wall are the remains of a fireplace and south of it a four-centred archway (pl. 39). At this corner there are fragments of a staircase, which possibly communicated with the gatehouse range.

The conversion of the building into a farmhouse during the eighteenth century has obscured many features. An extra storey was formed below the roof and a square wing was built at the north-west angle, partly, perhaps, on old foundations but with a greater projection to the north. Beneath this wing there is a well. The break in the roof is deceptive; there is no corresponding break in the masonry of the walls, and the gable end may have been built up at the time of the eighteenth-century alterations; as the southern part of the range was left for storage purposes, it seems to have been roofed at a lower level in order to save the trouble of building up the walls to their full height. A puzzling feature is a tall stone panel high up on the north wall of the tower; it has been suggested that it was used for a cresset to light wayfarers seeking the ford across the river, but this explanation is anything but convincing.

After the death of Sir Guy de Bryan in 1391 Woodsford descended by heiresses to James Butler, Earl of Ormonde and Wiltshire, who was executed after the battle of Towton. On the same occasion a knighthood was bestowed on his wife's cousin, Sir Humphry Stafford of Hooke, and the manor seems to have been conferred on him. Eight years later he incurred the same fate as Butler, being arrested and be-headed at Bridgwater for deserting the Yorkist cause, although only three months previously he had been created Earl of Devon. His three cousins were his co-heiresses, one of whom, Alianor, by marrying Thomas Strangways, brought Woodsford to his family. From him it has descended as part of the Strangways estates to the present Earl of Ilchester. When *The Survey of Dorset* was written, about 1630, the castle was already 'allmost ruinated.' The writer mentions a local tradition that 'it was besieged and beaten down with Ordnance,' the villagers pointing out a spot called Gunhill, 'where they sawe the Ordnance planted.' There is no record of any such siege, but the story might have been a tradition of an assault on the castle during the Wars of the Roses. The building was restored about 1850 under the direction of John Hicks. For some years before the Second World War the house was occupied by the late Mr Ralph Bond of Tyneham.

Winterborne Clenston (4 miles S.W. of Blandford). Dorset, like Wiltshire, possesses a number of chalk streams that flow only in the winter, and two of them have passed on their names to a string of villages threaded along their courses. The northern Winterborne, rising in the heights about Bulbarrow, makes its way down to join the Stour at Sturminster Marshall, and in its leisurely progress baptises nine little hamlets. Houghton, Stickland, Clenston, goes the succession, Whatcombe, Whitchurch, Kingston, Anderson, Tomson and Zelstone. Clenston is actually the diminished survivor of three hamlets, two of which, Winterbornes Philipston and Nicholaston, have disappeared altogether.

As you enter the upper part of the valley from Whitchurch the road runs for nearly a mile beside Whatcombe Park before the downs on either side become bare of trees; then the old group of farm buildings, which was Clenston's manor house, appears on the right of the road, a great stone and flint barn coming first into sight. This barn is one of the finest examples in the county. It is of six bays, with great porches on either side, projecting like transepts, and within possesses a remarkable hammer-beam roof, the timbers of which its builders took the trouble to mould as though it were the roof of a church.[1] The little manor house stands father back, behind the stream that flows in front of it, and is built in the same manner with alternating bands of stone and flint (pl. 42). The plan of the house, if the later extension north of the gable coping be ignored, is an inverted T, in which the cross-stroke (the main part) is longer than the upright (the wing going back behind). Projecting from the centre is a most unusual form of staircase turret with its two outside angles cut off to give a half-octagon plan, but in the upper stage the splays are corbelled out by a series of moulded stone courses to support an overhanging gable (pl. 41). The object of this ingenious but top-heavy arrangement was to give headroom to the stair, a stone newel which serves the attic as well as the first-floor rooms. An eighteenth-century engraving shows that there was a similar fea-

---

[1] It has been suggested that the moulded roof timbers were brought from one of the domestic buildings of Milton Abbey after the Dissolution.

ture on the south front of Wolfeton, and at Bridport an early sixteenth-century house in the High Street, now used as the town Museum, has a projecting porch with a gable corbelled out in the same way.

The earliest surviving windows are of Tudor form, but the shell of the main portion of the house is probably at least as old as the fifteenth century, for in the attic a fine arch-braced open timber roof runs from end to end of it. It would appear that this was originally a great hall open to the roof and that it was divided horizontally in Tudor days. A similar rearrangement must have taken place to that found at Barnston, a heavy ceiling of finely moulded timbers being introduced to take the floor above. The staircase turret was probably added at the same time and carried up a second storey to give access by way of the attic to the upper room in the wing behind, which, owing to the rise of the ground, is built at a higher level. At the south end of the east side of the house a two-storey bay was thrown out, again recalling that at Barnston, and showing that the Tudor hall was at this end. The oak ceiling runs unbroken the full length of the old part of the building, but a partition was probably made then, as now, to the left of the entrance passage. The south portion has been divided into two rooms in recent times. About 1600 further changes were made. The lights of the ground-floor windows were enlarged; the oak ceiling was decorated with plasterwork panels in the spaces between the beams, and leaf ornaments and bosses were applied at the points of intersection; on the first floor the northern of the two rooms was lined with wainscoting. There are also preserved fragments of rich plasterwork, of an intricate foliated pattern, which probably decorated the other first-floor room. An interesting feature at the end of the first-floor passage between the two rooms is a wall recess with a stone socket for a candle.

Clenston is remarkable in having passed in uninterrupted ownership from its earliest known possessors, the de Winterbornes, who held it as far back as 1230. From them it came by heiresses to the Heryngs and the de la Lyndes, John de la Lynde obtaining it through his wife in 1456. An ancestor of the de la Lyndes, who was bailiff of Blackmore Vale in the time of Henry III, was responsible for slaying 'the beautiful and goodly white hart,' of which a local story is told. The King came upon a white stag when hunting in Blackmore and spared it for its comeliness. The bailiff, encountering it later, gave chase and after an exciting hunt slew his quarry beside the King's Stag Bridge. His exploit, the story goes, so enraged the King that he laid a tax on the Vale, which came to be called 'the White Hart Silver.' In later days the de la Lyndes bore as their arms three harts' heads, and it is a curious coincidence that Hartley was the name of their earlier home in the Vale. It was probably Sir Thomas de la Lynde (died 1532) who carried out the Tudor

41. WINTERBORNE CLENSTON

The gabled staircase turret projecting from the west front, early sixteenth century.

42. WINTERBORNE CLENSTON
The manor house from the west.

43. PURSE CAUNDLE
The long south front of the manor house.

alterations to the house. On the death of his son the property passed to the Mortons of Milborne St. Andrew and from them to the Pleydells, who in the middle of the eighteenth century moved from Milborne to Whatcombe (p. 163), just below Clenston. While the Mortons' home at Milborne has gone, this older manor house of the de la Lyndes still survives. The present owner is Mrs Pleydell-Railston. In the 1861 edition of Hutchins' *History* a part of it is said to have been pulled down 'several years since,' but what portion is not stated.

Purse Caundle (4 miles E. of Sherborne). Of the four Caundle parishes, which lie together in the Blackmore Vale, Purse Caundle is the most northerly and is bounded on three sides by Somerset. A lane going southward from the main Sherborne–Shaftesbury road takes you between meadows and orchards to this quiet village whose old grey manor house stands on your right as you enter. One wing, with roses climbing up its walls, protrudes its buttresses into the street itself, and from its gable end hangs out a mediaeval oriel like a lantern to light passers-by. With its steep, stone-slated roofs, its many gables and mullioned windows, it is as picturesque a building as one can find. Seen from the meadow across the way (pl. 44), when the projecting wing and gables flatten out, the main front stretches a considerable distance along the line of the street, so that one is astonished to find, on entering the garden to the south, another, still longer front, extending back at right angles to the west (pl. 43). This second front, beautifully clothed with magnolias, clematis and ceanothus, and broken by three short wings, spreads out so far that from a photograph it might easily be taken to belong to another building. Indeed, the house rambles so delightfully and inconsequently that without a plan to help one is lost.

Let it be said, then, that the building is a fifteenth-century manor house, built probably during the reign of Edward IV. Its owners at that time were a family of the name of Long, whose arms are to be seen in a window of the church. The mediaeval house consisted of the great hall, which runs parallel with the street; a parlour and some other rooms at its north end; and, to the south of the hall, the wing projecting eastward, which contains in its upper story the great chamber with the oriel overhanging the road (pl. 45). Not many years later, perhaps in the time of Henry VII or VIII, a short addition was thrown out from the south end of this wing along the line of the street, leaving undisturbed the old corner buttress from which the extension begins. This addition (a wing added to a wing) forms the easternmost of the three projections of the long, low south front. Originally this far-spreading range appears to have stopped short a little to the left of the middle projection. Its westward prolongation probably dates from the early seventeenth century. On this front all

the windows are now of the Elizabethan or Jacobean form with flat heads to the
lights and dripstones over them; but in the north wing earlier forms of window
remain with labels of fifteenth-century design. The oriel (pl. 32), which may be
compared with the well-known examples at South Wraxall and Great Chalfield
in Wiltshire, is a beautiful survival and remains in excellent preservation. Its lower
portion, corbelled out from the wall, is ornamented with panels in which are set
four shields that, no doubt, were intended to be carved. The lights are cusped, showing that the window is certainly pre-Tudor. A date about 1460–80 may be reasonably
assigned to it, and this also fits the barrel form of roof in the great chamber which
the window lights.

The hall (pl. 46), which is probably of the same date as the great chamber, is
entered at its south end through a screens passage, on the left of which are the
buttery and pantry doorways, disclosed in the years between the Wars. The fine
fifteenth-century roof is of the arch-braced collar-beam type, reinforced by tie-
beams and curved struts serving as queen-posts; it has a band of quatrefoils running
above the wall-plate. It would appear that the east side of the hall was remodelled
in the first half of Queen Elizabeth's reign, since the initials of William Hanham
(died 1576) appear over the doorway to the right of the fireplace. The square bay
lighting the dais, with a room over it, as at Bingham's Melcombe, was added at
this period, and the entrance porch to the south of it seems to have been enlarged
and rebuilt at the same time. The two gable-ends so formed make a continuous front
to the street and are faced with dressed ashlar. North of the hall, behind the dais,
is a little parlour with Elizabethan or Jacobean wainscoting; and west of this room a
stout oak staircase of Charles II date gives access to the floor above. Formerly there
was a stone staircase leading from the hall to the south range; about half-way up
there is said to have been a well of water, supposedly inhabited by a fairy. The staircase was destroyed in the course of the last century, tradition says because the
family disliked meeting the apparition as they went to bed.

The owners of Purse Caundle in Plantagenet days were the Aleyns, who held it
by serjeanty 'of tending and lodging the King's sick or injured dogs for his Lord the
King's keeping when his Lord the King courses wild beasts in Blackmore,' and also
'of maintaining the fences of the park of Gillingham by rendering service annually
of 1d.' So John Aleyn was found to hold land here at his death in 1293. Purse Caundle
may be said to have been a royal dog hospital. Tradition makes it also a hunting
lodge of King John's; but, although that monarch found Dorset to his liking, there
is no record among his itineraries of his staying in the place. It is with Henry III
that Blackmore is associated over the story of the white hart, which has been mentioned in the account of Clenston. It is possible that John Aleyn may have tended

44. PURSE CAUNDLE

A fifteenth-century manor house with later additions. The east front from the meadow on the opposite side of the village street.

46. PURSE CAUNDLE

The fifteenth-century hall, looking south to the screen.

45. PURSE CAUNBLE

The south-east wing with its oriel overhanging the street.

Henry's hounds, since the first mention of him is in 1269, when his eldest son, Roger, was born. The child's uncle, the rector, recorded in his missal the date of the christening, and others remembered afterwards, when proof was required of the boy's coming of age, how bad the roads had been and how someone had fallen off his horse and broken his leg. In the reign of Henry VI the heiress of the Aleyns sold their property here to Richard Lang or Long, whose son it may have been who built the present house. The Longs were succeeded in the reign of Henry VIII by Hanhams, who were an elder branch of the family still seated at Deans Court, Wimborne. Their loyalty to the King lost them the estate during the Civil War, after which it was purchased from the Commonwealth Commissioners by John Hoskins. In the hall there hangs a portrait of Peter Mews, who was Bishop of Winchester from 1684 to 1706; he was born at Purse Caundle in 1618. Space does not allow of more detailed description of this beautiful old house and its rooms, scarcely two of which are on the same level, or of the gardens, cut in two by a little stream flowing through them, and the bowling green, overlooked by the long south front. Lady Victoria Herbert, who made the Manor House such a charming home, died in 1957. The present owner is Mr Oliver Barnes.

Childhay, a farmhouse in the parish of Broadwindsor, lying down in the valley of the Axe under Blackdown Hill, and within a few hundred yards of the Somerset border, was once the seat of the de Crewkernes, who, marrying into the de Childhay family in the time of Edward III, held it for nearly three centuries. On the west side of the house is a doorway with pointed arch, perhaps of fourteenth-century date, but the most interesting feature is the late fifteenth-century battlemented porch on the east front with its grotesque carvings and four-centred doorway (pl. 33). The building has been much altered, but the shell is largely mediaeval, including probably the wing to the right of the porch into which later windows have been inserted. The ground-floor room to the south of the screens passage, occupying the position of the mediaeval hall, has some early eighteenth-century painted panels over its fireplace; but the paintings—a landscape and two animals, apparently lions—are so thickly coated with varnish as to be scarcely visible. In the kitchen there is an original fireplace and a ceiling with the timbers exposed. Going up from the screens passage is a staircase with Jacobean balusters. In the first-floor room of the north wing is an open fireplace of Ham Hill stone. The last of the Crewkernes left as his heir a daughter, who married Sir Arthur Champernowne of Modbury, co. Devon. He was a friend of Richard Carew, the Cornish historian, and 'skilled in many ingenious arts, particularly architecture.' For a second husband his widow took Henry Drake, with whom, according to *The Survey of Dorset*, she lived on at Childhay as a tenant after having sold the property to the Bragges of Thorncombe and Sadborow. Childhay was already a farm in Hutchins' time.

Parnham ($\frac{1}{2}$ mile S. of Beaminster). From the circle of hills which encloses Beaminster the river Brit draws its waters for its short run of ten miles to the sea at Bridport. By the time it has reached Parnham it is already a fair-sized stream, flowing through a green and grandly timbered park which for a mile or more fills the valley. The fine Tudor house, for three centuries the home of the 'right antient and worshipfull family of Strodes,' is thus yet another of the many Dorset houses that lie low in the shelter of hills and trees. Its beautifully weathered stone front, plentifully clothed with flowering climbers, can be seen, at the end of a short drive, from the Bridport road soon after leaving Beaminster.

The house has suffered much, though not from neglect: the blurring of its outline is due to an excessive attention from its owners in the last 150 years. Round about 1810 John Nash was commissioned to carry out repairs and 'improvements,' which have resulted in a superstratum of Gothic Revival 'picturesqueness' overlying the Tudor work. The main front (pl. 47), is the least altered, but the copings and pinnacles of its gables are Nash inventions; the walls of Ham Hill stone, except at the back, where Nash added a dining-room on to the west side of the hall, are for the most part those of the Tudor house, although the south front was re-designed by Nash in the romantic style of his day (pl. 48). The plan included a great hall, entered from the porch through a screens passage, north of which were placed the kitchen and offices, according to the usual mediaeval arrangement. But the changes in houseplanning that came in with the Tudors are reflected in the limitation of the height of the hall, which has rooms over it, and in the striving after symmetry in the design of the front, which, though irregular in outline, achieves a certain balance. The porch (pl. 49) is made much more prominent than it is at Athelhampton, for instance; it is definitely a central feature, three storeys high and given a fine double-tiered oriel corbelled out on a rich series of mouldings, like those at Forde Abbey and Cerne Abbas. Between the upper and lower window there is a seventeenth-century cartouche carved with the quartered shield of Strode. As at Creech Grange, there is a square projection for a staircase at the side of the porch, and the left-hand wing ends, as there, in a two-storey bay finished with stone water-tabling.

Parnham came to the Strodes in the time of Henry VI and remained in their possession until 1764. Richard de Strode, who married Elizabeth Gerard, the Parnham heiress, was seated at East Hewstock, the neighbouring property; his family, once so famous in the West Country, had been associated with Dorset from as far back as the eleventh century and in all probability took its name from the Strode

47. PARNHAM
The entrance front.

48. PARNHAM
From the south-west. These two fronts with their battlements and pinnacles were designed by
John Nash about 1810.

49. PARNHAM

The entrance porch with its oriel, a beautiful piece of early Tudor stonework. The pinnacles
and coping of the gable are due to Nash.

a mile or two west of Parnham. In 1522 Robert Strode of Parnham married Elizabeth, the granddaughter of Sir William Hody, who had been Chief Baron of the Exchequer under Henry VII, and it may have been with the help of her money that he was able to rebuild his father's house some years later, after he had succeeded to the estate. He died in 1558. The hall, porch and greater part of the front are his work, but the north wing, altered about 1600, may have incorporated part of an earlier building. In Hutchins' time considerably more remained of the house and its surroundings than there is now. He mentions 'the school-house, the gatehouse, the wall about the inner court and the garden,' all of which he assigns to Robert's son and successor, John (died 1581): he also refers to 'the base court set up by Sir Robert Strode,' John's successor, and enumerates 'three orchards, outgardens and ponds,' comprising four acres. These facts he derived from a survey of the estate drawn up by Sir John Strode of Chantmarle (p. 97), who about 1628 succeeded his brother, Sir Robert, at Parnham. A great deal of litigation ensued, since his brother had married off his only daughter to a kinsman, Sir Richard Strode of Newnham, in return for £2,000, which he used to buy additional lands, and on the understanding that the property should go to their son. As matters turned out, they had no son, and Sir Robert went back on his word, altering the limitation and making his younger brother his heir. Sir John, a lawyer by profession, succeeded in maintaining his claim and died in possession, an old man of 81. But his widow was destined to a violent end. At the time when Cromwell 'had totally routed the enemy in the West,' to quote Sir Richard's version of the affair, 'one of his soldiers with his sword casually killed the said Sir John's wife in the same place Parnaham which she so unlawfully kept,' while her son 'was taken prisoner for the Parliament for his malignancy.' But Sir Richard failed to win his case, even with the party that he supported in power, and eventually Sir John's son was released and allowed his title after paying a composition for the sequestrated estate.

In 1764, when the male line of Sir John became extinct on the death of Thomas Strode, Parnham passed to Sir John Oglander, of Nunwell, in the Isle of Wight. For a time the place was deserted, and it was during this period that the gatehouse and other features mentioned by Hutchins disappeared. But at the beginning of last century Sir William Oglander made it once again a residence with the help of Nash. No doubt, they felt the romantic appeal of the house and were anxious to eliminate the Georgian features which had been introduced in the first half of the eighteenth century. Now, in its turn, nearly all Nash's work, so far as the interior is concerned, has been suppressed.

In 1896, after the death of the last of the Oglanders, Parnham was sold for the first time. The purchaser was Mr Vincent Robinson, during whose ownership the house became a kind of private museum for his immense collection of European furniture and woodwork. He and his successor, Dr Hans Sauer, who had Parnham from 1911 to 1914, made so many alterations that little original work in the interior has been left undisturbed beyond the fine armorial glass in the hall. But a curious story of exile and home-coming attaches to the hall door and the carved oak chimney-beam now placed above the hall fireplace. These were found by Mr Robinson in a house near Taunton, and he afterwards learned that they had actually come from Parnham, having been turned out at the time of the Nash alterations. Mr Robinson placed the fifteenth-century chimney-beam in the low parlour in the north wing; but it was moved by Dr Sauer, who altered the original character of this room by throwing the adjoining room into it. The rich early Tudor panelling and plasterwork which now have their place there came from a West Country house and were introduced by Dr Sauer. He, too, was responsible for the present lay-out of the terrace, the formal gardens, and their pavilions, the details of which are based on those at Montacute. After the First World War there was a period when Parnham was turned into a country club, but it again became a private residence in 1930, when it was bought by Mr Edward Bullivant. Further alterations were then made in the interior. Several rooms have seventeenth-century panelling either imported or re-set. The screen in the hall is composed of old woodwork brought from elsewhere. The sixteenth-century painted glass shields in the hall display the arms of various Dorset and Devon families. The quartered shield of Strode is dated 1559.

Parnham was acquired in 1955 by the National Association for Mental Health as a residential home for old ladies.

Wolfeton House (1 mile N.W. of Dorchester). The ancient seat of the Trenchards stands in the fields east of the Dorchester–Sherborne road, not far from the point where the Frome is joined by its tributary, the Cerne. Charminster is Wolfeton's parish church, and in it rest many generations of its former owners, who figure so largely in the Dorset of Tudor and Stuart days. Thomas Hardy describes the place in his *Group of Noble Dames* as 'an ivied manor house, flanked by battlemented towers, more than usually distinguished by the size of its mullioned windows.' Of recent years the ivy has been removed to reveal once again the beauty of the stonework. Though much altered and reduced in size, the house is still a beautiful and romantic building, and suggests vividly the proud rivalry that must have existed between the great Dorset families of the sixteenth century—Trenchards and Turbervilles, Horseys and Martyns.

The most famous event associated with Wolfeton was the visit paid in January,

50. WOLFETON HOUSE

For centuries the home of the Trenchards. The south front.

51. WOLFETON HOUSE

The east side of the gatehouse with its two round towers.

52. WOLFETON HOUSE

Early Tudor windows with carved labels in the south front.

53. WOLFETON HOUSE

Jacobean carved chimney-piece in the drawing-room. Early Tudor carvings of the Works of
the Months and the Signs of the Zodiac have been inserted round the fireplace.

54.   ATHELHAMPTON

Formerly the home of the Martyns. The entrance front and west wing.

1506, by the Archduke Philip of Austria and his Spanish wife, Joanna, the daughter and heiress of Ferdinand of Castile and Isabella of Aragon. The pair were on their way from the Netherlands to claim the throne of Castile, when they were caught by a storm in the Channel and forced to put in at Weymouth. Sir Thomas Trenchard, when he heard the news, rode down to welcome them and brought them back to his house at Wolfeton. Converse proved difficult, however, and so to help him out Sir Thomas sent for his kinsman, John Russell, of Berwick, near Bridport, who had travelled abroad and could act as interpreter. When, a few days later, the Archduke and his wife were invited to Windsor, Russell accompanied them, and his fine bearing and accomplishments won him a place at Court. This episode was not only the stepping-stone to a career that was destined to bring him great wealth, high office and eventually an earldom, but proved to be the foundation of all the subsequent fortunes of the ducal house of Bedford. There used to hang at Wolfeton two portrait medallions of Philip and Joanna, which they are said to have given their host as souvenirs, together with two Chinese porcelain bowls, possibly the earliest to have reached England. The portraits and the bowls are now in the possession of the Lanes of Bloxworth and Poxwell, the present representatives of the Dorset Trenchards.

Wolfeton came to the Trenchards in 1480 on the death of John Mohun, of Hammoon or Ham-mohun (p. 78), who had married an heiress of the Jourdains, its earlier owners. The Trenchards were of Hordle, near Lymington, and had long held lands in the Isle of Wight. As John Mohun had no son, Wolfeton passed through his daughter, Christian, to her son, John Trenchard, who died in 1495. He was succeeded by his son, the future Sir Thomas Trenchard, a boy of 16 at the time, who lived until 1550, serving twice as Sheriff of the county and for many years as a Commissioner of the Peace. In 1557 his great-grandson, George, who was knighted by Queen Elizabeth, entered on an even longer reign, which continued until 1630. He was Governor of Sandesfoot Castle, and at the time of the Armada was ordered to make an inventory of the stores in a Spanish ship that had been brought in to Portland. From the wills of John Trenchard and Sir Thomas it is evident that much of their wealth came from extensive sheep-farming.

Between them Sir Thomas and Sir George were responsible for the ancient parts of the house that remain, with the possible exception of the two round towers of the gatehouse (pl. 51). Eighteenth-century descriptions of Wolfeton show that the buildings were ranged round a courtyard, which was entered from the east through the gatehouse. On the north side of the court there was a chapel, which was pulled down in the first half of the eighteenth century. The west range, as shown in an old drawing in the house, was of three storeys with an arched doorway. This part of the building, which has also disappeared, may have contained pre-Tudor work; certainly there must have been a house on the site long before the days of the Trenchards, and it was probably protected by a moat. Now, besides the gate-house, only the south range survives; it originally extended farther east, connecting with the south-west corner of the gatehouse, as the engraving published in the first edition of Hutchins' *History* (1774) shows, but this end was pulled down in 1822. A bowling-green or pleasaunce lay in front of the south range, bounded by battle-mented walls, of which the western one remains.

As the two round towers of the gatehouse are of unequal size and have plinth mouldings of simpler section than those of the structure connecting them, it may be inferred that they were incorporated in it, having been built at an earlier date and perhaps left unfinished. They have arrow-slits commanding the entrance. In a recessed panel high up on a chimney-breast at the north end of the gatehouse there is an inscription which reads: '*Hoc opus constructum est anno domini MDXXXIIII.*' Though not in its original position, it is valuable in giving a definite date for Sir Thomas Trenchard's work. His initial, both singly and joined by a love-knot to that of his wife, Elizabeth, daughter of Henry Strangways, is to be seen on the west face of the gatehouse, where they occur as ornaments to the label of the four-centred arch. The T on two of the shields is a curious Gothic capital which has the same form when looked at upside down; it also occurs on the tower of Charminster church, which Sir Thomas Trenchard built. On the south side of the entry there is a spiral stair with steps of solid oak, each cut in a single piece so that their rounded ends take the place of a newel. The room over the gateway contained until recently a Jacobean stone fireplace flanked by Ionic pilasters.

The south range (pl. 50) consists of three portions. The east end is of early Tudor date, built by Sir Thomas Trenchard. The portion to the west of the little projecting turret, with the two tiers of large mullioned windows, was built or re-built by Sir George Trenchard about 1600. At the west end there is a lower range of offices dating from the seventeenth century, or perhaps earlier, but it has been modernised. The three Tudor windows at the east end of the south front are remarkable for their enrichments (pl. 52). The labels are ornamented with foliage, which in the upper window takes the form of a vine trail, and they terminate in carved figures; there is an inner enrichment of ribbon form, which is carried down the jambs; the spandrels of each arched light are carved, and the mullions are stopped with base mouldings.[1] The lower windows show signs of disturbance and the sill of one of them has been

[1] It has been suggested that Sir Thomas Trenchard may have employed a French mason, perhaps an *immigré*. Such ornamentation has parallels in early sixteenth-century domestic building in the north of France.

55. ATHELHAMPTON
The south front, restored by Mr A. C. de Lafontaine.

56. ATHELHAMPTON
The courtyard from the south, showing the gatehouse (*left*) removed in 1862. Lithograph
from Nash's *Mansions of England in the Olden Time*.

57. ATHELHAMPTON

The north side of the house and the round dovecote.

58. ATHELHAMPTON

Late fifteenth-century fireplace in the State Bedroom.

55. ATHELHAMPTON

The south front, restored by Mr A. C. de Lafontaine.

56. ATHELHAMPTON

The courtyard from the south, showing the gatehouse (*left*) removed in 1862. Lithograph
from Nash's *Mansions of England in the Olden Time*.

57. ATHELHAMPTON

The north side of the house and the round dovecote.

58. ATHELHAMPTON

Late fifteenth-century fireplace in the State Bedroom.

dropped. From the old descriptions of the house printed in the later editions of Hutchins it is clear that the hall occupied this part of the building and had windows facing south and east; it must have had a flat ceiling, for there was a long parlour over it. A drawing made by Mrs Rachel Gurney in 1811, before the range was curtailed, shows a short projecting wing at the south-east angle, set askew. The inscribed panel with the date 1534 was originally on this wing. The little projecting turret adjoining the Elizabethan portion of the range was a garderobe; its conical top is capped by a finial in the form of a seated figure playing some musical instrument. The Elizabethan building is of fine ashlar masonry, weathered to a lovely silvery tone. Its six great windows, which give such distinction to the front, have their mullions neatly stopped with base mouldings—a refinement that is also to be seen in the old manor house at Kingston Maurward. The two centre windows have been re-set; in the engraving in the first edition of Hutchins' *History* a bay window of half-octagon form is shown rising the height of both storeys, but this was removed in 1798 and the wall built up flush.

In this portion of the house there was a fine gallery, or great chamber, on the first floor, approached by a staircase on the north side and entered through a Renaissance doorway of carved stone, still *in situ* (pl. 8). It has been cut up into three separate rooms, in one of which is a stone chimney-piece in two tiers, flanked by pairs of fluted columns (pl. 14). As noted in the Introduction (p. 24), there are close parallels to it in two Somerset houses, Montacute and Wayford Manor. The three little reclining ladies carved on it were intended to typify Faith, Hope and Charity. The same trio, two seated and one reclining, occur on the chimney-piece in the great chamber at Herringston. That room is notable for its elaborately decorated barrel ceiling, and there was formerly a similar one in this gallery at Wolfeton, portions of which are believed to remain above the modern flat ceilings. The same craftsmen probably worked at both houses. There was much richly carved woodwork in this room, some of which is now in the two drawing-rooms below.

The larger of these drawing-rooms is entered through a passage, from which the early Tudor hall originally opened eastward. Carved woodwork and panelling of different dates are now assembled here. The passage and both drawing-rooms retain their original ceilings, which are ornamented with scrolling foliage, masks, grotesques and little reliefs of animals—sheep, horses, oxen, stags and unicorns. The larger drawing-room is entered through a doorway framed by remarkably elaborate woodwork, with flanking Corinthian columns; above it are two caryatids of a king and queen. A great carved wood chimney-piece (pl. 53), rising the full height of the room, is framed by another pair of Corinthian columns, within which two tiers of caryatid figures are prominently displayed. The three in the upper stage are male figures, which from their dress appear to represent the three degrees of knight, squire and serving-man; in the panels between them are symbolic figures of Hope and Justice. Filling part of the chimney opening are a series of early Tudor carved panels which have been inserted. These, though mutilated and arranged in no order, form part of a remarkably interesting set of carvings of the twelve Signs of the Zodiac and the Works of the Months; others from the series have been fitted above the two doorways in the entrance passage. In the second edition of Hutchins' *History* they are said to have been in a room adjoining the hall called 'Mr Trenchard's smoking parlour,' where they formed a continuous frieze round the top of the wainscoting. In the inner drawing-room there is a plaster overmantel (pl. 15) to which there is another close parallel at Montacute; the cartouche in the middle has a naïve representation of the contest of the three goddesses with Paris awarding the apple. The woodwork below it, on which the date 1652 occurs, was not originally in this position. In common with that framing the doorway to the right of it and some in the entrance passage incorporating twisted columns, it seems to have come from the gallery on the floor above, the decoration of which was probably left incomplete by Sir George Trenchard and finished by his son and successor, the second Sir Thomas, who inherited in 1630 and died in 1657.

It is melancholy to think how much the house has lost since the end of the eighteenth century. In the later editions of Hutchins a detailed account is given of the splendid armorial glass, which Dr Pococke in 1754 was able to see in almost every room in the building. Besides the Trenchard alliances which it recorded, it included shields of five abbeys—Bindon, Cerne, Milton, Sherborne and Glastonbury. The glass was removed by the last of the Trenchards to own Wolfeton and taken to their other house at Lytchet Matravers, but was packed so badly that much of it was broken in transit. Then followed the demolition of the west range and the east end of the house. The place was sold and remained in a forlorn state until bought in 1862 by Dr W. H. P. Weston. He heightened the south-east tower, originally a staircase turret with a gable,[1] and gave it its battlements, built one at the north-east corner to match it, linking it with a stone wall and passage to the gatehouse; he also added a Gothic porch on the north side in front of the entrance doorway. In the interior the wide stone staircase seems to owe its present character to him; unfortunately, in rearranging the woodwork collected from various parts of the house, he made a confusing pastiche of different dates so that it is difficult to

---

[1] The original appearance of this turret can be seen in the engraving of Wolfeton in the first edition of Hutchins' *History*. It was of a similar character to the gabled turret on the front of the manor house at Winterborne Clenston (pl. 41).

be certain how much is in its original position. In 1874 the house was bought by Mr Wynne Alfred Bankes, of the Kingston Lacy family, whose granddaughter, Countess Zamoyska, now owns it. Since the Second World War it has been divided into three residences.

Various stories are told of Wolfeton. The most gruesome is the experience recorded of a Justice who had been invited to dine by the owners. 'The company had no sooner sat down than his lordship, greatly to the surprise of everyone present, ordered his carriage and abruptly left the house. He told the Marshal on the way to Dorchester that he had seen standing behind Lady Trenchard's chair a figure of her ladyship with her throat cut and her head under her arm. Before the carriage reached Dorchester a mounted passenger overtook it with the news that Lady Trenchard had committed suicide.' There is also a strange anecdote of Aubrey's. Over the great chimney-piece of the hall there were carved the figures of fourteen English kings. On November 3, 1640, while the family and a number of guests were dining, the sceptre fell from the hand of Charles I. Aubrey notes that this was the day on which the Long Parliament began to sit.

Athelhampton (1 mile E. of Puddletown). As you leave Puddletown on the Wareham road, Athelhampton is to be found on your left, screened by trees and standing on low-lying land near the stream, which half encircles it. Like so many other Dorset manor houses, it is only a fragment of what it was in the past, but the two surviving early Tudor ranges, not quite at right angles to each other, compose into a picture of extraordinary charm that has made its appeal ever since topo- graphical artists in search of picturesque architecture began to explore the county. The richly detailed stonework has taken on lovely overtones through the weathering of time, so that the visual appeal cannot be separated from the romantic associations conjured up. Both house and gardens are in actuality a studied re-creation of the past after a long period of neglect.

Both without and within the house there are still plentiful reminders, in heraldic carvings and armorial glass, of its builders, the Martyns, who lie a mile off in their own chapel in Puddletown church. They came to Athelhampton from Waterston (p. 89) in the time of Edward III and possessed it until near the close of the sixteenth century. In its name the place must commemorate some Saxon noble, whom Hutchins liked to think was the Athelhelm who in 837 lost his life fighting against the Danes at Portland; but of its early owners nothing is recorded and its earliest known lords were de Loundres and de Pydeles, from whom the manor came to the Martyns by marriage. The family claimed a Norman ancestor in the person of Martin of Tours, who came over with the Conqueror and whose descendants flourished in Devon and Pembrokeshire. A fine of King John's reign shows that a William Martyn was at that time lord of the castle of *Pidela*, possibly the earlier home of the family at Waterston. The most distinguished member of the Athelhampton line was Sir William Martyn, who was Lord Mayor of London in 1493 and held the lucrative office of Collector and Controller of the Tonnage and Poundage in the City. He died in 1504, and was followed by his son, Christopher (died 1525). The last of the family was Christopher's great-grandson, Nicholas

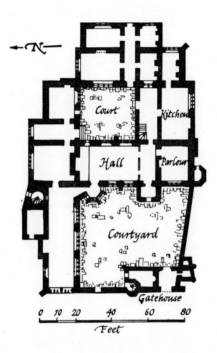

ATHELHAMPTON

Plan of the house before the removal of the gatehouse and demolition of the buildings east of the hall.

Based on a plan drawn by Buckler in 1828.

Martyn, on whose death in 1596 the property was divided between his four daughters. A description of the Martyn tombs in Puddletown church is given in Prideaux's *Some Dorset Manor Houses*.

The earliest surviving portion of the house is the embattled range lying north and south (pl. 54) and containing the great hall with its fine oriel and porch, built by Sir William Martyn, probably towards the end of the fifteenth century. The wing running out westward from the north end of the hall range and the demolished gatehouse were probably somewhat later additions, forming an outer court to what must originally have been a quadrangular house. Outside the gatehouse there was a large walled forecourt, on the south side of which stood the chapel. Of the inner quadrangle the north and east sides have disappeared, but their foundations are recorded in a plan made a hundred and thirty years ago by J. C. Buckler (British

Museum, Add. MS., 36,361). The hall, entered through the porch, which has a room over it, is 38 ft. long and 21 ft. wide, and is spanned by an open timber roof. The original screen has gone, but has been replaced by one, brought from an old house in Devon, which is remarkable for the length of its linenfold panels. The oriel, on the west side of the dais, is a beautiful piece of late Perpendicular work, its tall windows being divided externally by slender buttresses. The portion south of the porch was altered about the end of the sixteenth century, when a third storey under a gable was added, but the battlements are still there, embedded in the wall, and the staircase turret remains at the south-west angle. Of the south range (pl. 55), which now looks out on a walled expanse of lawn centring in a fountain pool, only part remained before Mr de Lafontaine reconstructed it. This formed the south side of the quadrangle and contained the kitchen and other offices. In the rebuilding the turret and gable on the left side of this front have been repeated to the right with happy effect.

Until 1862 a remarkable early Tudor gatehouse stood facing the porch on the west side of the outer courtyard. Its relation to the hall is shown by the coloured lithograph in Nash's *Mansions in the Olden Times* (pl. 56). At its north end it had octagonal angle shafts and finials similar to those of the west wing, and on its inner side, corbelled out over the archway, there was a finely moulded oriel, with a sculptured panel containing a shield quartering the Martyn arms with those of Kelway and bearing the initials R.M. and E.M. The Renaissance character of the carving links this with the sculptured panels of Bingham's Melcombe and Clifton Maybank; the initials date it between 1525 and 1550, the period of owner-ship of Robert Martyn, who married Elizabeth, daughter and heir of Sir John Kelway.

It was either at this time or a little later that the west wing was brought forward and rebuilt. That there was already a wing of some sort here is proved by the door-way giving access to it from the north side of the hall oriel (pl. 61). Garner and Stratton, in their *English Domestic Architecture of the Tudor Period*, ascribe the rebuild-ing of this wing to Nicholas, the last of the Martyns and the successor of Robert, on the ground of its similarity to Sandford Orcas (p. 75). 'The masonry details carried out in Portisham stone, with mellow-tinted Ham Hill for all dressed work, so closely coincide with those of Sandford Orcas Manor House, that there is little doubt that the same hands worked on both, and the similarity is even more marked in the diamond-shaped panels above the second-floor windows at Athelhampton and on the porch and gateway at Sandford Orcas, the section of the moulding and the modelling of the bosses of carving being so similar, and so unusual, that it is more than probable the same carvers executed both.' The probability is strengthened by the marriage connection between the owners of the two houses, Nicholas's sister Catherine having married Edward Knoyle of Sandford Orcas. The Martyn crest, a chained monkey,[1] which is carved over the outer doorway of the porch, reappears on the finials of the angle shafts of this wing.

After Sir Nicholas Martyn's death the Athelhampton property was divided equally among his four daughters, the eldest of whom married Henry Brune. The Brunes in the next fifty years acquired two of the other three shares, but the fourth remained with the Floyers, into which family the youngest of the four sisters had married. The partition of the property was so exact when it was made that not only was the estate divided into four parts but the house as well, and the Floyers continued to own a quarter of the house until 1848, when Athelhampton was bought by George Wood; this curious anomaly was then straightened out by means of a voluntary exchange. Meanwhile, a Brune heiress in 1661 had carried Athelhampton to Sir Ralph Bankes of Corfe Castle, who four years later sold it to Sir Robert Long of Draycot Cerne, Wiltshire. When bought by George Wood, it had descended through Sir James Tylney Long to the fifth Earl of Mornington.

George Wood has been severely criticised for pulling down the gatehouse and the old chapel and has even been accused of destroying the inner quadrangle, which had gone long before. The loss of the gatehouse is certainly most regrettable; but, in justice to him, it should be stated that it was sadly out of repair and darkened the windows of the house, and that he carefully preserved and re-erected the carved oriel in a little building[2] placed somewhat farther to the west. He also did much to repair the house, which had become very derelict, and was responsible for restoring the hall roof, retaining the unusual cusped design of the arched principals. But for his timely intervention Athelhampton might have become a complete wreck. The work of redemption was continued by Alfred Cart de Lafontaine after his purchase of the house in 1891. Stage by stage he restored the interior, introducing appropriate panelling and plaster ceilings and filling the rooms with old oak furniture. Some of the original heraldic glass recording the Martyn alliances remains in one of the east windows of the hall and in the rooms in the west wing; the glass in the other windows of the hall has been copied from the old. Between the hall and parlour is an ante-room, from which a newel stair ascends to the upper floors of the wing; this is partly of stone and partly of wood construction, resembling somewhat similar staircases at Sandford Orcas and in the gatehouse at Wolfeton. The long gallery,

---

[1] In heraldic language 'a martin sejant.' According to mediaeval legend, at the second naming of the beasts, when the Hare was called Wat and the Fox Reynard, the Monkey was named Martin. The motto of the Martyns was : 'He who looks at Martyn's ape, Martyn's ape shall look at him.'

[2] This was pulled down by Mr de Lafontaine, but the stones have been preserved.

59.
BINGHAM'S
MELCOMBE
The manor house
in its remote valley.

60.
BINGHAM'S
MELCOMBE
The bowling green
and ancient yew
hedge.

61. ATHELHAMPTON
The oriel in the hall, dating from Henry VII's reign.

62.
BINGHAM'S
MELCOMBE
The oriel in the two-
storey bay added on
the south side of the
hall about 1555.

63.
MELCOMBE
HORSEY
Early seventeenth-
century plaster ceil-
ing.

64. BINGHAM'S MELCOMBE

The south side of the hall range. The hydrangeas on the terrace are shown in Nash's lithograph about 1840.

which occupies the whole of the first floor of the wing, was reconstituted by Mr de Lafontaine. In the bed-chamber south of the hall is a late fifteenth-century fireplace in Ham Hill stone, carved with a series of quatrefoils, in three of which are shields, once no doubt painted (pl. 58); in the spaces below them appear the Martyn ape and the Faringdon unicorn—Sir William Martyn married a Faringdon as his first wife. The Elizabethan bed was at Montacute in Lord Curzon's time.

Mr de Lafontaine was responsible for the re-creation of the gardens, which were laid out for him by Mr Inigo Thomas. This was one of the most successful revivals of the old formal garden, divided by stone walls and yew hedges into a series of compartments, all united and composed into a coherent plan. The largest compartment is the south-west court with its pyramids of yew and its raised walls terminated by garden pavilions. Before the south front is the green court with its long pool set in the grass, and there is the rose court and the central 'corona,' a walled circle crowned with obelisks. North of the house a great expanse of grass stretches away to the bank of the little river Piddle, and here is an old circular dovecote (pl. 57), resembling those at Melplash and Bingham's Melcombe, and still possessing its revolving ladder.

Alfred Cart de Lafontaine died in 1944 and was buried at Athelhampton, but he had parted with the house in 1918. His successor, George Cockrane, built the north-east wing and recreated the solar at the north end of the hall. The present owner, Mr Robert V. Cooke, F.R.C.S., who acquired Athelhampton in 1957, has begun a careful restoration of the house and gardens.

Bingham's Melcombe. Lying in a far-away valley, ten miles from anywhere, Bingham's Melcombe is one of the loveliest, as it is also one of the oldest, of Dorset manor houses. Its 'combe' is a deep hollow carved out of the chalk uplands of mid-Dorset by a stream called the Dewlish (or sometimes the Devilish or Devil's) Brook, which runs southward down to Puddletown. Sheltered by the downs (pl. 59) and hidden among trees—great elms, sycamores and planes planted two hundred years ago—the manor house has little more than the church to keep it company, for the village has almost entirely disappeared.

The Binghams who gave this Melcombe their name were owners of the manor for over six hundred years. Early in the thirteenth century Robert Bingham married Lucy, the heiress of Sir Robert Turberville, to whose family the place had belonged from the time of Stephen or earlier. Robert was the second son of Sir Ralph Bingham of Sutton Bingham in Somerset; one of his uncles was Bishop of Salisbury from 1229 to 1246. By the end of the fifteenth century the family held lands in several

Dorset parishes; but none of them appears to have distinguished himself greatly
until Sir Richard Bingham made his name as a soldier of fortune in the days of
Queen Elizabeth. The long list of his military services in France, Scotland, the
Netherlands, under the Venetians at Lepanto and in Crete, and finally for his Queen
in Ireland, is recorded on his monument in Westminster Abbey. He died in Dublin,
as Marshal of Ireland, in 1598. It was not Sir Richard, however, but his elder brother,
Robert, who inherited Melcombe and remodelled the house in the time of Queen
Mary. Of later Binghams the most noted was John, great-grandson of Robert,
who sided with the Parliament in the Civil War. Bingham's Melcombe, in spite of
its remoteness, was chosen as the headquarters of the local Parliamentary forces, and
its owner was their commander at the second siege of Corfe Castle. After the
Restoration, Bingham returned to Sir Ralph Bankes 'a large bed, a singel velvit red
chair and a suite of fine damaske' which had been looted from the castle, but,
curiously, retained two portraits of Strafford and Laud, which used to hang in the
hall and presumably came from the same source. In the eighteenth century we meet
with George Bingham, the antiquary and friend of Hutchins, the county historian;
Hutchins was rector of Bingham's Melcombe from 1733 to 1744. The house remained in the possession of the family until 1895, when it was bought by Reginald
Bosworth Smith, a Harrow schoolmaster, author and naturalist. He was succeeded
by his daughter, Lady Grogan, after whose death in 1948 Bingham's Melcombe was
purchased by its present owner, the Hon. Sir Francis Hopwood.

   Unlike many Dorset manor houses, Bingham's Melcombe has been almost
continuously occupied and has never degenerated to the status of a farmhouse. It is
for this reason and because of the conservative instincts of its possessors that it has
been preserved in such perfection. An avenue of great elms, guarded by the stone
eagles of the Binghams, leads up to the house, the oldest portions of which are the
gatehouse and the range adjoining it. The gatehouse is of fifteenth-, or possibly of
late fourteenth-century date; it was built for strength, its walls in one place being
nine feet thick. But strength was no longer a necessity at the time when Robert
Bingham built the carved and gabled oriel bay of the hall, which confronts you inside
the courtyard (pl. 64). The buildings with wonderful irregularity range round
three sides of the court, the hall standing on a higher level with a little terrace in
front of it. On the terrace grow large clumps of hydrangeas, naturalised foreigners,
which, however, have been there for over a century now, as they are shown in the
lithograph in Nash's *Mansions in the Olden Time*. From the parlour gable west of the
hall, a lower mullioned and gabled range runs southward to the kitchen in the corner
of the court, and then turns eastward to join the gatehouse at an obtuse angle. To
the right of the porch, in the position where we should expect the kitchen and its

offices to have been, is a short two-storeyed wing with sashed windows, rebuilt in the seventeenth century and given Georgian features later on.

The hall itself probably incorporates work older by a century or more than the oriel bay, which can be dated within the five years of Queen Mary's reign, if, as it is reasonable to suppose, the heraldic glass in its windows is contemporary and not later. The design of this bay is unusual in being of two storeys. Warm Ham Hill stone is used for the decorative features with contrasting grey limestone for the walls.

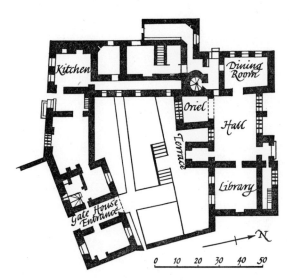

BINGHAM'S MELCOMBE
Ground-floor Plan.

A richly carved panel displaying the Bingham arms is skilfully introduced beneath the upper window, both being framed by slender pilasters set diagonally and carried up above the gable coping to end in twisted finials. The angle shafts, which terminate in the Bingham eagles, are in three stages, the second stage having the same curious band of volutes to be found at Athelhampton and Sandford Orcas. The character of the carving and the treatment of the sculptured panel so closely resemble the Clifton Maybank work, now at Montacute, that the same masons must have worked on both houses (see p. 21). Both in its composition and delicate detail, enhanced by the plain wall surfaces, this is one of the most beautiful pieces of Tudor stonework in the country.

The oriel bay is divided from the hall by a wide moulded arch of four-centred form springing from responds with carved capitals (pl. 62). In using the word 'oriel' to describe what is in effect a little room of its own, complete with a fireplace, we have the authority of Thomas Fuller, who before the Civil War held the living of Broadwindsor and so knew the local usage. 'Sure I am,' he wrote in one of those pleasant personal asides that enliven his writings, 'that small excursion out of gentlemen's halls in Dorsetshire (respect it east or west) is commonly called an oriel.'[1] As at Lytes Cary in Somerset, the oriel has developed from a bay into a deep recess, where the master and mistress of the house and their guests could, if they wished, sit and eat apart from the rest of the household in the hall. It thus represents an interesting transitional stage between the mediaeval custom of the whole household eating together in the hall and the Elizabethan practice of providing a separate dining-parlour for the owner and his family. The original fireplace in this oriel has recently been revealed behind a later one, which dated from about 1700. Its existence was inferred from the inventory of Robert Bingham's goods taken after his death in 1561. Under the heading 'In the Oryalle' there is the item, 'one payre of aun-dyrons,' valued at 3s. The other furniture of the oriel comprised a square table-board, two forms and a third form 'in the entry.' There are six roundels of armorial glass in the window, including the crowned shields of England and Spain (for Mary and Philip).

The hall has lost its original decoration. Three finely carved panels and four of linenfold were rescued from the servants' hall at the end of the last century and are now in one of the bedrooms. These were probably relics of the Tudor panelling banished from the hall. What was originally the parlour, at the west end of the hall, was heightened and redecorated about the middle of the eighteenth century. A new fireplace was inserted, and between the windows a charming pair of oval mirrors in carved frames were placed above marble-topped side tables supported by scrolls and rocaille work. Above the fireplace an Elizabethan or Jacobean over-mantel was retained, and, apparently, to keep it in countenance, the room was given a ribbed plaster ceiling of Elizabethan character. If this is contemporary with the Georgian decoration, as on careful examination it appears to be, it is an early in-stance of the conscious reproduction of work of an older period, not unique, how-ever, for a few other examples of Georgian-Elizabethan have come to light.

A spiral stone stair adjoining the oriel bay gives access to the first-floor rooms at the west end of the house, including the room over the oriel. The west range is probably part of the mediaeval house, but the three gables with their mullioned windows facing the court were added early in the seventeenth century, and the lean-to passage is an addition. The east end of the hall range has banded masonry of flint and stone, very neatly worked. Here there are sashed windows, and a Georgian staircase has been inserted at the north end of the screens passage. The lower room is lined with the bold bolection-mould panelling of Queen Anne's reign. In the middle

[1] *Church History of Britain* (1655), VI, ii, p. 285. At Purse Caundle the hall has an oriel recess similar to the one at Bingham's Melcombe (p. 56).

of the eighteenth century sashed windows were also inserted in the gatehouse, where, in the east room, there is another carved overmantel contemporary with the one mentioned above. The upper rooms of the gatehouse are reached by a newel stair of oak.

The gardens at Bingham's Melcombe provide the perfect setting for the house. Westward stretches a long bowling green, flanked by a gigantic yew hedge of immemorial age (pl. 60), at the end of which is a Georgian alcove contrived in the high brick wall. On the far side of the hedge is a delightful old kitchen garden, which has at its east end a circular dovecote, recalling the one at Athelhampton. Immediately behind the hall there are two tiny enclosed plots, one of which is known as the Ladies' Garden; east of them, on the far side of a yard, is a long, picturesque range of thatched buildings. Bounding all to the north, an avenue of giant planes, sycamores and silver firs leads down to a wild garden, laid out with walks beside the little stream, and to three ancient fishponds.

Melcombe Horsey. In the same parish as Bingham's Melcombe, but about a mile and a half west of it, is another ancient manor place, which, however, long ago became a farmhouse. It lies in an amphitheatre of the hills, which close it in on three sides and culminate westward in the great camp-crowned summit of Nettlecombe Tout. The Horseys of Clifton Maybank inherited this manor by marriage with a Turges in the reign of Henry VIII, and bequeathed their name to it, although they held it for less than a hundred years. Sir George Horsey in the time of James I mortgaged the estate to his father-in-law, Sir Thomas Freke of Shroton. With his family it remained for a century, when it passed to the Pitts and Pitt-Rivers. Leland, writing shortly after Sir John Horsey had inherited, describes the manor as 'one of the fairest lordships in Dorset'; it was worth in his day £100 a year. Originally a courtyard house with a gatehouse on which were displayed the Horsey arms, it consists now of only two ranges in the form of the letter L. The eastern range contains the former chapel, built of alternate stone and flint courses. About the end of the eighteenth century it was divided into two floors and used as a brewhouse and laundry, but it preserves a fine waggon roof and its little stone bellcote. On the monument of Sir Thomas Freke in Shroton church (died 1633) it is stated that he built this chapel at Melcombe; otherwise it would be taken to be of fifteenth-century date. On the south side the windows have had their tracery altered, but one remains on the north with its Perpendicular tracery untouched. The waggon roof has moulded ribs and carved bosses. In the west range two of the first-floor rooms retain the Jacobean woodwork and plaster ceilings given them by Sir Thomas Freke. One of the ceilings is an elaborate example of its period, divided by broad moulded ribs with a running pattern on the soffit, and enclosing panels of varying shapes which are ornamented with conventionalised designs of plants (pl. 63). On some of these a Tudor rose and a thistle emerge from a single stalk in allusion to the union of the English and Scottish crowns. In the smaller room, which is lined with linen-fold panelling, the fireplace has some Jacobean carved woodwork as an overmantel and a pretty late eighteenth-century firegrate. The oak staircase dates from about 1700. The south end of the building was altered and done up in the neat farmhouse taste of the early nineteenth century. House and chapel have both been carefully repaired by the present owner.

Clifton Maybank (2 miles S.E. of Yeovil). Only a small portion of the great house of the Horsey family survives *in situ*, but dispersed about the neighbourhood are many fragments of this once splendid Tudor building, including its richly ornamented front and porch, which are now at Montacute, six miles away. In 1786 the greater part of Clifton Maybank was pulled down and the materials were sold. Edward Phelips attended the sale and, with an appreciation for 'Gothic' building rare at the time, purchased and transferred to Montacute the fine façade, re-erecting it against the west front of his Elizabethan house. He also bought six hundred feet of ashlar for his house at Cattistock. Other portions are said to have been taken to Brympton d'Evercy, and there are fragments of stonework made up into a gateway in the garden of the Manor House, Beaminster, as well as an heraldic finial at Compton House, near Sherborne. In 1800 the fine Jacobean gatehouse (pl. 66) was sold to Lord Paulet and re-erected in the park at Hinton St. George. What was left of the building was used as a farmhouse until the present century, but since 1906 it has once again become a residence and various additions have been made to the surviving portion. The Horseys, a Somerset family, obtained Clifton at the beginning of the fifteenth century through the marriage of John Horsey with the May-bank (or Maubank) heiress. A later John Horsey, who was an Esquire of the Body to Henry VIII and died in 1531, married Elizabeth Turges, who brought Melcombe Turges, now Melcombe Horsey (p. 73), to her husband's family. His son and grandson, both named John and both knighted, are buried in Sherborne Abbey under an early Renaissance tomb. The former, who died in 1546, purchased the abbey and its manor, and sold the church to the townspeople. The latter at his death in 1564 owned some 18,000 acres in Dorset and Somerset. His wife was Edith Phelips, and it was, no doubt, partly on account of this family connection that the eighteenth-century owner of Montacute purchased the Tudor front of the Horsey mansion. The fluted shafts, surmounted by heraldic beasts, and the pierced parapet are characteristic late Gothic features, but Renaissance detail appears in the remark-

65. CLIFTON MAYBANK
The surviving portion of the great Tudor mansion of the Horsey family.

66. CLIFTON MAYBANK
The Jacobean gatehouse, which was removed to Hinton St. George in 1800. From Hutchins'
History of Dorset (1774).

67. SANDFORD ORCAS

The west face of the gatehouse on the north side of the manor house.

able sculptured work above the archway of the porch (pl. 6). This shows a delicacy and refinement that suggest that it is from the hand of a foreign carver. Two *amorini* carved with great spirit hold aloft a hatchment-shaped panel, which encloses an elaborate achievement of arms.[1] The shield was originally that of the Horseys, but Edward Phelips substituted his own for theirs. As at Bingham's Melcombe (pl. 5), the composition is framed by two slender pilasters, set diagonally and delicately carved; they are carried up to end in Ionic capitals, supporting two further cherubs holding shields. In the triangular spaces above the 'hatchment' the initials, IH and EH, are set within circles surrounded by arabesque-like foliage. These must stand for Sir John Horsey and Edith Phelips, and the date of the work will, therefore, be between 1546 and 1564. This agrees with the probable date for the oriel bay at Bingham's Melcombe (1553–58), the sculpture of which is undoubtedly by the same hand.

The surviving portion of the house at Clifton seems to have formed the west wing. On the south front there remain three fluted shafts and a strip of pierced parapet (pl. 65). On the west side, high up under a central gable, there is a Tudor oriel, anticipating those which light the gallery at Montacute; the doorway and all the other windows in this front were inserted early in the eighteenth century during the ownership of the Harveys, by whom the house is stated to have been 'repaired, sashed and otherwise modernized'. Inside, there remain two original doorways and a fireplace and a late sixteenth-century staircase. South-east of the house stands part of an earlier house of late fifteenth or early sixteenth-century date. The Jacobean gatehouse, now at Hinton St George, was erected either by Sir Ralph, or his son, Sir George Horsey. Between them they dissipated their great estates so that nothing was left by the time of the Civil War; Sir George Horsey died penniless in a debtors' prison in 1644. The additions to the house, made by Mrs Daniell in 1906–7, bear no relation to its original form, but they were carefully carried out, and the smooth lawns and dark shapes of ilex against the stone walls make an attractive picture still.

Sandford Orcas (3 miles N.W. of Sherborne). Until 1896 Sandford Orcas belonged to Somerset, and by all rational rules should belong to it still. In gaining this narrow promontory of a parish Dorset has acquired a village of great charm, set in a fold of green, hilly country rich in pastures and orchards. The manor house, built of Ham Hill stone, stands beside the church at the far end of the village. It faces away from the street, its main front being approached up a steep incline at the

---

[1] The design was copied on the Horsey tomb in Sherborne Abbey (*circa* 1565), but it is obvious from the coarseness of execution that this was the work of a less skilled carver.

side of the churchyard and through a beautiful gatehouse attached to the north side of the building (pl. 67). It is an unusually well-preserved example of the smaller Tudor manor house, and appears to have been built all at one time. The date of its erection is uncertain; the fact that the windows have flat heads to the lights (and there is nothing to show that they have been altered from the arched form) suggests that the building may be as late as the middle years of the sixteenth century, but the occurrence of the arms of Henry VIII and Anne Boleyn in the south window

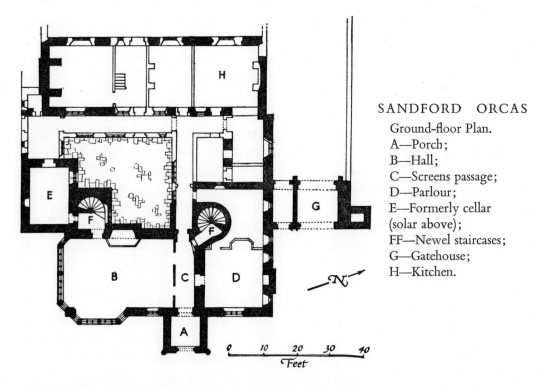

SANDFORD ORCAS
Ground-floor Plan.
A—Porch;
B—Hall;
C—Screens passage;
D—Parlour;
E—Formerly cellar
(solar above);
FF—Newel staircases;
G—Gatehouse;
H—Kitchen.

of the hall might be taken to imply that the rebuilding was carried out between 1533 and 1536.

At this time its owners were the Knoyles, whose ancestor, Thomas Knoyell, had acquired a moiety of the manor about the year 1400. The Norman lords of Sandford were a family of the name de Orescuiltz, of which Orcas is a corruption. The manor belonged to them for three generations before being divided between co-heiresses. Of the Knoyles, William served as Sheriff of Somerset and Dorset in 1492. The builder of the house was probably Edward Knoyle, who succeeded Leonard Knoyle in 1533. From the remarkable resemblance between the ornamental details and those to be seen on the north wing at Athelhampton (pl. 3 and 4) it may be inferred that the same master mason worked at both houses, and, as we have noted (p. 68), there was a link between their owners in the marriage of Edward Knoyle with Catherine, the sister of Nicholas Martyn. The unusual lozenge-shaped panels with carved bosses on the porch and gatehouse are almost identical with those at Athelhampton, and the gatehouse chimney and the angle shafts of the porch have the outward-curling scrolls that also appear at Athelhampton and are, perhaps, an attempt to reproduce the Ionic volute.

The house now encloses a small courtyard, but the range at the back containing kitchen and offices seems to have been built independently and was linked only at the north end. In the main building there is a wainscoted parlour to the right of the porch; to the left is the hall with unusually large bay windows facing south and east (pl. 68). An early seventeenth-century oak screen divides the hall from the entry; at the end of the passage, on the right, a newel staircase of stone goes up to the first-floor rooms. A second newel stair on the west side of the hall leads to a solar, placed in a small south range over a low room that was originally a cellar, and also to the great bedroom above the south end of the hall. The hall and parlour and some of the first-floor rooms retain their original stone fireplaces, and there is a good deal of sixteenth- and seventeenth-century woodwork. In the south window of the hall there is heraldic glass commemorating Knoyle alliances as well as the shield of Henry VIII and Anne Boleyn; other windows contain roundels and panels of Continental glass, mostly German. The left-hand gable of the front and that at the south end were rebuilt in 1872, when the house was carefully restored for Mr Hubert Hutchings by Henry Hall. A drawing by J. C. Buckler made in 1838 shows the front at that time with a hipped roof at its south end. The shield in the panel on the porch was carved with the arms of Knoyle impaling Fry. No alliance between a Knoyle and a Fry has been recorded, but in 1560 there was a conveyance made by Edward Knoyle to a Thomas Fry, who was, perhaps, a relation by marriage. The Edward Knoyle who succeeded in 1533 may have married a Fry and been the father of another Edward, who married Catherine Martyn. There were Knoyles living at Sandford Orcas up to 1732, although they had sold the property half a century earlier. In 1739 it was bought by Samuel Hutchings; there followed a period of a hundred and forty years when the house was let to farmers. It was then restored by Hubert Hutchings, who bequeathed it to his kinsman, Sir Hubert Medlycott, of Ven House, near Milborne Port, the father of the present owner. Some of the fine furniture from Ven is now at Sandford Orcas. Both within and without this is one of the most charming manor houses in the West of England.

After the division of the manor about 1480, the other moiety descended to the Gerards. Their name is commemorated in a house called Jerrards, which is of fifteenth-century date but altered and enlarged early in the seventeenth century. The arms of Gerard and the date 1616 appear on the porch.

Hammoon is an out-of-the-way village lying beside the Stour about two miles east of Sturminster Newton. Its little manor house is one of the most beautiful things in Dorset (pl. 70). Half its charm comes from its roof of thatch, covering the whole building and sealing up, as it were, the scars it must once have suffered; it is now a cottage manor house with only its Classic porch and a two-storeyed bay to the right of it to show that it was once a place of some account. This south end of its front has an octagonal angle shaft, probably once terminating in a heraldic finial, which with the mullioned windows of its bay goes to show that the house must have been yet another characteristic example of Tudor domestic work. The porch has a shaped gable with strapwork on either side suggesting an Elizabethan or Jacobean date. But the Classic doorway with its ringed columns seems to have been brought from elsewhere, since it is out of scale with the porch itself and the masonry framing it has evidently been disturbed. The left-hand portion of the front, overshadowed by a great sycamore, has been rebuilt in cottage style; on the south side a long wing goes back eastward. Hammoon is a phonetic spelling of Ham-mohun. At the time of the Domesday survey the great Norman family de Mohun held fourteen manors in Dorset, of which this was one; their chief seat was Dunster Castle in Somerset, and after the Luttrells succeeded them there, a younger branch of the Mohuns continued here holding the manor of the Luttrells. They were succeeded towards the end of the fifteenth century by the Trenchards. In Henry VIII's reign a William Hody was seated here, perhaps as a lessee of the Trenchards. The house contains some good Jacobean panelling.

Little Toller Farm ($1\frac{1}{2}$ miles W. of Maiden Newton). Although the two Tollers, Porcorum and Fratrum, are famous as place-name oddities, their Latin surnames are almost unknown to the local inhabitants, to whom they are just Great and Little Toller. The valley in which they lie comes down from the heights above Beaminster to join the Frome at Maiden Newton, a third village, Toller Whelme, marking the source of the rivulet. Toller 'of the Brothers,' which is about a mile farther down than Toller 'of the Pigs,' acquired its suffix from the Knights Hospitalers or Brethren of St. John of Jerusalem. It is sometimes stated that they had a Preceptory here; but there is no evidence for this, and the only connection with the Knights was the remote one that this manor belonged to the Priory of Buckland in Somerset, whose nuns were obedientaries of the Knights Hospitalers. The old stone manor house, known as Little Toller Farm, may incorporate portions of the mediaeval grange, but the

68. SANDFORD ORCAS

One of the loveliest of west country manor houses, probably built by Edward Knoyle
towards the middle of the sixteenth century.

69. SANDFORD ORCAS

From the north-east. The gatehouse is on the right.

70. HAMMOON

A thatched manor house near Sturminster Newton. In its name Hammoon perpetuates the memory of the Mohuns, who were succeeded as lords of the manor by the Trenchards.

surviving Tudor work can be assigned to John Samways, of Winterborne Martin, who purchased the property in 1540. The house stands to the west of the little church, its buildings forming three sides of a court. The low thatch-covered range on the east side (pl. 72) has for long been used as an outbuilding. A continuous string course runs above the windows, the heads of which are flanked by carved drops of Renaissance character, and in one place the initials of John Samways appear on a shield. Let into the wall is a carving of a man playing bag-pipes. The main body of the house has several Tudor windows with arch-headed lights, and at the south-east corner is an octagonal shaft, surmounted by a griffin, like those at Mapperton and Athelhampton. The south front (pl. 71) is interrupted midway by a projecting chimney-breast terminating in two twisted chimney-stacks, which were rebuilt about 1933. But the carved finial between them is original—a chained monkey holding a mirror. What its significance may have been it is difficult to guess: a chained monkey was the crest of the Martyns of Athelhampton, who had no connection with Toller Fratrum; possibly, it is a punning allusion to the Samways' earlier home, Winterborne Martin or Martinstown. Over the porch is another heraldic finial—a lion with a shield bearing the royal arms; it probably once surmounted a gable. The house was much altered and modernised about a hundred years ago, and internally it preserves little of interest beyond an arch-braced collar-beam roof, below which there used to be a barrel ceiling, running the whole length of the first floor. Three Samways were owners of Toller Fratrum—John (died 1586), Robert (died 1621) and his younger brother, Bernard (died 1645 at the age of 96). The property then passed by marriage to the Fulfords of Great Fulford, Devon, remaining with them for over a century. In 1867 it was sold to Lord Wynford.

Mapperton (2 miles S.E. of Beaminster). It is odd to find Hutchins describing as a 'neat and elegant fabric' what is one of the most picturesque manor houses in Dorset. With its grey walls and roofs stained with lichen, its mullioned windows, twisted chimneys and heraldic finials, Mapperton to our eyes is as far removed as a house can be from what an eighteenth-century writer usually meant by those two adjectives. Perhaps he liked the symmetry of the front with its forecourt and balancing ranges of stables, and indeed this note of formality adds much to the charm of the house, which, however, the retention of the Tudor wing has saved from becoming too self-conscious, too 'neat.' But even more delightful is the unusual approach. A straight avenue of tall elms leads down to the house (pl. 76), with the high garden wall on its left, and the drive makes its entry through stone gate-piers placed between the house and the stables. It is not until the last moment that the front of the building and the whole charming lay-out of forecourt and stable-court reveal themselves.

Like Bingham's Melcombe, but unlike so many Dorset manor houses, Mapperton has a long history of unbroken occupation in a continuous descent that was only terminated in the present century. From the Bretts, who owned the manor in the time of Edward I and probably earlier, it passed by heiresses successively to the Morgans, Brodrepps and Comptons, the four families between them covering more than six centuries. A pleasant record has been preserved of a Robert Morgan in the fifteenth century, who received a patent from the youthful Henry VI 'to use and were his bonnet on his hed' at all times in the King's presence, 'forasmoche as wee bee credibly enformed that our welbiloved Robert Morgan, esquier, for diverse infirmities which he hathe in his hedde, cannot convenyently, without his grete daungier be discovered of the same.' It was a later Robert Morgan who undertook the rebuilding of Mapperton, probably some time between 1540 and 1560. Hutchins records that the following inscription was to be seen in the hall: 'Robert Morgan and Mary, his wife, built this house in their own lifetime and at their own charge and cost.

> What they spent, that they lent;
> What they gave, that they have;
> What they left, that they lost.'

He also notes that there hung in the parlour a portrait of the builder, dated 1560 and giving his age as 51. Of his house, planned in the form of the letter L, only the north wing retains original features, and even so its north front has been classicised about the middle of the eighteenth century; none the less, enough remains to show that it must have been very similar in character to the early Tudor wing of Athelhampton and to Barrington Court, over the border in Somerset, where the same twisted pinnacles with heraldic finials at the angles occur. There are four of these heraldic finials, each carved with the Morgan griffin and admirably preserved.

The principal range (pl. 74) was rebuilt in the seventeenth century, perhaps on the old foundations and incorporating some earlier work. Hutchins ascribes this reconstruction to Richard Brodrepp, and it is usually assumed that he meant the first Richard Brodrepp, who obtained possession of Mapperton in 1618. The character of much of the work points to a date late in Charles I's reign or during the Commonwealth, but the date 1666 with the initials RB is to be seen on a stone within the porch. It has been suggested that the balustrade is an eighteenth-century feature, but the front was clearly designed to be finished with a parapet of some kind. The windows are of the common seventeenth-century type with crossed mullion and transom; only the hall bay (on the left) has a functional purpose, but symmetry demanded one to balance it on the right. Internally, the hall bay is entered through

71. LITTLE TOLLER FARM

Formerly the manor house of Toller Fratrum, owned in the sixteenth century by the
Samways. From the south.

72. LITTLE TOLLER FARM

The thatched stable range with Tudor windows and doorway.

73. MAPPERTON

The forecourt with its gate-pieces surmounted by eagles taking wing. On the right is the church.

a massive moulded arch with semicircular head and keystone somewhat similar to one in the hall at Herringston. Other features characteristic of the first half of the seventeenth century are the shell-headed niches in the porch and the form of the outer doorway with its label and four-centred head. Over this doorway there is a stone cartouche carved with the coat of the Brodrepps with its four swans. The inner doorway, however, displays in its spandrels the Morgan crest; this is evidently an earlier feature re-used. Shell-headed niches, possibly re-set, occur again in the

MAPPERTON

Ground-floor Plan of House and Church.

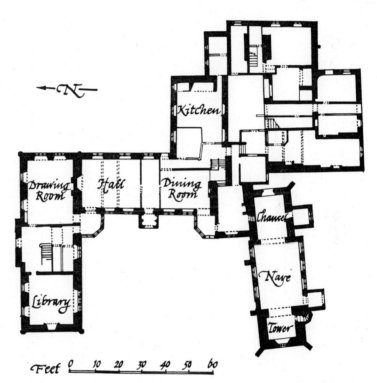

Feet

eagle-crested gate-piers (pl. 73), which, along with the wrought-iron railings and gates, probably belong to the Restoration period.

The second Richard Brodrepp lived until 1706. After the Restoration he built the two ranges of stables and coach-houses that face each other across the courtyard (pl. 75). The south range has his initials and the date 1670 cut on the keystone of an archway in the south wall. A rectangular dovecote south of the house, also built by him, is dated 1665. The remodelling of the north front was carried out by the fourth and last Richard Brodrepp, who died in 1774. This work probably dates from the decade 1750–60 to judge by the staircase which was introduced into the wing at the same time and by the rococo character of the ceiling above it. Fortunately, the parlour and bedroom at the east end of the wing were allowed to retain their six-teenth-century plaster ceilings. The designs consist of an elaborate network of ribs, in the upper room radiating from pendants (pl. 77); the fleur-de-lis, a favourite ornament of Elizabethan plasterers, occurs in the interspaces, but here it was used with particular appropriateness, since it formed part of the Morgan coat. In style the ceilings belong to the latter years of the sixteenth century, and they seem to be later than the frieze in the bedroom which has little profile heads set in garlands held by figures emerging from scrollwork. The early Renaissance character of this frieze also appears in the motives used for the modelled plasterwork over the two bedroom fireplaces in the wing which are contemporary with it. Neither the large Jacobean overmantel in the hall (pl. 18) nor a smaller one in the library at the west end of the north wing is original to the house; they were brought from Melplash in 1909, and, though interesting in themselves, are too large for the early Tudor fireplaces below them. The hall has a seventeenth-century screen and panelling, but the ceilings of the hall and screens passage are modern, having been introduced by the late owner, Mrs Labouchere. Since her death in 1955 Mapperton has been bought by Viscount Hinchingbrooke.

At the south-east corner of the house there is a seventeenth-century block, originally independent but now joined to the main building. A notable feature of the gardens is the great terrace between the upper and lower levels. The little church, which adjoins the house and makes a south side to the forecourt, was rebuilt in 1704. It is a humble unit in a group of buildings that blend perfectly together in spite of their diversity of style and date.

Melplash Court. This gabled stone building, which was for long a farmhouse, lies about a mile beyond Parnham on the road from Beaminster to Bridport, and is approached by a long avenue of elms. From a family de Melplash it passed by mar-riage to the Mores of Marnhull, and from Sir Thomas More, in Henry VIII's reign, to a younger son of William Paulet, Marquess of Winchester. The Paulet marriage is said to have been the result of an escapade which nearly brought Sir Thomas More into serious trouble. In 1533 he served his year of office as Sheriff of Dorset and Somerset, and one day he took it into his head to throw open the gaol at Dorchester and let out all the prisoners. Things might have gone badly for him had not Paulet intervened and procured him a pardon. The price of the pardon, however, was the hand of one of his daughters for Lord Paulet's second son, Thomas.[1] Until 1909 the

---

[1] This story is a curious corruption of the facts. Sir Thomas More got into trouble over an affair of gaol-breaking at Ilchester, not Dorchester. He seems to have had no concern in it apart from his official respon-sibility. See Dorothy Gardiner, *Companion into Dorset* (1937), pp. 122–5.

house contained two fine Jacobean plaster overmantels, which are now at Mapperton. The larger of the two, dated 1604, stood in the hall (pl. 18). In its centre is a splendid achievement of the Paulet arms, enclosed in a Garter, with their supporters, the crest (a hawk with extended wings) and the Paulet motto: 'AMES LOYAULTE.' The smaller one, removed from the parlour, has the royal arms of James I. The most interesting feature left in the interior now is the oak screen, with massive posts and moulded bands of Tudor times (pl. 80). What remains of the original house is only one range of a larger building; and only the north (pl. 78) and east sides retain their old gables and windows. In 1693 the property was bought by Richard Brodrepp, and for over two hundred years descended with Mapperton, the house becoming a farm. In 1922 Mrs Gundry restored the house and added a new wing at the west end; the architect was Mr E. P. Warren. An old barn, which stood behind the house, provided the material for this addition. Near the south-west angle stands a circular dovecote similar to those of Athelhampton and Bingham's Melcombe (pl. 79). Melplash is now the home of Mr P. Tiarks.

Puncknowle (5 miles E. of Bridport). The tiny village of Puncknowle, corrupted in local speech to Punnel, lies on the southern slope of the Bride valley, about a mile from Swyre, backed by a ridge of downland that separates the valley from the sea. Church and manor house are both on a miniature scale, and they stand close together, forming a charming group, when seen from the east. The front of the manor house (pl. 81) is at right angles to the church and is approached between a pair of stone gate-piers on the south side of the churchyard. Though of sixteenth-century date with mullioned windows having arched heads, the front is symmetrical and there is a central projecting porch of unusual width. It is probable that the hipped roofs were the result of alterations made late in the seventeenth century or early in the eighteenth. The first-floor rooms contain overmantels and painted panelling of this period.

From Tudor to Georgian times the manor belonged to the Nappers or Napiers, whose ancestor settled at Swyre, the adjoining parish, in Henry VII's reign. He came from Scotland, and his name is given as James Napier on the monument in Swyre church which his descendant, Sir Robert, of Puncknowle, had put up to commemorate him in 1692. There he is stated to have been 'brother of Sir Alexander Napier of Merchiston' and to have 'supplied the several adjacent Abbies with fish'. In the Heralds' Visitation of Dorset in 1623 he appears as John Napper, of whom it is merely noted that he 'came out of Scotland'. Until the family became conscious of their Scottish ancestry, the Dorset and Somerset branches spelt and pronounced their name as Napper. John (or James) of Swyre married Anne, daughter of John

Russell in that parish, by whom his descendants could claim kinship with the Dukes of Bedford (see under Kingston Russell, p. 156). Of their four sons, Nicholas, the youngest, established the line that settled in Somerset, at Tintinhull, near Montacute, while James was common ancestor of the Nappers or Napiers of Baglake in Long Bredy, of Puncknowle, of Middlemarsh in Minterne Magna and, later, of Crichel (see p. 165). In the church at Puncknowle there are monuments to several members of the family, including one with three admonitions, in Greek, Latin and English, erected by Sir Robert not long before 1700 and signed by the carver, John Hamilton, who described himself as 'Scoto-Britannus'.

Creech Grange (3 miles S. of Wareham). Lying under the northern flank of the Purbeck Hills, half-way between Corfe and the point where they break off in the cliffs of Worbarrow Bay, Creech Grange has a setting as beautiful as any house in Dorset. Here, on the lower slopes of the Downs, is a narrow strip of country forming a green hem to the brown and purple heathlands stretching away north towards Wareham. Just to the east Creech Barrow raises its conical top, breaking forward like a bastion from the hill wall; at its foot nestles Grange, hidden in the seclusion of its woods. The grey gables of the entrance front are momentarily glimpsed from the road that comes from Wareham, and a quarter of a mile farther on, as it climbs the steep hillside, the trees open to give a vista of the south front (pl. 83), looking on to a lawn guarded by double ranks of sturdy yews (pl. 84), the parade ground of peacocks. To the west of the house lies the Little Wood, on the fringe of which is a charming formal garden with a grass-verged pool (pl. 86). This, the wood itself and the southward vista are all part of an early eighteenth-century lay-out, the formality of which has been modified by later generations. One of its features is the curious stone screen—Grange Arch—on the crest of the down, meant to terminate the vista from the south windows of the house. But the Great Wood on the hillside has since grown up to hide it.

Originally a grange or farm of Bindon Abbey, the estate was granted at the Dissolution of the monasteries to Sir John Horsey of Clifton Maybank, who promptly sold it to Sir Oliver Lawrence, brother-in-law of Henry VIII's Lord Chancellor, Wriothesley. Lawrence, through Wriothesley's influence, acquired a considerable fortune, which he invested in lands in the Isle of Purbeck; one of his offices was Collector of the Customs in the Port of Poole. Between 1540 and his death in 1559 he rebuilt the house at Creech, but of his work to-day only the two-storey bay on the left of the entrance front (pl. 82) and a large window lighting the kitchen remain undisturbed. His son, Edward Lawrence, who lived until 1601, may have added the three-storeyed wing on the right. The whole of the front was taken down and

74. MAPPERTON
The entrance front, remodelled in the seventeenth century.

75. MAPPERTON
One of the late seventeenth-century ranges of stables flanking the outer court.

76. MAPPERTON

Looking north up the avenue by which the house is approached; on the right is the Tudor wing.

77. MAPPERTON

Mid-sixteenth-century ribbed ceiling with pendants and fleur-de-lis ornaments.

78. MELPLASH COURT

The north front. Melplash in the sixteenth and seventeenth centuries belonged to a branch
of the Paulet family.

79. MELPLASH COURT.
The round dovecote.

80. MELPLASH COURT
The hall screen.

81. PUNCKNOWLE

A little manor house, east of Bridport, formerly the home of a branch of the Napper or Napier family. The entrance front framed by a pair of late seventeenth-century gate-piers.

rebuilt in 1846. It comprised a great hall, which had been much altered, however, and divided into two storeys; the porch had the usual angle shafts of Tudor date, but had been dressed up with a classic doorway and pediment. The rebuilding was unusually successful for its time, and recaptures in all but details the spirit of the local Tudor style.

The Lawrence ownership came to an end in 1691, when John Lawrence, the sixth of his line, disposed of the property to Nathaniel Bond of Lutton. He had sold the reversion five years previously, and three years before that Nathaniel Bond had also purchased Tyneham (p. 86). The association of the Bonds with Purbeck goes back to the time of Henry VI, when a Robert Bond, of Hatch Beauchamp, in Somerset,

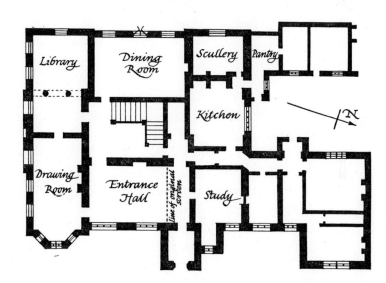

CREECH GRANGE
Ground-floor Plan.

married the heiress of Lutton, a farmstead lying on the south side of the hills, between Tyneham and Steeple. The family fluctuated in wealth and importance, one member, John Bond, making a fortune as a merchant in London in the time of Queen Elizabeth. From a brother of his was descended Sir Thomas Bond, who gave his name to the famous street in London, which at the time when he laid it out proved such a ruinous speculation. Nathaniel Bond was the youngest of five sons, and made his fortune at the Bar, eventually becoming a King's Serjeant. His father, Denis Bond, had supported the Puritan party during the Civil War, sitting as member for Dorchester. His death occurred four days before that of Cromwell, occasioning a popular saying that 'the Devil had taken Bond for Oliver's appearance.' Nathaniel bought out his brothers' interest in the Lutton estate and so became the senior representative of the Purbeck branch of the family.

Considerable alterations to the house were carried out by Denis Bond, Nathaniel's son and successor. He was responsible for the lay-out of the grounds, and between 1738 and 1741 he lengthened and classicised the south wing. This south front (pl. 83), like the side façades of Edmondsham and Mapperton, is a modest country version of the current Palladian style. A book of accounts in Denis Bond's handwriting shows that he spent £1,300 on 'building about the house.' His architect was Francis Cartwright of Blandford, who, besides supervising the work, supplied three chimney-pieces. The drawing-room in this south wing, whilst retaining the Tudor bay at one end, has some good Georgian decoration, including a chimney-piece in the style of William Kent; beyond it is the library, its south end divided by a screen of Ionic columns. Although in the course of these and the nineteenth-century alterations the house has lost most of its original character, it is still a charming place in very lovely surroundings. Lieut.-Colonel A. R. Bond is the present owner.

Tyneham (5 miles W. of Corfe Castle). 'After Creech Grange it is natural to consider another Purbeck house which has been in the Bond family for two hundred and fifty years. Tyneham is on the opposite side of the Purbeck Hills to Grange, set in the deep fold that runs between the chalk ridge and the limestone ridge and which meets the sea in Worbarrow Bay. The house lies encircled in its trees more than a mile inland from the shore at Worbarrow, its grey front looking eastward across a level lawn up an avenue of tall limes. To the south the ground rises steeply above it to break off suddenly in the abrupt crags of Gadcliff, perhaps the grandest feature in the wonderfully varied coastline of the mythical island. The main part of the building is Elizabethan with a front of Purbeck ashlar, which has the beauty of simple and unpretentious workmanship (pl. 87). Three gabled dormers are carried up to the level of the roof-tree, giving a large and varied expanse of sloping roofs which retain their old covering of Purbeck stone slates. In the centre projects a little gabled porch with an Early Renaissance doorcase bearing the date 1583. This symmetrical block was built at right angles to the hall of an earlier building, which still survives at the back of the house. From the exterior its age would hardly be suspected—it has been divided into two storeys and used for a time as a cottage—but within it still retains a portion of its original open timber roof. This was of the arch-braced collar-beam form with cuspings to the collar-braces as well as to the wind-braces and a pierced quatrefoil in the space above the collar. The surviving details suggest a date about the middle of the fourteenth century.'

At that time Tyneham was owned by the Russells, who may have been a younger branch of the Kingston Russell family. There have been links with other Dorset families. After passing by heiresses from the Russells to the Chykes and from them to John Pope, Tyneham was bought in 1523 by John Williams, who ten years previously had purchased Herringston, near Dorchester (see p. 88). He settled the estate on his younger son, Henry, who between 1567 and 1583 rebuilt and enlarged the mediaeval house. His initials and the former date were once to be seen on an arched doorway leading to a newel staircase in a part of the building, lying east of

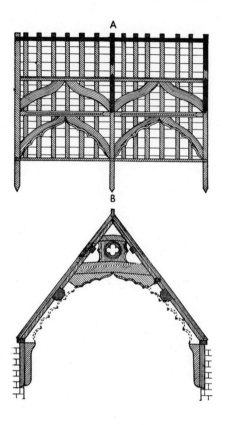

TYNEHAM

Roof of the fourteenth-century hall. Two bays and section (AB) with missing portions conjecturally restored.

the old hall. This was pulled down about 1820, when a two-storey block containing the dining-room was erected on its site. The Williams family continued to own Tyneham until the middle of the seventeenth century, when Jane Williams brought it to Sir Robert Lawrence of Grange. His son, John, sold it to Nathaniel Bond in 1683, three years before doing the same with Grange. While Grange became the seat of the senior branch of the Bond family, Tyneham was settled by Nathaniel Bond on his younger son, John. Later, it passed to the Rev. William Bond, fourth son of Nathaniel's grandson, John Bond of Grange, whose descendants remained at Tyneham until the Second World War.

The description in the first paragraph, written in 1934, has been left as a record of the house now left derelict and abandoned. Tyneham during the last war was brought within the area requisitioned by the War Department for military training, and, in spite of undertakings given at the time, it has not been restored. An Elizabethan chimney-piece and panelling, saved from one of the bedrooms, were installed in 1952 in the Council Chamber of the Museum at Dorchester as a memorial to the late William Ralph Garneys Bond of Tyneham. Some heraldic glass from the house has been placed in the Dorset Field Club's library in the same building.

Herringston ($1\frac{1}{2}$ miles S. of Dorchester). Herringston is one of the southern group of Winterborne villages, which lie along the course of the stream that flows eastward past Maiden Castle to join the Frome below Dorchester. The place takes its name from the family of Harang or Herring, which was also established at Chaldon Herring, near Lulworth, and exchanged land there for Herringston with the Abbot of Bindon in Henry III's reign. In 1337 Walter Heryng had license to crenellate and fortify his manor house of Wynterbourn with stone walls. Somewhere about the end of the fourteenth century Herringston passed either by marriage or purchase to the Filiols, and in 1449 we find John Filiol granting a lease of the manor to John Hogies, the latter covenanting to 'well and fully maintain support and repair all the Houses and buildings . . . especially one building called the Gatehouse.' In 1513 the manor was sold to John Williams of Dorchester, and ever since it has remained continuously in the possession of his descendants.

Until the beginning of last century Herringston was a courtyard house, the entrance to which was through a gabled range on the north side bearing the date 1582. This, together with the adjoining parts of the east and west sides of the quadrangle, including the chapel, was pulled down soon after 1803, when Thomas Leverton was commissioned to design a new front, which was built across the old quadrangle on the north side of the hall range, so converting the house into a solid block. Most of Leverton's work is in the manner of Robert Adam, but here he attempted a Gothic façade. The exterior is uninteresting, though the south front retains the large mullioned and transomed windows of the Tudor hall. The outstanding feature of the house is the great chamber with its carved wainscoting and elaborately decorated barrel ceiling (pl. 88). Sir John Williams, grandson of the purchaser, whose canopied tomb stands in St Peter's Church, Dorchester, was responsible for this work, which can be dated between 1612 and 1617, the year of his death. In one of the panels of the ceiling the Prince of Wales's feathers appear with the initials C.P., and as Charles did not become Prince of Wales until 1612, the ceiling cannot be earlier than that date. There are twenty-four of these square

82. CREECH GRANGE

The entrance front. A successful nineteenth-century reconstruction of the Tudor manor house.

83. CREECH GRANGE

The south side of the house, which was re-fronted between 1738 and 1741. Architect:
Francis Cartwright of Blandford St Mary.

84. CREECH GRANGE

A bodyguard of yews. In the distance, to the south, are the Purbeck Hills.

85. CREECH GRANGE

A glimpse of the house in springtime: daffodils growing below an ilex.

86. CREECH GRANGE

The formal garden and pool with a peacock posing in the foreground.

87. TYNEHAM

Formerly the home of a junior branch of the Bond family of Creech Grange. The east front, dated 1582, from a photograph taken in 1934. The house was allowed to fall into ruin when Tyneham was compulsorily evacuated during the second World War.

panels arranged in the rectangular pattern of broad, decorated bands, most of them filled with representations of animals, birds and winged creatures taken from books of emblems and the bestiaries. There is a swan, a gryphon, a boar, three interlaced fishes, the pelican in her piety; there is also an angel holding a scroll with the letters G.I.E.D. (*Gloria in excelsis Deo*), and balancing the Prince of Wales's badge are the arms of England. The intervening spaces between the framing bands contain conventionalised renderings of flowers and fruit. The wall space above the frieze at the north end of the room shows further quaint reliefs of animals—including a camel, a rhinoceros, an elephant—and a naïve attempt to depict trees. Of the five pendants that are placed along the ridge of the ceiling and are modelled on metal cores three are of openwork form. The middle one is more elaborately treated than the others, being ornamented with four caryatids springing from a boss, on which two little figures sit dangling their legs. The excellence of the modelling, as well as the wealth of fancy and invention displayed in this ceiling, though not unique, place it among the finest examples of its period. Perhaps the nearest parallel to it is the ceiling of the long gallery at Lanhydrock in Cornwall. Some thirty years ago the timbers of the roof supporting the ceiling were found to be in an advanced state of decay, but the damage was made good without injury to the ceiling itself. The carving of the wainscoting is even more elaborate than the ornament of the ceiling, each panel depicting a scriptural or allegorical subject (pl. 89). A chimney-piece, of extraordinarily crude form and entirely out of scale with the decoration of the room, shows how little the provincial craftsman understood even at this date the principles of Classic design. On it appear, in uncomfortable attitudes, three emblematic ladies, Faith, Hope and Charity, who are also represented on a chimney-piece at Wolfeton (see Introduction, p. 24). Hope, who is much smaller than her sisters, had to be fitted in, almost as an afterthought, in a half-reclining posture. The splendour of this room makes it doubly regrettable that so much else in the house that survived until 1800 has gone, as, for instance, the 'grotesque figures' on the wainscot of the hall, presumably early Tudor panels, of which only a few remain to indicate their character.

Waterston Manor ($1\frac{1}{2}$ miles W. of Puddletown). For a manor house of its modest size Waterston has about it an unusually distinctive architectural character, in spite of having undergone more than the usual number of vicissitudes that befall old houses. Besides going through the usual farmhouse period—Hardy described it in its unregenerate days as the home of Bathsheba Everdene—it was all but gutted by a fire in 1863. It was then rebuilt by the fifth Earl of Ilchester in a manner not unsympathetic considering the time when the work was done, though with some unnecessary elaborations of the original design. Finally, it was acquired by

Captain G. V. Carter, who commissioned Mr Morley Horder to remove the less fortunate Victorian features, replan the interior and lay out an appropriate garden setting. The fire of 1863 spared the south front of the house and the east gable with its Classic frontispiece. This feature, which forms the subject of one of the lithographs in Nash's *Mansions in the Olden Time*, bears the date 1586, and so can be assigned without any doubt to the time of Thomas Howard, second son of the first Lord Howard of Bindon.

The manor of Lower Waterston (or Walterston) had belonged to the Martyns before their migration to Athelhampton on the other side of Puddletown. The last Martyn to live here died in 1377, and thereafter the manor descended by marriage, first to the Govis family, and eventually through the Newburghs and their successors, the Marneys, to the first Lord Howard of Bindon, who married the East Lulworth heiress. Waterston seems to have been given to Thomas Howard as a younger son's portion, and he must have proceeded to enlarge the existing house. His Classic frontispiece, displaying the three Orders (pl. 91), shows him anxious to be in the new architectural fashion, which Elizabethan builders were learning from the Netherlands. It is an attractively naïve composition. The three-light window proved a problem, ingeniously solved by treating its mullions as little Ionic columns. The space below was, no doubt, filled by an heraldic shield, and the usual shell niches flank the entrance. Of the three allegorical figures one represents Justice with her scales, and a second, a gentleman with palm branch and staff, symbolises Contempt of the World; the third is unidentified. The sculptor was at greater pains to get their attributes than their anatomy correct.

The fire and the subsequent rebuilding make it impossible to reconstruct the original plan of the house. The south front (pl. 90), which is built of brick and has its upper storeys plastered, appears to be rather later than the dated gable. Perhaps Thomas Howard did not get very far with his alterations to the older house, for in 1590 his infamous brother died, and he succeeded him as the third Lord Howard of Bindon. Fifteen years later his estates passed to his kinsman, the Earl of Suffolk, who may have bestowed some attention on his Waterston property before selling it in 1641 to Sir John Strangways. This is a charming little front with its three gables united by scalloped arches to let the rain off the roof, its projecting bow rising out of the square porch, and its tall mullioned and transomed windows. The pilasters framing the lower windows and the pediments, which seem to have got stranded over the upper ones, are features more characteristic of the time of Charles I than of Queen Elizabeth. From 1641, for over two and a half centuries, Waterston belonged to the owners of Melbury until bought by Captain Carter.

Various architectural features were utilised by Mr Morley Horder in reconditioning the house. Two Renaissance arches now flank the south front, and another pair have been built into the end of an old range of cottages, which now forms the gatehouse (pl. 92). These arches and a niche in the garden show that much has been lost in the fire and that the house may once have possessed an arcaded loggia like those at Warmwell and West Stafford House. Both inside and out Mr Morley Horder's work makes its effect by its unobtrusiveness; the wing on the right of the east front is an addition quietly in keeping with the rest of the house. A peculiarity of the building is that the two gables of the east front are not in line with one another. This raised a problem in the lay-out of the garden on this side, but it needs a sharp eye to detect that the little water garden that runs out from the Classic frontispiece is not axial to it, but planned to centre on a fine copper beech opposite. Beyond the garden enclosure to the east are traces of old fishponds, while just to the north of the house runs the little river Piddle.

Waterston was sold by Captain Carter in 1936. It is now the home of Colonel H. W. Woodall.

Kingston Maurward. *The old Manor House.* This beautiful stone house stands on the eastern edge of Kingston Park, about a quarter of a mile from the new house which was built to supersede it in the reign of George I. For several generations Kingston was the home of the Greys, who about the end of the fourteenth century acquired the manor by marriage with the heiress of the Maurwards, to whom the place owes the second part of its name. In spite of the vicissitudes through which the building has passed—it has been a farmhouse, 'a home for poor widows,' and was latterly divided into separate dwellings—its exterior has been preserved in a remarkably unspoiled condition (pl. 93). In the perfect symmetry of its E-shaped front it may be compared with Anderson Manor, which, however, is probably somewhat later and is built in brick. Here there was room for intermediate gables between the porch and the wings, giving a five-gable composition, clear cut and well proportioned. There is some uncertainty as to the date of erection. In Hutchins' time there was still armorial glass in some of the windows, and a shield in the hall bore the date 1591, which might have recorded the year of its completion. In that case the builder will have been Christopher Grey, who was a minor at his father's death in 1567 and himself died in 1607. Over the entrance doorway, which, it may be noted, is unusually low, there appears the shield of Grey impaling Stawell, recording the marriage of Angel Grey with Katherine Stawell of Cothelstone in the time of Charles I. This shield may have been set up subsequently, although a date as late as this for the house need not be ruled out. An interesting characteristic is the curious treatment of the mullions of the windows, which are given little moulded bases, rather like the later windows at Wolfeton, suggesting that the same masons worked on both houses. The raised terrace before the main front may well be original, but its balustrade has disappeared. Within, practically all the original features have gone, including the glass mentioned by Hutchins. The later house at Kingston Maurward is described on p. 154.

Poxwell (about 6 miles N.E. of Weymouth). Lying in a hollow of the downs almost equidistant from Weymouth and Dorchester, this long, low manor house stands discreetly back from the high road (pl. 94). A grove of ashes and sycamores overshadows its brick gatehouse, making it look even more like a toy than it appears in a photograph. When first visited by the present writer, the house was still in its unregenerate state. Many of its windows were blind; long grass grew in its forecourt; a rambler straggled across the arch of its porch. Inside, all to the left of the screens passage showed bare, damp-stained walls; for generations this part of the house had been abandoned for dwelling purposes and used, if used at all, for storing apples. The hall still retained a part of its panelling, and under the windows stood the wreck of a long refectory table contemporary with the house itself, its once massive board riddled with rot and worm. But the old building had all the romance surrounding fallen fortunes, and the hand of decay had not been left altogether to work its will: both front and gatehouse had been stripped of their ivy and the structure was for the most part sound. In 1934 thorough repairs were put in hand, entailing the renewal of much decayed woodwork, and Poxwell then became the home of Mr E. F. C. Lane of Bloxworth.[1]

In the Middle Ages Poxwell, or Pokeswell, was a possession of Cerne Abbey, after the dissolution of which it was granted by Queen Elizabeth to Thomas Howard of Lulworth and Bindon. He did not hold it for long, selling it in 1575 to John Henning, a merchant of Poole, whose son was Sheriff of Dorset in 1609. Over the arch of the gatehouse (pl. 96) appears the date 1634. But the house is earlier, since the author of *The Survey of Dorset*, writing about 1625, mentions it as already in existence, 'faire' and 'newe.' The change from stone to brick is curious, but, as Anderson shows, the use of brick was already beginning to penetrate into Dorset, richly supplied with stone as the county was—and is. This gatehouse is only a memory of the defensive gatehouse of mediaeval times; it has shrunk to the proportions of a gazebo. But with its little pyramidal roof and thimble-topped turrets it forms a charming prelude to house and forecourt, the low wall of which, with its broad coping, curves up on both sides as if to receive it. The porch of the house (pl. 95) is decorated, as so often, with a pair of shell-headed niches, and two further pairs

[1] The death of Mr E. F. C. Lane occurred when these pages were already in print.

88 and 89.　HERRINGSTON.　(*Above*) Ceiling of the great chamber (*circa* 1615)
and (*below*) detail of carved woodwork.

90. WATERSTON MANOR
The early seventeenth-century south front.

91. WATERSTON MANOR
The east front with a Classic frontispiece dated 1586.

92. WATERSTON MANOR
The approach through the gatehouse.

93. KINGSTON MAURWARD
The five-gable front of the old manor house, probably built by Christopher Grey.

are placed inside. In one of them appears the date 1613. The screens passage runs between stone walls, and a round-headed arch leads into the hall on the right. At its far end a similar arch leads to the staircase, which retains its oak balustrading, and to the long wing containing kitchen and offices that projects at the back. Upstairs, there is a little panelled room in the angle formed by the wing with the front range, and what was, no doubt, the great chamber contains a rudely carved chimney-piece with allegorical figures and its original gilding still on the stone. The front and the long wing form two sides of a courtyard, which is completed by picturesque ranges of farm buildings.

Poxwell continued in the possession of the Hennings until after 1800, although in 1699 Elizabeth Henning as heiress carried it to her husband, Colonel Thomas Trenchard of Wolfeton. Their daughter married her cousin, George Trenchard, but in 1727 they re-settled the Henning estates, and at the end of the eighteenth century Poxwell was the home of Edmund Henning, banker of Weymouth, who several times entertained George III at the manor house. A two-handled cup presented to him by the King in 1800 is in the possession of a descendant living in Australia.[1] After the failure of the Henning Bank, Poxwell passed to the Pickards of Bloxworth and followed the descent of that house (p. 101). As the representatives of the Trenchards of Wolfeton, the Pickards inherited some of the Trenchard family heirlooms, and these passed to Mr Lane through his mother, who was the daughter of Colonel Jocelyn Pickard-Cambridge of Bloxworth. They include the portrait medallions of the Archduke Philip of Austria and Joanna, his wife, and the silver-mounted Chinese porcelain bowl, traditionally gifts presented to Sir Thomas Trenchard of Wolfeton in gratitude for his hospitality. The story of their visit to Wolfeton is told in the account of that house (p. 60).

Warmwell lies within a mile and a half of Poxwell, on the north side of the Dorchester–Wareham road and close to the point where it is joined by the road from Weymouth. An avenue of horse-chestnuts leads down to the house, which looks southward up smoothly rising parkland, and is sheltered to the east by a copse of beeches, foiling the grey stone of its walls and roofs. The manor was acquired in 1526 by Sir Thomas Trenchard of Wolfeton, having previously belonged to the Newburghs and before them to a family taking its name from the place. In 1618 Sir George Trenchard settled Warmwell on his third son, John, and it was about this time that the building was given its present curious shape. It is an early example of a house planned as a sun-trap, with balancing wings set obliquely to the centre

[1] See a letter from Edmund Thomas Henning, of Newcastle, New South Wales, printed in *Country Life*, Sept. 5, 1936, p. 261, where a photograph of the cup is reproduced.

(pl. 97); but this unusual form seems to have been dictated in part by the desire to preserve portions of an earlier building. To this older house, no doubt, belongs the spiral stone stair on the west giving access to the long gallery on the first floor. The later staircase is on the east side of the house; it has massive balusters of stone, and is carried up in an extraordinary fashion on a kind of bridge. The plan of the building is almost impossible to unravel, scarcely a room in it possessing four right angles. The main front has three shaped gables, each flanked by a pair of round chimneys. The entrance is set back behind two round-headed arches, treated with amusing Classic detail, the whole forming a recessed loggia; on either side of the doorway is a shell-headed niche. Over the arches, in a panel set in the outside wall, is carved a lamb standing on a cap, the crest of Warmwell's later owners, the Richards, one of whom must have placed it there in the eighteenth century. Between 1662 and 1674 the place belonged to John Sadler, the Orientalist, who married John Trenchard's third daughter, Jane. During the Commonwealth he was Master of Magdalene College, Cambridge, and held other offices, all of which he lost at the Restoration, along with the estates that he had acquired in Bedfordshire. His house in Salisbury Court was burnt in the Fire of London, whereupon he retired to Warmwell and 'lived privately till his death, having been much disordered in his senses long before.' The Richards' ownership lasted from 1687 to 1806; in the latter year Warmwell was sold by William Richards on succeeding to Smedmore (p. 162). It then passed by marriage through the purchaser's daughter to Captain Augustus Foster and continued in the Fosters' ownership until 1935. In 1936 the late Lord Ellenborough acquired the estate. Warmwell is now the home of Colonel H. Crawley Ross Skinner.

The mullions in many of the windows were replaced about 1850 by Captain Foster, who also added the bay window at the south-west end of the house. In a few of the rooms, notably the gallery, there remains some Jacobean carved woodwork and wainscoting. On the east side of the house are two Perpendicular windows, which were probably brought from the church at the time when the chancel was rebuilt. Terraced gardens with flights of stone steps rise to the east between the house and the beech grove on the hillside above. Warmwell is famous for its rookery; there is a delightful description of the evening gathering in *Bird Life and Bird Lore*, by the late Reginald Bosworth Smith.

Hanford House ($4\frac{1}{2}$ miles N.W. of Blandford). Where the river Stour has made a breach in the chalk range of mid-Dorset, the two camp-crowned heights of Hod Hill and Hambledon Hill stand out into the vale, with a narrow gap dividing them, through which runs a wooded lane leading from Stepleton Iwerne to Child Okeford. Between the lane and the river lies the many-gabled manor house of Hanford, which has been the property of the Seymers since it was built in the time of James I. This old West Country family, which probably has a common origin with the ducal house of Somerset, purchased the manor in 1599; but they had been established at Hanford as early as Edward IV's reign, probably as tenants of the nunnery at Tarrant Crawford, to which the manor belonged before the Reformation. The present grey stone building is due to Sir Robert Seymer, whose father had purchased the estate. He was a Teller of the Exchequer and a man of note in his day; he was knighted in 1619. An inscription records that he rebuilt the house in 1604, but the date 1623 appears on the lead pipes on the front, which may have been added then to complete the courtyard. Hanford is remarkable for a house of its time in having been designed on the quadrangular plan, which by then was being generally abandoned for the block plan to be seen at Anderson and Kingston Maurward. The mediaeval court-yard house usually consisted of four ranges loosely disposed around a quadrangle. Here a later age that loved symmetry has produced a compact and uniform design. The main front of three gables faces north-west (pl. 98). In the centre is a two-storey Classic frontispiece, framing the arch that leads into the court. The stout oak doors with their wickets still remain in place, and within the entry shell-headed niches are set in the walls on either hand. About 1880 the courtyard was roofed in, so that the projecting porch in the range opposite the gateway now stands under cover in the large hall so formed. This, formerly the real entrance to the house, is dignified by a pair of Ionic pilasters and a large square panel above, in which are displayed the Seymer arms (pl. 99). On the north-east front of the house are four gables, surmounted by round chimneys arranged in pairs, and at either end are two capacious bay windows with five sides to them.

As originally planned, the hall will have been in the inner range, approached no doubt through a screens passage from the porch. In this range there is now a fine staircase, introduced about 1680 to 1700, with twisted balusters and a handrail ending in the fat scroll and thick newel characteristic of the Blandford joiners. An older staircase, contemporary with the house itself, goes up from the north corner of the court; its broad treads are of elm and its newels and stout balusters have the massive character of Elizabethan joinery. From the first-floor landing are reached two rooms which still retain their contemporary ribbed ceilings. The finer of the two is in the larger room, which is at the north end of the entrance range and takes in the deep five-sided bay. The geometrical pattern of its ribs is embellished with pendants and conventionalised designs of flowers, which include the fleur-de-lis and the Tudor rose. The stone chimney-piece in this room (pl. 100), the work of a carver making a brave attempt to interpret designs taken from the Dutch and Flemish pattern-books of the time, belongs to the group discussed in the Introduction (p. 23).

Two caryatids emerging from pedestals of an extraordinarily wayward form flank the chimney opening, over which appears a design of carved strapwork. The overmantel is composed of three shell-headed niches, each ensconced in a frame of stubby Corinthian columns, while between them are set two half-length reliefs of Roman soldiers. The crude and clumsy character of such work helps us to realise how great a revolution in taste Inigo Jones was effecting at this very time.

Close beside the house stands its chapel, a little building that has lost most of its interest. At the back is an enclosed garden with trim box hedges. But the great charm of Hanford is its setting under the steep slope of the hill, on the crest of which the great lines of ramparts are seen breaking the smooth sky-line. The Dorset 'clubmen,' under the leadership of a local parson, were the last warriors to occupy the ancient Camp in a brave but futile attempt to stem the advance of the Parliamentary troops during the Civil War. Hanging like a dark cloud on the hillside is a venerable thicket of yews, many of which are old enough to have furnished long bows for the mediaeval archer. The park itself boasts numbers of magnificent trees; a group of giant planes stands eastward of the house, while an old avenue of horse-chestnuts lines one of the approaches. The male line of the Seymers died out in 1864, but Hanford is still owned by a descendant, who has taken the Seymer name. For many years the house had been let on lease, and since 1947 it has been occupied by Hanford School.

Upcerne (1 mile N. of Cerne Abbas). Pleasantly situated on the side of a hill, this picturesque manor house looks southward down the valley to Cerne Abbas. Anciently a part of the Sherborne estates of the Bishops of Salisbury, the manor was included in the grant of lands made to Sir Walter Raleigh, who parted with it to the Mellors of Winterborne Came (p. 158). The house was built by Sir Robert Mellor, who died in 1624; he was still living when the passage about Upcerne in *The Survey of Dorset* was written. The irregular character of the masonry and various fragments of carving found in the walls make it probable that stone from the ruins of Cerne Abbey was used in their construction. Until the early years of last century the house contained much fine woodwork and plasterwork and some heraldic glass, all of which, except for a few pieces of carving, was destroyed or removed about 1830. The upper room, lighted by the bay window on the left the of east front, was a great chamber; it had a frieze of carved griffins and heraldic shields surrounding the wainscoting, and a barrel ceiling with stucco reliefs on the wall spaces at either end, representing the Judgment of Solomon and Abraham's Offering of Isaac. The right-hand bay on the east front was added at the time of the alterations, made about 1830, to balance that on the left. On the entrance front,

94. POXWELL

The manor house and brick gatehouse before restoration.

95 and 96. POXWELL

(*Left*) The porch of the manor house and (*right*) the brick gatehouse, dated 1634.

97. WARMWELL

The manor house from the south-west. The front is unusual in having the sides set obliquely
to the centre.

98. HANFORD HOUSE

A quadrangular house built by Sir Robert Seymer. It was begun in 1604, but the front
bears the date 1623, perhaps marking the year of completion.

99. HANFORD HOUSE

The inner doorway on the far side of
the court now roofed over.

100. HANFORD HOUSE

Chimney-piece with a curious
assemblage of Classic motives.

101. CHANTMARLE

Built by Sir John Strode, a younger son of the Parnham family. The porch, dated 1612.

facing west, there are four gables, below one of which is the porch (pl. 109); the windows have lights with arched heads, as at Chantmarle. A later wing, incorporating part of an earlier building, runs out northward. The Mellors were succeeded at Upcerne by the White and Batten families.

Chantmarle. This beautiful house, built of Ham Hill stone, stands on the western side of the upper Frome valley 'distant more than a great mile from Cattistock.' An admirable example of early seventeenth-century stone building, it is in some respects archaic for its time and shows how long traditional forms persisted in out-of-the-way parts of the country. Except in the archway of the porch and its flanking niches (pl. 101), Renaissance features nowhere appear. For the windows the old-fashioned arch-headed lights of early Tudor character were used, and the internal doorways are of late Gothic form. The house is dated by an inscription on the keystone of the porch: 'EMMANUEL 1612.' Its construction is unusually well documented for a house of the time, for Sir John Strode, its builder, has left in a manuscript book, now at Nunwell in the Isle of Wight, particulars of the building of the house and former chapel, extracts from which are given in the third edition of Hutchins' *History*. From it we learn that 'Gabriel Moore my surveyor, born about Chinnock[1] in Somersetshire, had of me 20s. monethly, with his dyet, for his paines only, to survey and direct the building to the forme I conceived and plotted it.' Owners in those days often laid claim to the design of buildings of which they merely indicated the general form and plan. Sir John may have drawn a 'plott,' but, no doubt, Gabriel Moore fulfilled all the functions of an architect. The names of the chief masons are also recorded: they were Joseph and Daniel Rowe, 'of Hambdon Hill,' where, perhaps, they owned a quarry. The whole cost of the house amounted to £1,142.

Sir John Strode was a younger son of the family seated at Parnham, and a lawyer by profession. He bought Chantmarle in 1606 from the mortgagees of Christopher Cheverell, who had been compelled by financial difficulties gradually to dispose of his considerable estates. The Cheverells had become possessed of Chantmarle early in the reign of Henry VI by marrying a co-heiress of the original family to which the place owes its beautiful name. Sir John pulled down the greater part of the Cheverells' home, but retained a portion of a wing, which joins his building obliquely at the

---

[1] There are three Chinnock villages—West, Middle and East—all lying south-west of Yeovil and within two or three miles of Ham Hill. One would suppose that Gabriel Moore was related to Robert Moore, freemason, who in 1607 received £5 6s. for cutting the arms of the royal founder over the doorway of the School House at Sherborne, now the School House dining-hall (J. Fowler, *Mediaeval Sherborne* (1951), p. 355).

back (pl. 105). In his diary he tells us that 'there did anciently belong to the manor house an oratory or chapel scituate within the house', but 'being inconveniently placed in the house, low-rooft, little and dark, I therefore in the new building of Chantmarle House did erect and dedicate to the service of God a new oratory or chapel eastward upon the right hand comeing to the house, in a place where formerly was a garden of herbs.' Perhaps out of feelings of reverence he spared that part of the building containing the old chapel, which was identified, at the time when the house was restored, by the discovery of a piscina and of a four-light window blocked up in the east wall. His own chapel, the building and consecration of which he describes in detail, has entirely disappeared, although it survived in a desecrated condition until last century. He laid the foundation-stone in 1612; it was 'finished and covered before the rest of the dwelling house.' It must have possessed a splendid plaster ceiling, 'fretted over with the sun, moone, starrs, cherubims, doves, grapes and pomegranates, all supported with 4 angells in the 4 corners of the roofe.' This work, he says, 'was wrought by Eaton of Stoke-gursey [Stogursey] in Somersett'; the woodwork was fashioned by Edward Batten of Salisbury.

The house was formerly planned '*in forma de littera E, sc. Emmanuel, id est, Deus nobiscum in eternum.*' The E-shape was a common one for houses of the time, but Sir John Strode, with the love of conceits and emblems that characterised his age, gave the letter an esoteric meaning, which he caused to be carved over the entrance. A drawing which J. C. Buckler made in 1828 shows the ruined walls of the south wing still existing. Mr Arthur Stratton, misunderstanding a sentence of Hutchins, doubted whether the wings were ever finished; but in the first edition of the county history there is an engraving of Chantmarle showing both wings entire (pl. 104); moreover, Sir John Strode's memorandum definitely states that the structure was completed in the form of an E. It is probable, however, that he never entirely fitted up the interior, for, as we have seen, he not long afterwards succeeded his brother at Parnham (p. 59). Chantmarle from that time on became only an occasional residence of the family, and in course of time, descending with Parnham to the Oglanders, degenerated to a farmhouse, and eventually the wings were pulled down.

Chantmarle remained a farm until 1910, when it was bought, restored and enlarged by Mr F. E. Savile. He introduced carved woodwork and ornamented ceilings to take the place of the lost fittings, some of which had been removed to Parnham, and he was responsible for re-creating the gardens. These were designed and laid out by Mr Inigo Thomas, and are perhaps his finest achievement. The sloping site called for a different treatment from that Mr Thomas had devised for Athelhampton. The gardens are on three levels, with connecting flights of steps, and diversified by architectural features in character with the house (pl. 103). A long canal (pl. 102), recalling the moat which, according to Strode, 'there was some time invironing the house,' forms the base of the plan, running north and south below the main expanse of garden, from which it is separated by a retaining wall; pairs of obelisks on this wall are related to the cross-axes. Mr C. H. St John Hornby, who bought the property in 1919, extended the gardens and made some further alterations to the house; believing that the best work of all ages can keep happy company, he brought together some notable examples of contemporary craftsman-ship—furniture by the Barnsleys, pottery by the Powells and books printed at the Ashendene Press—which took their place side by side with furniture and ceramics of earlier centuries. At the beginning of the approach to Chantmarle are two charm-ing thatched cottages designed by Mr Alfred Powell. From here one has a view of the house on the far side of the valley, with its pine trees partly screening it and the hill rising up steeply behind.

In 1950 Chantmarle was acquired by the Ministry of Works for use by the Home Office as a police training centre.

Wraxall Manor House. There is a Wraxall in Wiltshire and a Wraxall in Somerset; the Dorset Wraxall lies north-west of Cattistock, and consists of two separate hamlets, a Higher and a Lower. Lower Wraxall claims the church, Higher Wraxall the manor house, which is set in a valley of its own high up in the hills. It is best approached from the Crewkerne–Maiden Newton road down through the woods, when the back of the house is first seen; the front looks eastwards down an avenue of limes. Its seventeenth-century owners were the Lawrences, lessees of the manor farm here, and one of them—perhaps the William Lawrence who died in 1640—may have built the house round about 1620. The regular, stone-built front (pl. 106) has four gables, large mullioned and transomed windows, and a projecting porch in the centre with a smaller and lower gable. The composition is a variant of the three- and five-gable designs of Anderson and Kingston Maurward. The placing of the chimneys on the gable ends must have produced difficulties with the flues, but it is a practice commonly found in Dorset and Somerset houses of the time. A second William Lawrence, born here in 1611, was a lawyer of some emi-nence. A work of his, *Marriage by the Morall Law of God*, is said by Anthony Wood to have been written 'on a discontent arising from his wife (a red-haired buxom woman) whom he esteemed dishonest to him.' In another book he argued in favour of the Duke of Monmouth's claim to the succession. From the time of Henry VIII the manor was divided into two moieties, held by the Stawels and the Bampfields, which were not reunited until the beginning of last century.

In the course of alterations made in recent times a wing was added linking the main building with a detached block at the back of the house. The present owner is Major P. E. Inchbald.

Wynford Eagle ($1\frac{1}{2}$ miles S.W. of Maiden Newton). The old manor house of the Sydenhams stands in one of those deep valleys carved out by the chalk streams, most of them nameless, that feed the Frome in its upper reaches. In Norman times it formed part of the vast estates, held of 'the Honour of the Eagle,' which Gilbert de Aquila ruled from his castle at Pevensey. An eagle to-day crowns the porch of the house in allusion to Wynford's ancient overlordship, but as early as Henry III's reign the Honour had been escheated to the Crown, and it was of the King that the St. Maurs and the Zouches held this manor in the fourteenth and fifteenth centuries. Thomas Sydenham, who purchased Wynford in 1545, was of an old Somerset family, seated originally at Combe Sydenham, near Stogumber. It was his great-grandson, William Sydenham, who rebuilt the house in 1630, the date which appears on the porch. The main front (pl. 107), of dressed Ham Hill stone, faces west across the valley. In the centre a porch rises the full three-storey height of the front, and is flanked on either side by wide gables whose outer side is carried down almost to the level of the upper string course. The north wall of the house shows a surprising change to masonry of alternate flint and white limestone courses; possibly this is a relic of an older house retained at the time of the rebuilding. The entrance has a round-headed arch with projecting keystone and rude capitals to the jambs. Inside, most of the original features have disappeared, except from the north-east bedroom, which is lined with panelling said to be of chestnut but grained; above the open Ham Hill fireplace is an overmantel framing two arched panels with painted landscapes. A large transomed window lights the staircase at the back of the house.

When the Civil War broke out the five sons of William Sydenham were active in support of the Puritan side, and at least four of them fought in the army of Parliament. Colonel William Sydenham, the eldest of the brothers, was made Governor of Weymouth and played a leading part in subduing the local Royalist forces. Afterwards he was one of the founders of the Protectorate, and Cromwell appointed him a member of his Council. Thomas, the fourth of the brothers, was the famous physician, whose *Medical Observations* won him a European reputation. The end of the Sydenham ownership came about in a curious fashion. William Sydenham, the third, put up his estate at a private lottery, making some arrangement whereby the lucky ticket should fall to a friend of the family. It fell, as had been foreseen, to a young lady, but unfortunately she proved a dark horse. Being in love with a neighbouring squire, Doyly Michel of Kingston Russell, she thought the estate

102.   CHANTMARLE

The front of the house seen from the far side of the canal. The gardens were designed by Inigo
Thomas.

103.   CHANTMARLE

Stone piers and Irish yews framing the porch.

To Sir William Oglander of Parnham Bart. this South Elevation of Chantmarle House, Engrav'd at his Expence is respectfully inscrib'd by his obliged humble Servant The Author.

104. CHANTMARLE

The front of Sir John Strode's E-shaped house before the demolition of the wings. An engraving from Hutchins' *History of Dorset* (1774).

105. CHANTMARLE

The back of the house, showing on the left the old wing of the Cheverells' house which Sir John Strode retained.

106. WRAXALL MANOR HOUSE
Built by one of the Lawrence family about 1620.

107. WYNFORD EAGLE
The old manor house of the Sydenhams, dated 1630 on the porch.

108. BLOXWORTH HOUSE
Built by George Savage early in the seventeenth century.

109. UPCERNE MANOR HOUSE
The entrance front.

110. EDMONDSHAM HOUSE
An Elizabethan building, dated 1589 on the porch, with early Georgian wings.

would be a handsome portion to bring him; they married and promptly sold the property to another neighbour. Sydenham, called upon to make a formal surrender, refused, and was committed to Dorchester gaol, where nine years later (in 1718) he ended his days. Lord Wynford, the eminent judge, took his title from Wynford Eagle. The new house, the seat of the present peer, stands about half a mile higher up the valley.

Edmondsham House (1½ miles S.E. of Cranborne). The picturesque front of this manor house (pl. 110), which stands close behind the church, is a happy blend of the work of two different periods. The centre portion, with its shaped gables and mullioned windows, is a part of the Elizabethan house, and the wings are Georgian additions. The date 1589, which is to be seen on the centre gable over the porch, falls within the ownership of Thomas Hussey, who had bought the manor a quarter of a century earlier from its previous owners, the Servingtons. A finely carved escutcheon of the Husseys surmounts the doorway of the porch, the lower stage of which is of stone. The greater portion of the house, however, is of brick, which on the main front has been plastered over. The elevation of the west wing, with its pediment and sashed windows, recalls the similar side façade at Creech Grange, but here an unusual respect was shown for the older work in the treatment of the gable ends, which are of semi-circular outline and decorated with vases, harmonising quite successfully with the centre of the entrance front. These alterations were probably made by the third Thomas Hussey, after whose death in 1745, when the male line of his family became extinct, Edmondsham descended through Frys and Bowers to its present owners, the Monros. The interior of the house has been much altered, but a good solid oak staircase of late seventeenth-century date still remains.

Bloxworth House (6 miles N.W. of Wareham). This is a brick house of Jacobean date, but it has been much altered in the eighteenth and nineteenth centuries. Its situation is a delightful one in a beautiful park on the edge of Bere Wood, which screens it from the heaths that stretch away to the south. The wood covers the rising ground behind the house and effectively protects it from south-westerly gales. The long creeper-covered front is broken by three gables, but only the left-hand one remains unaltered (pl. 108). This and the walling at the back of the house are the only portions of the exterior left undisturbed. The date 1608 is to be seen in the attic room over the porch, to which time much of the existing building can be assigned; the stable range is dated 1649 and 1669. There must have been a house here from very early days. From the year 987 until the Dissolution of the Monasteries the manor was owned by the abbot of Cerne, who seems generally to have leased it to tenants. In 1547 it was sold to Richard Savage, whose descendant, George Savage, built the present house. After the Restoration Bloxworth was purchased by Sir John Trenchard, younger son of Thomas Trenchard of Wolfeton, who was Secretary of State for the Northern Department under William III. His son, George, sold the estate to Jocelyn Pickard of Lincoln's Inn, who had married his daughter, Henrietta Trenchard. The additional surname of Cambridge was assumed by their grandson, the Rev. George Pickard, under the terms of a relative's will, and when the Trenchards of Wolfeton and Lytchet died out, the Pickard-Cambridge family became their representatives in Dorset, as noted under Poxwell (p. 93). The late Mrs Lane of Bloxworth was the only daughter of Colonel Jocelyn Pickard-Cambridge. The house is now the home of her son, Lieut.-Colonel P. G. G. Lane, a younger brother of the late Mr E. F. C. Lane of Poxwell. On higher ground behind the house is an outbuilding with round arched doorways composed of brick voussoirs. This was a brewhouse; pipes running from it into the main building were discovered some years ago.

Anderson Manor (3 miles N.E. of Bere Regis). There are, perhaps, a dozen among the smaller Elizabethan and Jacobean manor houses of England which by the accomplishment of their design stand in a class by themselves. Of these Anderson is certainly one, ranging itself in the mind with such buildings as Cold Ashton near Bath, Nether Hambleton in Rutland, or Lake House near Salisbury. In the Winterborne Valley, in which it lies, one is on the edge of the region where brick building becomes more usual than stone: Anderson is brick-built, with fine stone dressings. The beautifully balanced front, which faces south, owes much of its charm to the lovely texture of the brickwork and the subtlety which made every third course one of flared bricks burnt a dark purple (pl. 111). But the composition itself gains its effect from the shadow contrasts of the recessed centre with the wings and the projecting bay of the porch. The latter, designed as a half octagon and carried up two storeys, is a refinement on the cylindrical bow at Waterston (pl. 90). Besides this effect of depth and fine-drawn shadows, there is the nice sense of proportion, the harmony between verticals and horizontals, and the perfect symmetry, completed by the twin groups of chimneys rising behind the roof-ridge. Like so many houses of its time, Anderson has been ascribed to Inigo Jones, but though quite unfounded, the attribution at least pays tribute to the quality of the design.

John Tregonwell finished his building in 1622, setting the date and his arms on the rainwater heads; and a few years later, when *The Survey of Dorset* was being written, the author was able to say of Anderson: 'where of late Mr Tregonwell has built him a faire house near the church.' A pleasant house it must have been to retire into, as he did in 1624, forsaking the glories (and the expenses) of Milton, which he handed over to his eldest son, newly married. The rise of this family to great estate in Dorset is told elsewhere (p. 109); here we are only concerned with the history of Anderson. Its early chapters are uneventful. 'Winterborne Fyveash,' *alias* Anderson, first crops up in a record of 1294, when the manor was held by William de Stokes of the heirs of John de Burgo. In the following century the great Turberville family were in possession, and retained it until about 1450, when it passed to the Mortons of Milborne. It was from Sir George Morton that John Tregonwell purchased in 1620. But if he sought here a quiet old age, his expectations were destined to be rudely shattered. When the Civil War broke out, his younger son, Thomas, who lived with him, joined the King's side, and in 1645 the old man was threatened with sequestration of his house, 'with imprisonment and plundering and that his bones should lie by it,' unless he compounded. And so 'he was obliged to retire from his usual place of abode, being eighty years of age and very infirm.' Seizure of house and goods followed, and only after payment of a fine of £3,735 was a pardon forthcoming. On the old man's death, Anderson went to the younger son. It remained in the hands of his descendants until 1910, but it had then long ceased to be a place of residence. From its fallen fortunes it was rescued by Mrs Gordon Gratrix, who carefully repaired the building and revealed much in the interior that had been hidden by later accretions. The arrangement of rooms is the traditional one of mediaeval houses, but accommodated to a block plan. From the porch you enter one end of the hall, to which the projection of the right-hand wing serves as a bay. On the left, divided from the hall by a screen, is the old kitchen, now the dining-room, with a great open fireplace. The oak staircase, in the north-west corner of the house, has slender turned balusters and its original dog-gate. The parlour was placed in the middle of the house, on the first floor, having the bay over the porch as an embrasure. Its ceiling has a centre-piece in plaster ornamented with the rose, shamrock, thistle and a fourth obscure emblem, presumably for Wales. Excavation assisted in the rehabilitation of the garden lay-out and forecourt; the old foundations of the terrace were thus discovered and also those of the garden houses. A straight approach through wrought-iron gates and brick gate-piers takes you up to the main front (pl. 112), crossing the stream by a bridge. The formal garden, with its knots of box and yew, lies to the south-east (pl. 111) and is a charming example of its kind; it is bounded to the east by a raised walk of pleached limes. On its north side a thick yew hedge shuts off the bowling green, which runs up to the east side of the house, where the dark form of a great ilex foils the pale brickwork. The kitchen garden lies behind the house, while round to the north-west are grouped the offices in the old brewhouse, cider mill and granary. Mrs Gratrix was followed as owner by Mr J. C.

Tabor and Mr R. H. Cholmondeley. The latter sold Anderson in 1952. It is now the home of Mr Eric Bullivant.

Woolbridge Manor House. From the part it plays in Hardy's *Tess of the D'Urbervilles* this has become the best known of all Dorset manor houses. 'They drove by the level road along the valley to a distance of a few miles, and, reaching Wellbridge [Wool], turned away from the village to the left, and over the great Elizabethan bridge which gives the place half its name. Immediately behind it stood the house . . . whose exterior features are so well known to all travellers through the Froom Valley; once portion of a fine manorial residence and the property and seat of a D'Urberville.' With only a slight change of spelling, Hardy introduced the story of the Turbervilles, the ancient Dorset family to which Woolbridge at one time belonged, and of which he made Tess a humble descendant. Their principal seat was at Bere Regis, where they were established in the time of Edward II or earlier. What remained of their manor house at Bere, which lay to the east of the church, was pulled down early in the nineteenth century. It was a younger son, Thomas Turberville, who early in the reign of Queen Elizabeth acquired the manor of Wool-bridge, which before the Dissolution of the Monasteries had been a possession of Bindon Abbey. Later on, when the elder branch died out, his son succeeded to the principal estate at Bere as well, and both houses continued in his family until the extinction of the male line in the time of Queen Anne. The last Thomas Turberville left as his heirs twin daughters, who lived all their lives together and died at Fulham in the same house on the same day at the age of seventy-seven.

Hackneyed though it is from innumerable photographs, the picture formed by the old house (pl. 114) with the bridge and the river beside it is one of great charm. The lovely blend of stone and tile and old mellowed brick has gained further subtleties of colour from the moss and lichen which have been allowed to grow freely on roofs and gables, so that it would be difficult to find a building that can rival it for loveliness of texture. What we see to-day is probably only a part of the Elizabethan house, which is said to have been garrisoned in the Civil War. The front (pl. 115) faces north, and on its porch is a stone with the letters I.T. and a date which might be 1635 or 1653. If the latter, it may record a rebuilding, perhaps in consequence of damage sustained in the wars during the ownership of Sir John Turberville, who was Sheriff of the county in 1652. The front is an interesting example of seventeenth-century brickwork, but the stone gables at either end of the range are certainly older. The fine brick chimneys, with their pairs of arched niches, seem also to date from the time of the remodelling. Hutchins records that in his day there were to be seen over a door in the hall the arms of Turberville impaling Howard

111. ANDERSON MANOR
From the south-east.

112. ANDERSON MANOR
Looking up the drive to the front of the house framed by the piers of the entrance gates.

113. ANDERSON MANOR

Built by John Tregonwell of Milton in 1622. A beautifully balanced front of brick with stone dressings.

of Bindon. (John Turberville, died 1623, married Lady Anne Howard.) While these have gone, there still remain the faded portraits of the two Turberville ladies whose features caused Tess to shudder. As the charwoman explained to Angel Clare, 'Owing to their being builded into the wall, they can't be moved away.' On the old thatched barn by the road there has been worked into the gable a little cinquefoil window, which may have come from the ruins of Bindon Abbey.

Trent Manor (3 miles N.W. of Sherborne). Much altered as this old house has been, it preserves historic memories that make it among the most romantic in Dorset. For here, in the guise of William Jackson, came Charles II on his flight from Worcester field, and was sheltered by the Wyndhams while plans were made for his escape from Charmouth. The exciting story has often been told, and there is not space to repeat it in detail here. After the King had ridden over to Charmouth

Hiding Place.   Interior.

and spent an anxious night at the inn, the carefully laid plans were found to have miscarried, and he was obliged to return to Trent. Here he remained for several days more before going on to Heale House, near Salisbury, from which the final journey was made to Brighthelmstone (Brighton), where the escape was at last effected. Altogether Charles was at Trent for about nineteen days. He was lodged in Lady Wyndham's chamber, in a part of the house that remains comparatively

C.H.D.—14

unaltered. Below it was the kitchen, and in the wall are two secret panels, through which the King is said to have received his food; he is supposed to have maintained communication with his friends by a string suspended in the kitchen chimney. Adjoining this panelled room is a secret chamber with a hiding-place below the floor boards, from which it was formerly possible to find a means of escape through the brew-house chimney. It is unlikely that the King had to spend much time in this secret chamber, although it may have been used during moments of alarm. A sketch of the hiding-place by the late Sidney Heath is reproduced.

The existence of a hiding-place in the house is a reminder that the Gerards, who owned Trent in the time of Queen Elizabeth and James I, were Roman Catholics, and it was, no doubt, originally contrived to shelter a priest in an emergency. We shall come across the Gerards again at Waddon Manor (p. 147). The most distinguished member of the family was Thomas Gerard, the antiquary (1593–1634), who was the author of *The Survey of Dorset*, for long ascribed to John Coker of Mappowder (see Introduction, p. 43). The Gerards acquired Trent in the time of Henry VIII through the marriage of William Gerard with Mary Storke, to whose family it had previously belonged. Thomas Gerard's second daughter, Anne, brought Trent to her husband, Colonel Francis Wyndham, and it was they who sheltered the royal fugitive. A large part of the house, including the entrance front, only dates from last century, but the portion of the building in which Charles II lodged is of great age and preserves mediaeval features. A wing at right angles to the old part of the house, running eastward, is dated 1706. Like Sandford Orcas, Trent was formerly in Somerset; it was transferred to Dorset in 1896.

114.   WOOLBRIDGE MANOR HOUSE

Formerly a seat of the Turbervilles, seen from across the Frome.

115.   WOOLBRIDGE MANOR HOUSE

Seventeenth-century brickwork on the north front.

116. MILTON ABBEY

The west front of Lord Milton's mansion designed by Sir William Chambers and completed by James Wyatt. Intended to harmonise with the abbey church, it is a Classic composition in a Gothic dress.

117. MILTON ABBEY

The fourteenth-century Benedictine church from the south-east, now used as the school chapel.

CHAPTER TWO

Milton Abbey, Forde Abbey
and Melbury

ORSET was more fortunate than most counties in the destinies of her religious houses after their surrender to Henry VIII's Commissioners. Three of the great churches were spared—Sherborne, Wimborne and Milton—and there are also some remains to show at Abbotsbury and Cerne, in the gigantic tithe barn of the one, and the porch-tower and guesthouse of the other. It seems little enough, however, when one realises that in proportion to its size Dorset was as richly endowed with monastic foundations as any county in England. Besides the four important Benedictine monasteries of Sherborne, Milton, Cerne and Abbotsbury, there was also the great Benedictine nunnery at Shaftesbury, the foundation of King Alfred, whose daughter was its first abbess. Its ground plan has been uncovered in part, to give one some faint idea of the glorious sight the town must have presented when the abbey crowned its precipitous hill. Of the two Cistercian houses Tarrant was a nunnery, founded by Bishop Poore of Salisbury; in its church was buried a Queen of Scotland, Joan, the sister of Henry III, but hardly a trace of its buildings now remains. Bindon Abbey, the Cistercian monastery, preserves a few ivy-covered walls and the lovely beech-shaded moats which surround a Calvary Mount. Forde, also a Cistercian house, belonged to Devon until the changes made in the county boundary just over a century ago.

Only Forde and Milton, the two abbeys which had their domestic buildings converted to secular use, fall within the scope of this book. Both have undergone great changes, Forde in the middle of the seventeenth century, Milton a hundred years later, when all but the abbot's hall was pulled down to make way for the 'Gothic' mansion which Sir William Chambers designed to harmonise with the abbey church. Melbury is grouped with these two buildings, as a third house which combines the work of more than one period. Sir Giles Strangways, its builder, was, like Tregonwell, who purchased Milton, one of Henry VIII's Commissioners; he, too, availed himself of the opportunity of acquiring church property by purchasing Abbotsbury; and as he must have been building Melbury much about the time when Abbot Chard was adding new grandeur to Forde, an interesting comparison that is not without its irony is set up between the work of the two men.

Milton Abbey. Although its remote and lovely setting would suggest that of a Cistercian foundation, Milton, in contrast to Forde, was a Benedictine abbey. The romantic solitude of its surroundings is deceptive, for the woods and lawns and lake that made this valley so enchanting were in reality only an eighteenth-century creation. Buck's view of 1733 shows the downs as bare as they still are farther south towards Milborne before their slopes begin to close in, and at that time the abbey, like other Benedictine houses, had the dwellings of a township clustering round it. It was owing to the high-handed action of its Georgian owner that Milton acquired its seclusion and beauty, standing in its amphitheatre of hills, though some of the glory has departed since the surrounding woods were felled. About 1770 Joseph Damer, Lord Milton, decided that he would remove the village, which had once been a prosperous little market town, so that it should not be visible from the windows of the new mansion he had resolved to build. All the houses but one were razed to the ground, and the inhabitants were rehoused in the model village of thatched cottages which runs up the hillside well out of sight. It is hardly surprising to find the author of this drastic project described by Horace Walpole as 'the most arrogant and proud of men.'

There is space to give only the bare outline of the abbey's history. It owed its foundation to King Athelstan, though the exact date is unknown. According to one story, he founded it as an act of expiation for having caused the death of his brother; another makes it a thankoffering for his victory over the Danes at Brunanburgh in 938. No traces remain either of the Saxon or Norman church. The present building (pl. 117) was erected after the fire of 1309 that destroyed its predecessor. Most of the existing work dates from the reigns of Edward II and Edward III. It is unusually simple and restrained for its period, the purity of its outline and the beauty of its mouldings recalling the style of the previous century. The Black Death seems to have caused an interruption, for the tower and the north transept are early Perpendicular in style. They were added in the fifteenth century, when Ham Hill stone was introduced. The contrast of its golden hue with the grey stone of the earlier work is still as striking to-day as five centuries ago. The Lady Chapel has gone, and so have all the domestic buildings with the exception of the abbot's hall. The nave, it is thought, may never have been rebuilt, since no traces of its foundations could be discovered when excavations were made in 1865 at the time of the restoration by Sir Gilbert Scott, but it is worth noting that a church with three spires, implying that there was a nave with western towers, is shown on the seal of the abbey.

The interior has suffered from the 'restoring' zeal of James Wyatt and by the removal of much of the original furniture in the eighteenth century; but the same beauty of line and proportion prevails within as without. Only in the lierne vaulting of the crossing, contrasting with the simple ribbed vault of the choir, and in the high reredos with its elaborately canopied niches, filling the whole width of the wall below the east window, is there a note of richness. The reredos, which for a long period was entirely concealed by plaster, was restored by Wyatt; an inscription below the second tier of niches records that it was painted at the expense of Abbot William Middleton and Master Thomas Wilkin, vicar, in 1492. On the south side of the altar are the sedilia with richly carved canopies. The stone screen remains under the eastern arch of the crossing, but has been partly rebuilt. Against it stand two canopied stalls, under which are crude paintings of Athelstan as donor and his mother or his queen with a hawk in her hand. These are all that remain of the mediaeval paintings with which the church was once enriched. Twelve painted panels of apostles, which were removed from the abbey in 1774, are now in the church at Hilton. But one exceptionally interesting and very rare piece of church furniture has been preserved. This is a late Gothic carved wood tabernacle, or hanging pyx, which is now in the south transept. The splendid seven-light window with reticulated tracery in the south wall of this transept contains excellent glass by Pugin, inserted in 1849. On the exterior of the north transept traces of the cloister are visible. After the surrender of the monastery four bays of the cloister were removed and taken to Hilton church, where they were re-erected to form a range of windows for the north aisle. That church contains other carved stonework which probably came from Milton, including perhaps the fan vault of the south porch.

At the Dissolution in 1539 the abbey was granted to John Tregonwell, one of the Commissioners for the surrender of the monasteries, who paid £1,000 for the property. The transaction seems to have been carefully arranged beforehand with the assent of the Abbot, John Bradley, who was appointed Suffragan Bishop of Shaftesbury. Tregonwell, who came of a Cornish family, had been bred to the law and had been chosen one of the King's Proctors in the Divorce Case. He was subsequently knighted and died at Milton in 1565. His altar tomb of Purbeck marble stands in the north aisle of the church; the brass is the latest extant example showing a man wearing a tabard.[1] Tregonwell made over the abbey church to the parishioners; the domestic buildings he converted into a house, which remained with his descendants for a hundred and fifty years. His great-grandson, John Tregonwell III, purchased Anderson and built the fine Jacobean house there (p. 102), leaving Milton to his eldest son. John Tregonwell V as a child had a miraculous escape when he fell uninjured from the roof of the abbey church. He owed his life to the fact that

[1] There are others at Puddletown of Christopher Martyn (died 1524) and at Melbury Sampford of Sir Giles Strangways (died 1562).

he was wearing a full dress made of nankeen, which, blowing out in the wind, acted as a parachute, completely breaking the force of the fall. 'As a thankfull acknowledgement of Gods wonderfull mercy,' he bequeathed in his will a library of books to the church.

After the death of this Tregonwell, Milton passed by his daughter to Sir Jacob Bancks, son of the Swedish Ambassador to the Court of Charles II. In 1752 it was sold to Joseph Damer, 'the heir of Swift's old miser and usurer,' Damer of Winterborne Came (p. 158). He married a daughter of the first Duke of Dorset and was created Baron Milton in 1753 and Earl of Dorchester in 1792. It was he who with such a bland disregard for the inhabitants of Milton transplanted the whole village, rebuilt the abbey house and carried out the magnificent landscape planting which has made the park one of the glories of Dorset. For some years after his purchase he contented himself with refacing and remodelling the old buildings, which were ranged round an irregular courtyard with the great hall on the south side. When Dr Pococke visited Milton in October 1754, he noted about the house: 'Lord Milton is casing it all round in a beautiful modern manner.' In addition to the great hall he mentions 'a room called the Starchamber, from the wooden cieling in compartments adorn'd with gilt stars.' A description of the old house is given by Hutchins, who states that Jacob Bancks, Sir Jacob's son and successor, shortly before his death in 1737, began to rebuild the part west of the hall 'in order to make some new apartments, but he lived only to finish the shell, and they were completed by Lord Milton.' John Vardy, William Kent's associate, was engaged for this work. In the library of the Royal Institute of British Architects there are a number of his drawings for Milton. One of them, dated 1755, is a section 'for the Great Room one Pair of Stairs at Milton.' There are also alternative designs for a Gothic and Classic treatment of a building seven windows wide with an additional bay at each end. If one of these was carried out, it would probably have formed a new west front, having the 'Great Room' in the middle on the first floor.

Between 1763 and 1770 Lord Milton employed Capability Brown to create the landscape park.[1] Then, perhaps on Brown's advice, he decided to pull down most of the old house and to build a new mansion in a Gothic style harmonising with the abbey church. Sir William Chambers was approached for designs, and his work extended over the years 1770–74. Chambers seems to have disliked the commission as much as he did his client. In his correspondence[2] he writes of 'this vast ugly Gothic

[1] Dorothy Stroud, *Capability Brown* (1950), pp. 81–2.

[2] Letter-books in the British Museum, Add. MSS. 41,133–36. These extracts are quoted by H. M. Colvin in his account of Chambers in his *Dictionary of English Architects, 1660–1840*.

118. MILTON ABBEY

Looking down on the church from St Catherine's chapel. A photograph taken before the felling of the woods.

119 and 120. MILTON ABBEY

(*Left*) The porch of Abbot William Middleton's great hall (1498). (*Right*) The grass staircase leading up to St Catherine's chapel.

121. MILTON ABBEY

Interior of the great hall, built by Abbot Middleton in 1498, looking towards the screens or 'speres'. A photograph taken in the Hambros' time.

house in Dorset' and 'this unmannerly imperious Lord, who had treated me, as he does every body, ill.' The courtyard plan of the old house was retained but enlarged northward, and it is possible that the Vardy building, if executed, was incorporated as the centre of Chambers's west front, but with the elevation redesigned. The Gothic treatment of the exterior is not even skin-deep. To give the house a mediaeval flavour reliance was placed on the furbishings—the parapet,[1] answering that on the church, the angle shafts and pinnacles, the shapes of windows and doorways: the massing and symmetrical composition are characteristically Georgian (pl. 116). The entrance is in the north front under a 'Tudor' arch set between three-sided bays—the whole forming a well-designed central feature vaguely reminiscent of a Gothic gatehouse. In the interior the mediaeval pretence was dropped altogether. Here Chambers seems to have done little. The staircase and dining-room may have been designed by him, but in 1775 James Wyatt was called in, and he was responsible for the decoration of most of the important rooms, which he treated in the fashionable manner of the brothers Adam. The finest of them, the saloon, in the centre of the long west front, on the first floor, may have been 'the Great Room' for which Vardy had made his design twenty years earlier. Wyatt gave it a segmental ceiling and delicate stucco ornament. His drawings for this room, described as 'the Gallery,' are dated July, 1776. These, with designs for other rooms by him, are also in the R.I.B.A. library, where, besides, there are many drawings for chimney-pieces at Milton by Thomas Carter and Richard Westmacott senior. The marble fireplace in the saloon was carved by Westmacott from Wyatt's design. Later, in 1789, Wyatt was employed by Lord Milton on the restoration of the abbey church.

In rebuilding the house Lord Milton was sensible enough to preserve the abbot's hall on the south side of the courtyard (pl. 121). This was kept as a genuine piece of mediaevalism and forms a transition both in style and date between the true Gothic of the church and the feigned 'Gothick' of the house. It is interesting to compare this fine Tudor hall with the somewhat later and still more elaborate example at Forde. It was built by the last abbot but one, William Middleton or Milton (1481–1525), whose rebus, a mill over a tun, appears in several places on the building. The date 1498 is to be seen both on the stonework and on the screen. The latter, carved with panels of tracery and quatrefoils, consists of three portions—two projecting from the walls and an isolated screen standing in the centre. In mediaeval documents

---

[1] The plate of Milton Abbey in the first edition of Hutchins (1774) shows the house with battlements all round and with some differences in fenestration. If this can be trusted, it would seem that some modifications to the design were made later by Wyatt. He added the pierced parapet to the tower, aisles and north transept of the church; the parapet on the house corresponds.

the two lateral sections of this type of screen are often referred to as the 'speres.'[1]
The cusped ogee-shaped cresting is an addition, but the groups of pinnacles above
the uprights appear to be original. The roof is a massive example of hammer-beam
form, a type that is seldom met with in the West of England. The nearest parallel
to it is the hall roof at Weare Giffard in Devon, where the detail is even richer than
here. The brackets supporting the hammer-beams are carried down on to wall
shafts terminating in sculptured angels holding shields. Further shields with heraldic
devices are carved beneath the windows, on the wall over the dais, and in the bay
window. On the porch (pl. 119) appear the arms of England, those of the abbey and
its founder, along with the monogram and rebus of Middleton (in the spandrels of
the arch).

The first Earl of Dorchester died in 1798. In the north transept of the church is
the fine monument by Carlini, in which he is represented leaning inconsolably over
the body of his wife. His eldest son, who married the sculptress, Anne Seymour
Conway, committed suicide in 1776; the second son succeeded, and on his death
in 1808 the earldom became extinct. A sister, Lady Caroline Damer, then came into
the property, which passed subsequently to the second Earl of Portarlington. His
successor in 1852 sold Milton to Baron Hambro.

To the east, high above the abbey and approached by a flight of some two hundred grass-cut steps, is the little Norman chapel of St Catherine (pl. 120), once a
place of great sanctity for pilgrims. From here a superb view is obtained of the
church and the house beside it, and away beyond, over the lawns and down the park
to the wooded slopes on the far side of the valley (pl. 118). Unfortunately, the fine
beeches which clothed the hill on which the chapel stands were felled after the break-
up of the estate in 1933, as were those on the southern slope above the eighteenth-
century village. It is uncertain whether the village was planned by Chambers or
Brown. Both seem to have prepared plans for it. Pairs of cottages, roofed with thatch
and standing each in its plot of ground, wind up the hill out of sight of the house;
between them, evenly spaced, horse-chestnuts were planted and allowed to grow to
a great size. A Gothic church, consecrated in 1786, an almshouse and a communal
well completed this early example of village planning. Until 1933 the whole village
street in its sylvan setting was perfect and unaltered, but blemishes were not long in
appearing after it had passed out of the care of the Hambros.

In 1932 the Benedictines of Downside were anxious to acquire the house for a
preparatory school and to restore the abbey church to monastic use, but it was found
that the parochial rights in the church had not been extinguished, although for

---

[1] Similar screens of this type may be seen in the hall of Chetham's Hospital, Manchester, and at
Wortham, in the west of Devon, where, however, the hall has a flat ceiling.

122. FORDE ABBEY

From the south-west. On the left is Abbot Chard's early sixteenth-century great hall with its porch-tower. The chapel, originally the chapter house, is on the extreme right.

123. FORDE ABBEY
The great hall, built by the last abbot, Thomas Chard, about 1528.

150 years it had been used as a private chapel. The house, the church and a portion of the park were eventually sold to the Ecclesiastical Commissioners and Milton became a centre for faith-healing. In 1953 the house was threatened with demolition, but a new use has been found for it as a public school for boys, and Milton is now again full of life and activity. The church has become the school chapel and the abbot's hall is the dining hall. Early in 1956 the east side of the courtyard was seriously damaged by fire, but it has since been carefully restored.

Forde Abbey. If Forde preserves no vestige of its abbey church, the greater part of its domestic buildings remain, including the extensive additions made by its last abbot, Thomas Chard. At the time of the Surrender this work of Chard's was but a few years old, and it must have seemed to the lay owner to whom the abbey was granted both too new and too fine to demolish along with the church. A hundred years later Forde was still a covetable possession when Edmund Prideaux, Cromwell's Attorney-General, purchased it and spent money lavishly in remodelling its interior. His work has been attributed to Inigo Jones, but on no reliable foundation. The introduction of seventeenth-century Classicism into this monastic setting is a strange anomaly; but time has softened the disharmony, and the stately suites of rooms, with their fine woodwork and rich plaster ceilings, are among the most splendid examples of their period.

Forde was a Cistercian abbey and one of the earliest houses of the order to be established in England. The story goes that in 1136 Richard de Redvers, Earl of Exeter, founded an abbey at Brightley within his lordship of Okehampton, to which an abbot and twelve monks came from Waverley. In the following year their patron died, and the little community, after struggling on as best they could for four years, abandoned their new home and, half starving, set forth on foot to return to the mother-house in Surrey. As they were passing through Thorncombe on the borders of Devon and Dorset, they met Adelicia, the sister of their founder, whose home Thorncombe was. Moved by their plight, she gave them her house and manor with its rich lands beside the winding Axe, and here, at a spot where there was a ford across the river, they built their monastery, which soon gained a reputation for the learning and asceticism of its inmates. To the time of Baldwin, the third abbot, who afterwards became Archbishop of Canterbury and died in 1190 in the Holy Land on the third Crusade, the earliest surviving portion of the abbey probably belongs. This is the vaulted chapter house, which is now the private chapel, at the east end of the long south front which the house presents. The foundations of the church lie below the lawn; the domestic buildings were laid out on the north side between the church and the river and they remain substantially intact, except for the greater part of the west range and the east, west and south walks of the cloister. The west range came forward from the arcaded portico to the right of Chard's tower to join the north side of the church; originally it must also have extended northward and provided accommodation for the lay brothers as well as the cellarer's quarters. The north walk of the cloister remains between the portico and the east range. Northward from the chapter house runs out the monks' dormitory, a range 168 feet long, carried on a vaulted undercroft. This is of early thirteenth-century date, as is shown by the character of the vaulting and the long line of lancet windows, which on the west side have been left unaltered. On the north side of the cloister quadrangle is the former refectory or frater, built, according to the Cistercian rule, at right angles to, instead of parallel with, the line of the nave. This building, originally longer, was divided into two floors in the later days of the monastery; it is covered by a fine fifteenth-century roof of the arch-braced collar-beam type. A recess in the east wall near the north end marks the position of the frater pulpit. Immediately to the west of the refectory is the kitchen, which still fulfils its original function.

The great additions which Abbot Chard made in the last days of the monastery formed a new range prolonging westward the north range of domestic buildings as far as the fifteenth-century gatehouse. He built in this position a new Abbot's Lodging of great splendour with a porch-tower three storeys high and a great hall exceeding in size the monks' refectory (pl. 122). An inscription in Gothic lettering on the tower records that the work was completed in 1528. It has been suggested that here, as at Fountains, the abbot and monks, scenting the dangers ahead, determined to lock up as much as possible of their money in new buildings. Actually, Chard's magnificent hall can have been in use for only a dozen years, while the cloister which he began to rebuild was never completed, and it was left to the Elizabethan owner of the house to finish off with plaster ribs the vault of fan tracery intended for it. Some of the ornament on the tower was also left unfinished; the central boss of the vaulting of the porch, for instance, remains uncarved. Chard's building has the delicacy and rather feminine charm that characterise much early Tudor work; the plain wall surfaces enhance the carved detail and the centuries have given a lovely patina to the golden Ham Hill stone. In all but a few details it is late Perpendicular Gothic; but in the frieze of panels running below the battlements Renaissance motives make their appearance, showing that among the carvers there was at least one familiar with the new Italian ornament then becoming fashionable. It is interesting to compare the porch-tower with that of Cerne, which was built by Abbot Sam about twenty-five years earlier. The feature of both these porches is the double-tiered oriel carried on richly moulded corbelling (pl. 2). The great hall was deprived of its two western

124. FORDE ABBEY

Interior of the chapel, originally the chapter house of the Cistercian abbey.

125. FORDE ABBEY

Tapestries in the saloon, woven at Mortlake from the Raphael cartoons bought by
Charles I.

127. FORDE ABBEY

The dining-room in the block at the west end of the great hall which was remodelled by Prideaux. Mid-seventeenth-century panelling and plasterwork.

126. FORDE ABBEY

The great staircase formed in 1658 by Edmund Prideaux, who was Attorney-General during the Commonwealth. A fine example of the type with openwork carving in the balustrade.

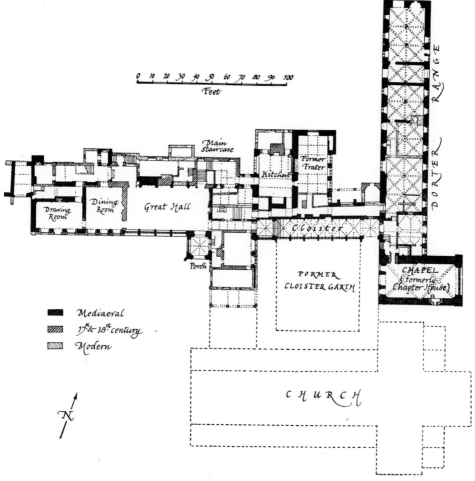

Scale: 0 10 20 30 40 50 60 70 80 90 100 Feet

Labels on plan: Main staircase · Former Frater · Kitchen · DORTER RANGE · Drawing Room · Dining Room · Great Hall · Cloister · Porch · FORMER CLOISTER GARTH · CHAPEL (formerly Chapter House) · CHURCH

Legend: ■ Mediaeval · ▨ 17th & 18th century · ▧ Modern

N

FORDE ABBEY

Ground-floor plan of the house. The approximate position of the destroyed church
is indicated.

bays when the space was utilised in the seventeenth century for forming additional
rooms, but even in its curtailed form—it now measures 55 ft. by 28 ft.—it is a splendid hall, retaining its original panelled ceiling, painted and gilded and ornamented
with stars (pl. 123). The panelling is early eighteenth century and fine work of its
date, though one may regret the loss of the original Tudor panels which, no doubt,
it superseded.

Abbot Chard surrendered the monastery on March 8, 1539. It was granted by
the King to Richard Pollard, one of the many sons of Sir Lewis Pollard of King's

Nympton in Devon. Later, Forde passed successively to Sir Amyas Paulet and William Rosewell. In 1649 the property was bought by Edmund Prideaux, a lawyer of great ability, who for ten years held the office of Attorney-General under the Commonwealth. His legal practice brought him a large fortune, part of which he spent on remodelling and decorating the house he had purchased. The name of Inigo Jones, as we have noted, is traditionally associated with his work at Forde; but as the King's Surveyor-General was a confirmed Royalist, it is unlikely that he would have placed his services at the disposal of Prideaux; moreover, the woodwork and plaster ceilings for which the house is remarkable, though following his style, fail to come up to his exacting standards, and most of the alterations were carried out after his death, which occurred in 1652. The date 1658 appears on the staircase ceiling, and the arms in the centre of the ceiling in the saloon record the marriage of the Attorney-General's son in 1655. Edmund Prideaux himself died in 1659 and, no doubt, his son completed what remained unfinished. Until recently it has been usual to attribute to John Webb most of the Commonwealth houses formerly believed to be by Jones, but Webb himself used the Palladian style with the scholarship and much of the sensitiveness of his master, whereas in many of the Commonwealth houses the Classic system of proportions which Jones observed so scrupulously receives scant regard and there is a liberal admixture of Flemish detail lacking refinement and sometimes crude. Mr Howard Colvin's discovery that Thorpe Hall, Northamptonshire, which was formerly attributed to Webb, was in fact designed by Peter Mills, a London builder, has thrown fresh light on the houses built by men who held high office under the Protectorate. Thorpe was the seat of Oliver St John, who was Chief Justice of the Common Pleas, and the new Wisbech Castle, which was probably also by Mills, was commissioned by John Thurloe, Secretary to the Council of State. The woodwork, chimney-pieces and plasterwork at Forde show closer analogies with their counterparts at Thorpe than with any of Webb's authentic work, so that Prideaux, like St John and probably Thurloe, may have employed Mills to make his alterations. It would seem that the plasterers were given a fairly free hand in applying ornament to the ceilings, for while the main lines of their designs correspond with the types introduced by Inigo Jones, the decoration is exuberantly rich and elaborate, and some of the detail still has a Jacobean flavour about it.

The Prideaux alterations involved the formation of new rooms in the space cut off from Chard's hall and the remodelling of the block immediately to the west. Here is the dining-room (pl. 127), and beyond it the small drawing-room, both possessing Classic chimney-pieces, rich ceilings and large-scale panelling, hung in the latter room with tapestry. In the reconstruction of this end of the house Classic windows were substituted for Gothic, but here, as in the chapel block, the battle-menting was preserved, and what incongruity there is comes from the later replace-ment of leaded lights by octagonal and lozenge panes in the 'Gothick' taste of Horace Walpole. The most important of Prideaux's alterations was the formation of the saloon on the first floor, in what had been the west range of the cloister court, and the introduction of a great staircase leading up to it from the north door of the hall. The staircase, treated in the grand manner with a balustrade composed of large panels of open-work carving, is an early example of a type that first appears in houses of the Commonwealth period and only became fashionable after the Restoration (pl. 126). There is one of the same kind at Thorpe Hall. On the wall side the pattern of the carving is repeated in a dado of painted panels. The great saloon, placed immediately to the east of Chard's tower, is a splendid room. It has a ceiling of fifteen compartments, in the centre of which is a curiously quartered shield, heraldically incorrect but managing to record the marriages of Edmund Prideaux senior and junior by setting the impaled arms of one above the other. The oak panelling, divided by tall Corinthian pilasters, is partly concealed by the five great Mortlake tapestries (pl. 125) after the famous Raphael cartoons.[1] These tapestries are said to have been given by Queen Anne to her minister, Francis Gwyn, who in-herited Forde by marrying the Prideaux heiress. The chimney-piece has an elabor-ately carved overmantel, but the marble fireplace is modern. In the suite of rooms east of the saloon is a bedroom with another rich ceiling. Further rooms were fitted up over the cloister and above the chapel (the old chapter house), and the chapel itself was provided with its handsome screen, a characteristic example of mid-seventeenth-century carving (pl. 124). With its Norman walls and ribbed vaulting, its Perpendicular east window and its seventeenth-century screen and pulpit, the chapel epitomises the three most important phases in the history of the building. Against the north wall is placed the Prideaux family monument.

Very little change has come over Forde since the Prideauxs' time. Francis Gwyn, who married Margaret Prideaux in 1680 and succeeded his father-in-law in 1702, set up on a rainwater head on the south wall of the chapel his name and office: 'SECRE-TARY AT WAR TO QUEEN ANNE, 1713.' This position he held in the Tory ministries of Harley and Bolingbroke. In the expectation of a visit from his sovereign, which never materialised, he carried out extensive refurnishings, and fitted up for her reception the bedroom above the dining-room, which is still called Queen Anne's room. As already mentioned, the tapestries in the saloon were a gift to him

---

[1] The original cartoons were bought by Charles I on the advice of Rubens and are now in the Victoria and Albert Museum.

from Queen Anne. They were put up for auction, but bought back, when in 1846
the abbey was sold by John Fraunceis Gwyn to John Miles of Bristol. Much of the
Prideaux and Gwyn furniture was dispersed at that time, the Queen Anne bed
with its crimson velvet hangings going for no more than £8. In 1864 the Abbey
was bought by Mrs Bertram Evans, who spent large sums on its restoration. On the
death of her daughter in 1906, it was left to Mrs Freeman Roper, mother of Mr
Geoffrey Roper, the present owner.

In the space at our disposal it has only been possible to touch on a few aspects
of this beautiful and historic house, which, to describe it adequately, would require
a book to itself. Besides the richness and variety of its architectural interest, Forde
can claim many historical associations. The younger Prideaux entertained Monmouth
here in 1680 on his progress through the West; he was, therefore, arrested five years
later, after Monmouth's failure at Sedgemoor, and had to pay Judge Jeffreys £15,000
for his release. In the early part of the nineteenth century, when Jeremy Bentham
tenanted the abbey, John Stuart Mill paid several visits, and the two men used to sit
for hours writing at different tables in the saloon. The beautiful grounds of the house
are notable for their gardens, fine lawns and trees, the series of ponds, once the
monks' fishponds, and the presence of the Axe winding through the pastoral valley.
The present owner has re-made the long pond west of the house, erected new gates
to the east and carried out many other improvements, besides planting extensively
on the estate.

Melbury. Seldom before the seventeenth century were great houses built on high
sites: the older manor houses almost invariably nestle in the shelter of valleys. But
Melbury is an exception to this rule. Even Horace Walpole, who was nothing if
not critical, thought it 'a sumptuous old seat in a fine situation.' The magnificent
deer park, which boasts some of the finest timber in Dorset, great oaks, limes and
chestnuts and a noble avenue of sycamores, covers a vast extent of the high ground
north of Evershot, where the chalk ridge throws out a series of promontories overlooking the Vale of Blackmore. From Bubb Down, a little to the east, it is possible
to see on a clear day both the Quantocks and the Mendips, and even to pick out the
towers of Wells Cathedral.

There are three Melburys in this part of Dorset. Melbury Sampford now com-
prises little more than the great house and the cruciform church lying a short distance
to the east of it. With it has usually gone Melbury Osmond, lying lower down the
slopes to the north, although for a century and a half in later mediaeval times the
manors were divided. The Sampfords, who gave their name to the place, held it
in the second half of the thirteenth century; the manor subsequently passed by

129. MELBURY

Tombs of Brunings and Strangways in Melbury Sampford church.

128. MELBURY

An octagonal garden house with an eighteenth-century Gothic doorway.

130. MELBURY

The south front of the house seen across the lake. The nineteenth-century additions are on the left.

131. MELBURY

From the south-west. An early Tudor house altered towards the end of the seventeenth century.

marriage through Foliots and Maltravers to the Brunings. A fine alabaster effigy of William Bruning rests on a canopied tomb under the north transept arch of the church (pl. 129); it was erected by his widow in 1467.[1] In 1500 his grandson, another William, sold the reversion of Melbury Sampford to Henry Strangways for 600 marks. This is the only occasion on which the property has passed by sale, but as Henry Strangways had married the widow of the last William Bruning's uncle, there was a link connecting the two families.

Henry Strangways died within four years of this transaction, and it was his son, Sir Giles Strangways, who set about rebuilding the Brunings' old home. He was one of Henry VIII's Commissioners for the surrender of the Dorset monasteries, and in 1542 obtained a grant of the Abbey of Abbotsbury with its manor, lands and the famous swannery, which have ever since remained with his descendants. Leland, writing about 1540, mentions how 'Mr Strangeguayse hath now a late much buildid at Mylbyri *quadrato*, avauncing the inner part of the house with a loftie and fresch tower.' Another passage relates how he 'caussid thre thoussand lode of fre-stone to be fetchid from Hamden quarre nyne myles of thither.' The older part of Melbury can thus be assigned to the latter half of Henry VIII's reign. The word *quadrato* used by Leland has been interpreted as 'with squared stone,' i.e. ashlar, but it is much more likely to mean 'in a square,' that is to say, in the form of a quadrangle, which would explain the words 'inner part' applied to the position of the tower. The house is in fact a hollow square, with the tower rising from the centre of the west range and having a wing projecting from its base westward (pl. 131). The entrance was originally in the middle of the east range. In the regularity with which the building was set out it was in advance of its time, and the hexagonal lantern tower is unique. But the character of the early Tudor work is typical of the group of Dorset and Somerset houses in the region of the Ham Hill quarries, which includes Barrington Court and Clifton Maybank. Barrington, built by Henry, Lord Daubeney, must have been going up at the same time as Melbury. The gable ends have the usual fluted angle shafts terminating in twisted finials with ogee-shaped caps, and the same type of finial is used for the pinnacles of the tower; the copings of the gables are ornamented with crockets. The chimneys are of octagonal section with a rather uncommon form of zig-zag design. The tower (pl. 132) rises from a square base and has a stair turret at the north-west angle; the other three angles are sloped back to the sides of the hexagon and are covered with stone weatherings, while internally the corbelling is given a rich suite of mouldings. The room inside the lantern was evidently designed as a belvedere, and must have been one of the first erected in

---

[1] Under the south transept arch there is a similar monument erected to commemorate a Bruning but appropriated to Sir Giles Strangways the elder (died 1547).

England. The view from the room and from the leads above is a magnificent one, extending far over the surrounding countryside.

When *The Survey of Dorset* was written, about 1630, there was still 'much old building' remaining beside Sir Giles Strangways' 'faire and stronge house', but no part of it now survives, unless the present entrance hall, which used to be the kitchen, lying north-west of the tower, incorporates in its walls work dating from the Brunings' time. Sir Giles Strangways (died 1547) was succeeded by his grandson, Sir Giles the younger, whose father had been killed at the siege of Boulogne in 1544. Sir John Strangways, the grandson of Sir Giles II, suffered severely during the Civil War. He was taken prisoner at the surrender of Sherborne Castle, and with his son, Colonel Strangways, was committed to the Tower. He afterwards compounded for his liberty, but was obliged to pay a huge fine, for which his son was kept as hostage. Nevertheless, he managed to send Charles II £100 to assist him in his escape when he was in hiding at Trent.

The seventeenth-century alterations and additions to Melbury were made by Thomas Strangways (1643–1713), the grandson of the Royalist, Sir John. The whole of the east front and the central portions of the north and south fronts between the gable ends were redesigned with Classic features, balustraded parapets and upright windows having keystones. Portland stone was used for the dressings. At the same time the courtyard was much reduced in size by the introduction of a staircase hall on its east side and connecting corridors on the north and south sides. Much of the interior was redecorated at this period. The identity of the architect responsible for these additions presents a problem so far unsolved. Hanging in the staircase hall is a portrait inscribed 'Mr Watson architect to Thomas Strangways Senr Esq who enlarged and adorned the house 1692.' Horace Walpole, however, in his notes on Melbury states that the house was modernised 'under the direction of Thomas Sutton, styling himself Architect to Thomas Strangways Esq.' Walpole may have misheard or misread the name; on the other hand, the inscription on the portrait may have been added later and given incorrectly. A Samuel Watson from 1690 onwards worked at Chatsworth, and executed much of the carving in wood and stone there, both inside and outside the house. He was a sculptor, however, and there is no evidence that he acted as an architect as well, whereas the portrait of 'Mr Watson' shows a man with paper and compasses and no attributes of a carver. The Classic façades of Melbury, whoever was their author, are of a somewhat tentative character, the work, one would suppose, of a provincial mason aspiring to be an architect. The centre of the east front (pl. 133) has superimposed orders of Doric and Corinthian columns, above which sits a quaint pediment having little architectural relation to them. Its sides are unusually steep, and its main purpose is to

132. MELBURY

Sir Giles Strangways' 'loftie and fresch tower' (*circa* 1530–40). Built of Ham Hill stone and hexagonal in plan, it rises from the middle of the west range of the courtyard.

133. MELBURY

The east front (1692). Provincial Classic of William and Mary's reign.

134. THORNHILL HOUSE

The north front, remodelled by Sir James Thornhill after he had re-purchased the home of his forbears.

serve as a frame to a finely carved achievement of arms. This displays Strangways impaling Ridout for Thomas Strangways and his wife, Susanna, daughter and heir of John Ridout. On the north and south fronts pilasters are used, instead of the attached columns, to ornament the central portion between the gable ends.

The interior of the house shows work of many dates. In the spandrels of several of the Tudor doorways the initials of Sir Giles Strangways, the builder, are to be seen, and some of the original linen-fold panelling remains. The first-floor room in the range running south from the tower has an elaborate Elizabethan or early Jacobean ceiling of a geometrical pattern, with scrolled designs, animals, birds and insects modelled in the compartments, and there is a contemporary overmantel framing the arms of Strangways with many quarterings. In the bay window of this room and that of the breakfast room below it are twelve armorial shields which formerly adorned the room in the tower. The walls of the breakfast room are hung with Mortlake tapestries of the Labours of the Months, which came from Redlynch, the Fox seat in Somerset, along with the eighteenth-century overmantel and the chimney-piece of coloured marbles in the saloon. The saloon, which occupies the whole of the central portion of the south range, contains some interesting examples of lacquer furniture noted by Walpole, and many of the finest pictures in the house are in this room, among them two admirable Ruysdaels. The adjoining room at the south-east angle is hung with green silk damask brought from Redlynch, for which it was obtained in 1735. Here is a replica of the Marc Gheeraerdts picture at Sherborne Castle showing Queen Elizabeth being carried in a litter to Blackfriars on the occasion of the marriage of Lord Herbert. Among other pictures in this room is a half-length version of Holbein's Henry VIII and Alan Ramsay's charming portrait of Lady Susan Fox-Strangways. In the old entrance hall in the centre of the east front there are two remarkable carved overmantels, one displaying trophies of musical instruments, the other of game and fish. Horace Walpole ascribed them to Grinling Gibbons, and their technical accomplishment certainly warrants the attribution. The carved festoons and drops over the fireplace in the south-east room are by a less-skilled hand. Behind the old entrance hall are two staircases, inserted by Thomas Strangways and arranged back to back. The grand ascent, the southern one of the two, has balusters carved with acanthus and a moulded and enriched hand-rail. The ceiling above it, representing the Council of the Gods, was formerly thought to be by Thornhill but can now be assigned to Lanscroon, who painted the underside of the first-floor landing with a composition of cherubs on clouds encircled in a garland which he signed and dated 1701. There are also two grisaille paintings, and a representation of Fame blowing a trumpet underlies the third flight of the staircase.[1] A large canvas by Thomas Hill, showing Thomas Strang-ways senior, with his wife and family, covers the whole of the north wall above the dado. One of the little girls in the picture eventually succeeded to Melbury after the death of her brother in 1726. She married Thomas Horner of Mells, and their only daughter became the wife of Stephen Fox, who subsequently added the name of Strangways to his own. In 1741 he was created Viscount Ilchester and in 1756 was raised to an earldom. His younger brother was the Henry Fox who became the first Lord Holland and whose younger son was Charles James Fox, the statesman.

Melbury was greatly enlarged during the nineteenth century. The third Lord Ilchester added the great hall, designed by Salvin, where among other pictures hang two full-length portraits of Sir John Strangways, the Royalist (1584–1666), and his wife, Grace Trenchard. The late Lord Ilchester in the eighties extended the house still farther by building a west range beyond the hall, ending southwards in a tower; the architect of these additions was George Devey. Close to the tower stands an octagonal garden house crowned with battlements and pinnacles (pl. 128). Walpole refers to it as 'ancient,' but its interior had been 'newly adorned with shields,' and the 'Gothick' arch was evidently inserted at the same time. The east range of the large stable court lying north-west of the house formed part of the 1692 additions. In an old painting it is shown balanced by another range projecting from the north-east corner of the house. The main approach was then from the east by a ten-arched bridge crossing the deep declivity on that side, which was filled with a large canal. Canal and bridge were both abolished when the surroundings of the house were laid out in the landscape manner popularised by Capability Brown. The great lawn on the south side of the house slopes down to a lake, from the farther bank of which the whole extent of the house is best seen, silhouetted against the sky and framed on either side by tall trees (pl. 130).

[1] There is another painted ceiling in the north-east room, where the design consists of festoons of fruit and flowers and birds flying between them.

CHAPTER THREE

Cranborne Manor House, Lulworth Castle and Sherborne Castle

A S THE hunting-lodges of three great Elizabethans, these three houses have a certain kinship, which may be held to justify their segregation into a chapter by themselves. The old manor house at Cranborne was enlarged and fitted up by Robert Cecil, Earl of Salisbury, largely for the purpose of entertaining King James when he came to hunt in the Chase. Lulworth Castle, begun by the Lords Howard of Bindon, passed to their kinsman, the Earl of Suffolk, better known as the Lord Howard who was with Sir Richard Grenville 'at Flores in the Azores' and whose five ships escaped the fate of the *Revenge*. Suffolk succeeded Cecil as Lord Treasurer and, like him, entertained his master at his Dorset hunting-lodge. As a 'lodge,' too, the present Sherborne Castle was built by Sir Walter Raleigh, though it was after-wards enlarged by the Earl of Bristol who, as Sir John Digby, acquired it in 1617. While all three houses are fine examples of Elizabethan and Jacobean building, they differ in appearance and character as much as did their possessors. About all the more fashionable buildings of the time there is a great diversity of form and plan—a reflection of the restless and inquiring spirit of an age that also went questing after the whimsical and the fantastic. Lulworth and Sherborne are really make-believe castles, the whims of a generation that loved conceits in architecture hardly less than in literature. Cranborne, on the other hand, takes us into that exquisite romance world of the Elizabethans, which was indifferently Italy or Illyria—a world in which loggias, arcades, pleached bowers and terraces evoked the same sort of thrill as later on did mediaeval ruins for the generation of Horace Walpole and William Beck-ford.

Cranborne Manor House. 'The loveliest manor house in Dorset'—as one writes the words, one is assailed by doubts. Visions of Mapperton, Athelhampton, Bingham's Melcombe, and half a dozen other places, rise before one; yet, if the apple must be awarded, it will have to go to Cranborne. Here Time and Nature have left on old walls their unimaginable touch; there is nowhere a jarring note. Neglect there may have been in the past, but its banishment has not brought in the opposite extreme of too much carefulness. Time has been allowed to marble the stonework;

Nature has added the delicate shadows of moss and lichen: these touches have brought to perfection the harmony between the building and its setting. Walled enclosures of gardens, lawns and orchards form the ordered but not too rigid framework. And the house itself gains much of its beauty from this same easy poise between discipline and freedom. But it is the addition of the two loggias, with their suggestion of southern breezes playing through their arches, that has lent a magical quality to the building. Applied to these mediaeval walls, they have an air of fantasy, as if they had been intended for the background of a Jacobean masque or one of Shakespeare's comedies with Italy as the setting.

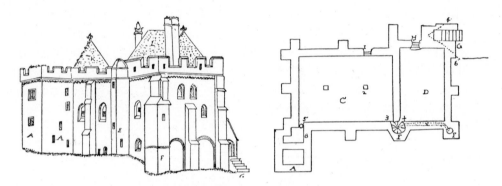

CRANBORNE MANOR HOUSE

View from the south-east and plan before Robert Cecil's alterations and additions. From a Survey made in 1605 by John Norden.

Much more practical, no doubt, were the thoughts of Robert Cecil when he gave the building the form we now see. With the manor he purchased the rights of Cranborne Chase, and his first concern when fitting up the half-derelict hunting-lodge was to be able to provide entertainment for his sovereign. The main fabric of the building is often said to be the hunting-lodge of King John; but although he visited Cranborne on fourteen separate occasions, the manor under the Plantagenets was held by the Earls of Gloucester, and the existing walls are in any case not earlier than the fourteenth century. The condition of the building, before Cecil began his repairs and additions, is known from a drawing and plan which John Norden included in the survey that he drew up in 1605 to Cecil's order. The main body of the house consisted of a hall and solar raised up on a vaulted kitchen (c) and cellar (D) and approached by an external staircase (G) at the north-east corner. A newel stair in the south wall (E) provided communication between the offices and the main floor. At the south-west corner there was a projection forming a kind of low tower

135. CRANBORNE MANOR HOUSE

The house and its walled gardens viewed from the church tower; looking west.

136. CRANBORNE MANOR HOUSE

The south front. A mediaeval hunting lodge enlarged and remodelled by Robert Cecil, Earl
of Salisbury.

137. CRANBORNE MANOR HOUSE
The north front, framed by Classic gate-piers.

138. CRANBORNE MANOR HOUSE
The hall, lined with old oak wainscoting and tapestries.

139. CRANBORNE MANOR HOUSE

The north loggia, built about 1610; William Arnold was the master mason employed by
Cecil for his alterations. The Italian forms and Flemish ornaments have been used to create
a fantasy of extraordinary charm.

(A). Cecil heightened this tower, and built a south-east tower to match it; added low wings to the east and west (the east wing was pulled down at a later date); and ornamented the north and south fronts with the charming loggias. The whole house was re-fenestrated and an extra floor inserted, but the battlements, the stair-turret and the buttresses were retained.

These alterations were effected between 1607 and 1611. Cecil had obtained possession of the manor before Queen Elizabeth's death, but it was not until James I was on the throne that he started work on the house. Created Viscount Cranborne in 1604 and Earl of Salisbury the following year, Cecil from the first became the minister whom James liked and trusted most. 'My little beagle' was the King's nickname for him, on account of his diminutive stature and untiring zeal in tracking down conspiracies. The first royal visit to Cranborne was made in 1607, before the alterations and additions had been begun, and it is doubtful whether much had been done by the time of the second visit in 1609. The surviving building accounts, preserved at Hatfield, start in the year between the two visits. Cecil's architect, as we have seen (Introduction, p. 26), was William Arnold, whose first recorded appearance at Cranborne was in July, 1609. In December of that year he received £5 for 'drawing a plott for Cranborne house,' and in the following year was undertaking the building of 'a tarryce and a kitchene.' The plan is probably the one at Hatfield (pl. 149) showing the terrace and new kitchen, also the two loggias and the additions at either end of the house. No specific references to the loggias have been found in the accounts, but in 1610 work was going on at the west and east ends,[1] and it is reasonable to assume that the loggias were built then or soon afterwards. In 1610 Arnold had begun the building of Wadham College, Oxford, and the infrequency of his visits to Cranborne delayed the work. It can barely have been completed when Cecil died. The south loggia, with its three rusticated arches resting on would-be Doric columns, the frieze above and the shell-headed niches, has a close parallel at Wayford Manor, Somerset (pl. 9 and 10). On this side of the house there are twelve roundels, formerly filled with carvings representing the signs of the Zodiac, of which only two (on the loggia) survive. The doorway, it may be noted, shows no Renaissance features, but is of the late Gothic type with a flattened four-centred arch. The north loggia (pl. 139) is a more sophisticated and accomplished piece of work, with bolder arches and strapwork ornaments of Netherlandish inspiration as well as the shell-headed niches. In the spandrels of the arches there are lion masks, recalling those at Lulworth Castle. The carved panel surmounting the parapet has the arms of Cecil with the supporters he assumed after he had been created Earl of Salisbury. To harmonise this Renaissance addition with the Gothic

[1] I am indebted to Mr Lawrence Stone, of Wadham College, Oxford, for this information.

structure behind, the mediaeval buttresses were embellished with pairs of pilasters arranged in three tiers.

In planning the gardens Cecil sent down Montagu Jennings and John Tradescant, who also laid out and stocked the gardens at Hatfield. The main lines of the lay-out are still preserved, but the dispositions have been reversed. The original approach was from the north, up what is now the walled garden, to the terrace and north loggia (pl. 137); the present forecourt, approached through the arch between the brick lodges, was 'the courte garden' (pl. 136); to the west beyond the lawn there was a 'mount.' The whole scheme comprised an extensive walled enclosure divided into nine rectangles, of which the house, 'the courte' and 'the courte garden' formed the middle section. The reversal of the approaches has meant no loss of beauty; indeed, the transformation of the old approach into a secret garden of exquisite herbaceous borders, sloping down from the loggia and its terrace, and looking out through stone gate-piers to the little stream beyond the walls, is a delight as rare and lovely as any English manor house can show.

The fine hall (pl. 138), which, though it has rooms over it, is of lofty proportions, is entered from the screens passage, above which is a gallery. The walls are wainscoted to half their height, and the spaces between the windows are covered by tapestries, which were found stored away in the house after long disuse. The older of the two towers (the western) was reconstructed by Cecil to take the main staircase —a picturesque piece of Jacobean joinery with turned balusters and newel posts united by columns with linking arches. There is a somewhat similar staircase at Audley End. Some of the woodwork in the house has been renewed, but the bold oak chimney-pieces in the west wing are original and in their exaggerated architectural treatment resemble some of those at Hatfield. A payment to 'Geyners' for 'wynescote' suggests that Jenever, the joiner at Hatfield, was responsible for them.

The first Earl died in 1612. But the furnishing of the manor house was continued on the most extravagant scale by his successor, as the surviving accounts show. The King was still a frequent visitor, coming five times between 1615 and 1623, always during the month of August. At the outbreak of the Civil War the second Earl, after some hesitation, threw in his lot on the side of Parliament, so that when in 1643 some 4,000 Royalists under Prince Maurice were quartered in the town, they showed little respect for his property. The house was plundered and considerable damage was done, though Salisbury had taken the precaution of having most of the household gear removed beforehand. Four years later Thomas Fort was sent down to survey the damage and report on the necessary repairs. To this time belong the stone gate-piers of the garden gateway (pl. 137) and the high hipped roof of the east wing (pl. 153). The latter, one of the earliest of its kind in England, is known from Fort's report to have been designed by a Captain Rider,[1] who later on did some work at Gorhambury, near St. Albans. He seems to have been employed by the Earl of Pembroke at the time, for he twice rode over to Cranborne from Wilton, which was burnt in 1647 and was soon to be rebuilt by Inigo Jones and John Webb. After the Restoration there is a long period of obscurity. The building was kept in some sort of repair, but was rarely visited; gloom enveloped the house, tenanted only by a housekeeper, until in 1863, after nearly two centuries of neglect, renovations were at last begun by the second Marquess. Since that time the manor house has been given a renewed loveliness; and, looking back, one may bless the long interval of years when, if little was done to mend, nothing was done to mar.

Lulworth Castle. From a distance the towers and battlements of Lulworth are still seen 'bosom'd high in tufted trees,' but it is an empty and roofless castle that now looks out of the woods down the vista of lawns and meadows to the sea at Arish Mell. Even before the fire which gutted its interior in the summer of 1929, this curious building wore an air that belied its age (pl. 140); and now that it stands uninhabited, with the sky showing through its windows and jackdaws circling its towers, it appears more than ever the creation of an eighteenth-century mind with an eye for 'the picturesque.' It might almost be mistaken for one of those 'Gothic' ruins of the kind that Sanderson Miller built at Hagley and Wimpole; certainly to Horace Walpole it would have seemed to possess 'the true rust of the Barons' Wars.' Such romantic ideas, however, are liable to be rudely shattered by the sight and sound of tanks firing on the adjacent terrain.

In *The Survey of Dorset* the building of the castle is attributed to Thomas, the third and last of the Lords Howard of Bindon. Hutchins, however, states that it was begun in 1588 but that the exterior was not finished until 1609. If this is correct, its originator will have been the second Lord Howard, to whom the property came through his mother, one of the Marney co-heiresses. It was Sir John Marney, of Layer Marney in Essex, who, by marrying the heiress of the Newburghs, a family which from the time of King John had held large estates in this part of Dorset, came into possession of Lulworth. Dying in 1526, he left two daughters, one of whom married Sir Thomas Poynings, the other Thomas Howard, second son of the third Duke of Norfolk. Lady Poynings died childless, and settled her Dorset property on her sister, whose husband in 1559 was created Viscount Howard of Bindon. Since their elder son, Henry, died in 1590, eight years after his father, the building of the castle cannot have proceeded very far by that date, if it was begun in 1588. The

---

[1] Richard Rider, or Ryder. In 1668 he was appointed Master Carpenter to the King and held the post until his death in 1683. See H. M. Colvin, *Dictionary of English Architects, 1660–1840.*

picture we have of him is not of a very flattering character. We find his father complaining to the Council of his son's outrageous behaviour and begging that his wife may 'be protected from the practices of him and of the naughty quean he keeps, she having been already beaten most pitifully and many ways else misused.' Among other faults, besides wife-beating, that he was accused of, was association with pirates and other ill company. As he left no son, he was succeeded by his brother, Thomas.

Whoever began the building, it must have been the third Lord Howard who determined its form, 'mounted on highe,' as the *Survey* has it, 'with Turrets at each

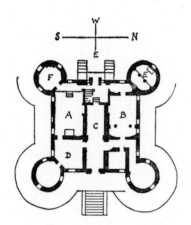

LULWORTH CASTLE

Plan of main floor (above cellars) before the fire of 1929.
A, Drawing-room; B, Dining-room;
C, Hall; D, Billiards-room;
E, Small chapel; F, Boudoir.

Corner, well seated for Prospect and Pleasure; but of little other Use.' In its construction, material from Bindon Abbey and Mount Poynings, a house built by Sir Thomas Poynings, is said to have been used, and the makeshift character of the walls, part brick, part rubble, as revealed by the fire, certainly confirms the tradition. The form of the building, though unusual for its time, is not unparalleled. There are several Elizabethan and Jacobean houses that are castellated, and the corner towers recall those of Longford, where the plan is a triangle. Like Cranborne, the house was intended primarily as a hunting-lodge, and after the Earl of Suffolk had acquired the property, he more than once entertained King James at Lulworth, 'who chose it to disporte himselfe in the Parke.' Suffolk was the builder of Audley End; he followed Cecil as Lord Treasurer, and also succeeded him in the exacting duty of providing sport for his sovereign on his Dorset estate. It is interesting to note certain resemblances in detail between Lulworth and Cranborne. The same shell-headed niches appear on both houses, and the lion-masks beneath the windows—apparently outlets for water basins set in the window embrasures—are almost identical with the lion-mask spouts on the north loggia at Cranborne. Although Lulworth is earlier

140. LULWORTH CASTLE

From the south-east, as it appeared before the fire of 1929. 'Four grey walls and four grey towers.'

141. LULWORTH CASTLE
The terrace and stone staircase leading up to the main entrance in the east front.

142. LULWORTH CASTLE
The upper drawing-room or ball-room, decorated soon after 1775. Destroyed in the fire of 1929.

than the Cranborne loggias, we have seen it was not completed until 1609, and the finishing details may well be contemporary. The sophisticated character of this Elizabethan castle suggests that it was designed by a London man, perhaps one of the officials of the Queen's Works, but it is not unlikely that William Arnold, who in 1610 drew 'a plott for Cranborne House' and undertook the building of 'a tarryce and kitchene' there, was also the mason contractor at Lulworth. The balustraded terrace, reached by a broad flight of steps and forming a raised platform to the building, was confined originally to the east front, and it was extended round the north and south sides only in the eighteenth century. In the design of the balustrade there is a close resemblance to the one at Cranborne. The entrance has a Classic frontispiece with an Ionic order based on the form of the triumphal arch, and it is surmounted by two figures of Roman emperors, between which a rose window composed of seven circles makes an unblushing appearance, showing no concern for its Roman environment. The emperors and the six lead figures,[1] which occupy the niches on the east front (pl. 141), survived the fire.

The third Lord Howard of Bindon died in 1611, but six years previously he had sold the estate to his kinsman, the Earl of Suffolk, and it was he who completed the Castle. In 1641 Lulworth was bought by Humphry Weld, a member of an old Catholic family hailing from Cheshire and grandson of another Humphry, who in 1609 was Lord Mayor of London. From that time to this it has remained continuously in the possession of his descendants, who at various times have entertained three kings—Charles II, James II and George III—within its walls. At first, however, Humphry Weld's investment was anything but profitable. When the Civil War broke out, the building was seized by Parliamentary troops and the lead was stripped off its roof to furnish ammunition for the siege of Corfe Castle. Not until the Restoration period was the damage made good and the interior fitted up again. The fine decoration, which perished in the fire, belonged, however, to the following century. Edward Weld's accounts show that at intervals between 1740 and 1756 the Bastards of Blandford were paid considerable sums for decoration, furniture and chimney-pieces. The hall and the old drawing-room on the ground floor were among the rooms which they redecorated (see p. 37). Several bedrooms before the fire contained marble chimney-pieces of that time. The lead rainwater pipes bore the date 1754. But more important work was undertaken later. Edward Weld's elder son, Edward, seems to have consulted James Paine: two plans of the house that have been preserved have been endorsed 'Pain's Plans for Lulworth Castle' and 'Designed 1773.' These show the platform and balustrade and the basement rooms beneath extending round the north and south sides. The younger Edward died in 1775, and

[1] The pair flanking the entrance represent Music and Painting.

it was his brother, Thomas Weld, who commissioned the new decoration of the dining-room (on the entrance floor) and upper drawing-room (first floor). The latter had a ceiling decorated in the Pompeian manner (pl. 140), like that of Humphry Sturt's drawing-room at Crichel.[1] But the greatest individual loss was the royal bed, designed for George III, a gorgeous creation with a domed canopy, gilded cresting and hangings of royal blue. It is amusing to recall, as Fanny Burney did when she visited the castle, that Lulworth a few years earlier had been the home of Mrs Fitzherbert. Edward Weld, Thomas's elder brother, had taken as his second wife the young Mary Anne Smythe, who subsequently was to earn so much notoriety. One wonders what her future would have been if her first husband had not died in the year after the marriage.

The domed chapel in the grounds, which stands far enough off to have been out of reach of the flames, was built in 1786. It is an interesting little Classic building with an intriguing plan. In 1830 Lulworth once again entertained royalty in the person of the exiled Charles X, who was lent the castle for six months after his ejection from France. On catching his first glimpse of his temporary home he is said to have ex-claimed, 'Voilà, la Bastille !'

Sherborne Castle. 'The castle of Shirburne,' wrote Leland when he visited it towards the end of Henry VIII's reign, 'is in the east end of the toun, upon a rokky hillet. It has by west-north-west, and by est-south-est, morisch ground. Roger le Poure, Bishop of Saresbyri, in Henry the First tyme, buildid this castelle, and cast a great dike without it, and made a false mure without the dike. There be four great towres in the castelle walle, whereof one is the gate house. Every of them hath three lodgginges yn hight. The great lodgging is yn the midle of the castle court, very strong, and ful of voultes. There be few peaces of work yn England of the antiquity of this that standith so whole and so well couchid.'

To-day only the gatehouse on the south-west, fragments of the curtain wall and north gate, and the ruins of the keep and 'great lodgging' remain to testify to the strength and grandeur of the castle which Leland pictures for us. Recent excavations, however, have recovered the plan of the central buildings and the removal of a dense overgrowth of ivy has disclosed many features formerly hidden. The castle was built by Roger, Bishop of Salisbury from 1107 to 1139; he was Justiciar to Henry I and the chief supporter of Stephen after Henry's death. Leland seems to have confused him with Richard Poore, the later bishop who removed the see from Old

---

[1] In *The Weymouth Guide* (3rd ed., 1790) it is stated that the ceiling was designed by John Tasker and painted by 'Mr. Hague,' who did other work in the house. For this reference and for other information about the eighteenth-century alterations at Lulworth I am indebted to Mr H. M. Colvin.

143. SHERBORNE CASTLE

Begun as a hunting-lodge by Sir Walter Raleigh, about 1592 and completed in James I's reign by Sir John Digby, later Earl of Bristol. The plan with the Digby wings acquired the form of an H.

144.

SHERBORNE CASTLE

The south front.

145.

SHERBORNE CASTLE

An aerial view of the house and
the lake formed by Capability
Brown.

Sarum and founded the new city and cathedral. Roger's castle occupied a rectangular site of over three acres, having the angles splayed off, and it was defended by a deep ditch and outer rampart. The gatehouse, of four storeys with shallow buttresses, rises to its full height at the north-west angle, but less remains on the south. The keep formed the south-west angle of a quadrangular block of buildings in the middle of the bailey, regularly set out and enclosing a court with cloister alleys on all four sides. Such an arrangement is almost unique in a Norman castle, but may have been adopted also for Bishop Roger's castle at Old Sarum. The great hall probably occupied the south range, most of which has vanished. The north range had a vaulted substructure, but the 'voultes' of Leland's description have all fallen in. Its first floor is likely to have been the chapel. Much of the south wall survives, showing a wall arcade of intersecting arches externally and internally; in the east bay of the north wall there is a well-preserved window with rich chevron ornament. Not long before his death Bishop Roger fell foul of the barons supporting Stephen, and the King compelled him to surrender his castles. Sherborne remained in the possession of the Crown and was not recovered by the bishops until the reign of Edward III.

Some fifty years after Leland's visit Sir Walter Raleigh cast no less admiring eyes on the castle as he passed through Sherborne on his journeys between London and Devon. He begged Queen Elizabeth to be allowed it, and in 1592 the Bishop of Salisbury—under pressure, no doubt—granted him a ninety-nine years' lease of all the episcopal estates in and around Sherborne, which seven years later were conveyed to him in fee. He at once set about repairing the castle—some windows which he inserted in the keep and gatehouse still remain—but, altering his mind, he decided to build a new house on the site of an old hunting lodge on the hill rising to the south of the castle beyond the 'morisch ground.' His building operations must have been a source of distraction during the years when he was banished from Court after having incurred the Queen's displeasure by his secret marriage with Elizabeth Throgmorton. Raleigh's attainder on the accession of James meant the forfeiture of all his estates, but he had already conveyed his manor of Sherborne in trust for his son, Walter. After much legal argument, in the course of which a technical flaw was discovered in the deed of conveyance, the manor was declared forfeited to the King, who thereupon bestowed it on his worthless favourite, Robert Carr. The King, however, on Lady Raleigh's petition, granted her compensation in the form of an annuity of £400 for the lives of herself and her son, together with a capital payment of £8,000. After the downfall of Carr the manor was again forfeited, and in the following year, 1617, was granted for £10,000 to Sir John Digby, the statesman who was entrusted with the long and tedious negotiations for a Spanish alliance and who was soon to be created Earl of Bristol. The estate has remained in the possession of the Digbys ever since; but after the death of the third Earl in 1698 it went to the fifth Lord Digby, a descendant of the first Earl's elder brother, and in 1856, on the death of the second Earl Digby, it passed to his nephew, George Digby Wingfield, who took the Digby surname. The present owner is Mr Simon Wingfield Digby.

The house with its eight hexagonal towers has a curious appearance (pl. 143). The multiplicity of chimneys and heraldic finials gives its skyline a restless and broken effect. The plan takes the form of the letter H, with the cross-stroke running east and west. The main entrance is between the two wings on the south. Raleigh was responsible for the high central block with its four towers, a romantic castle conception of a kind that gave birth to a number of Elizabethan houses in the Midlands and inspired Lulworth Castle already described. In a collection of maps and architectural drawings preserved at Hatfield there is a plan entitled 'Sherborne Lodge' and signed by Simon Basil[1] with the date 1600 (vol. ii, No. 4). It would appear, however, that the building had been begun some years earlier, for, according to an account of the house published in 1797,[2] the date 1594 and the arms of Raleigh were then to be seen on the windows of the centre part of the building. It is only this centre part of the house that appears in Basil's plan, together with a walled forecourt to the south (pl. 150). If Maton is to be trusted, the plan will have been a survey made after Raleigh's building was completed; otherwise it would have been reasonable to conclude that Basil was his architect. The four wings and subordinate towers at their extremities were added after 1617 by Sir John Digby; he became Lord Digby in 1618 and Earl of Bristol in 1622. Some time after the Restoration the Classic windows were inserted in the outer face of the two north-east and south-east wings (pl. 143). Pope, who was often a guest at Sherborne in the 'Good' Lord Digby's time,[3] attributed this 'newer architecture with beautiful Italian window-frames' to the first Earl and amused himself by sketching a design for a Classic portico to be attached to the centre of this east front. Although these windows are not likely to have been inserted before the Restoration, Pope is certainly right in saying that the wings were built by the first Earl, and not, as is sometimes stated, by his successor from material obtained from the demolished castle. Otherwise, it would be impossible to explain the presence of the fine Jacobean woodwork in the Oak Room in the north-west wing besides other features which are in the style of the first half of the seventeenth

[1] Simon Basil was Inigo Jones's predecessor in the office of Surveyor of the King's Works, which he held from 1606 until his death in 1615.

[2] W. G. Maton, *Observations . . . of the Western Counties* (Salisbury, 1797), vol. ii, p. 9. Quoted in the third edition of Hutchins, vol. iv, p. 278.

[3] The fifth Baron Digby was so called. He inherited in 1698 and died in 1752 at the age of 91.

century. The first Earl, after the failure of Prince Charles's visit to Madrid, was recalled in disgrace from his embassy, and for many years afterwards played no part of importance in public life. Between 1624 and 1639 he spent a great part of his time at Sherborne and may well have found diversion in the enlargement of his house. Before the outbreak of the Civil War he returned to public life, and after making fruitless efforts to find an accommodation between King and Parliament threw in his lot with the Royalists. In his absence the old castle, by then in a state of decay, was twice besieged. In 1642 the Earl of Bedford made an unsuccessful attempt to take it. Lady Bristol, who was at the Lodge, was his sister, and it is said that when her brother ordered her to quit it she replied that if he persisted in his intention to destroy it, he would find his sister's bones buried in it. In 1645 Fairfax appeared with a large force and ordnance to reduce the garrison in the old castle; it surrendered on August 15 after a siege of sixteen days. After its fall orders were given for it to be demolished and the ruins were subsequently used as a quarry. The Earl's estates were sequestrated, and he retired to France, dying in Paris in 1653. His son, the second Earl, who became a Roman Catholic while abroad, recovered the estate at the Restoration.

The masonry of the house is largely of rubble, plastered over, Ham Hill stone being used for dressings and the ornamental features. The two courts formed by the wings are entered through archways (pl. 144), flanked by shell-headed niches and crowned with the Digby crest, an ostrich with a horseshoe in its mouth. The centre block is built over cellars, the walls of which form part of the previous Tudor hunting lodge. In the north-west room of this basement a large fireplace was revealed about 1930; it has a four-centred head, formed of two massive blocks of freestone. The hall occupies the western two-thirds of the south front and is shown by Basil's plan to have been entered originally through a doorway in the east face of the south-west turret. Few early features remain in the hall or other rooms on the ground floor of the main block, and the main staircase dates from 1860, but the first floor retains original fireplaces and ribbed plaster ceilings. The large first-floor room known as the Green Drawing-room (pl. 146) running across the east end of the block shows the Raleigh shield in the ceiling, which has a web of intersecting ribs ornamented with conventionalised fleurs-de-lis and pendent acorns. The fleur-de-lis often occurs in Elizabethan ceilings, but it is the coat of the Digbys, and it appears on the overmantel of the chimney-piece.[1] This is a large and sumptuous composition, flanked by pairs of columns in two stages. The achievement of arms

[1] It has been suggested that the Digby coat on the shield over the fireplace may have been substituted for that of Raleigh, in which case the whole achievement with its supporters and coronet would have been an alteration, and this is unlikely.

is set against an elaborate strapwork cartouche, probably derived from one of the current Flemish pattern-books. In the two recesses in the adjoining towers there are smaller chimney-pieces with flanking columns and panels having gadrooned borders enclosing the Digby arms (pl. 147). The painting and gilding of the ceiling and chimney-pieces may well preserve the original scheme of colouring. In Lady Bristol's Room on this floor there is another ribbed ceiling, but the most interesting survival here is the late seventeenth-century brass lock on the door in the west wall, which was noticed by Horace Walpole when he visited the house. It is engraved with a figure of a servant in relief and bears the inscription:

> If I had ye gift of tongue
> I would declare & do no wrong
> Who ye are yt come by stealth
> To impare my master's welth.

The lock is signed by its maker: 'Johannes Wilkes de Birmingham fecit.'[1] The man's boot was made so as to cover the key-hole.

Of the rooms in the early seventeenth-century wings the least altered is the Oak Room in the north-west wing. Its walls are lined with the original panelling, and at the south end are two of those internal porches or lobbies (pl. 148), which, though introduced for the practical purpose of excluding draughts, were often made the occasion for an elaborate display of carving. There are other examples at Melcombe Horsey and Winterborne Thomson, but it is most unusual to find two in one room. The heraldic beasts and open scrollwork above the cornice prominently display the Digby ostrich and fleur-de-lis. In the Red Drawing-room in the north-east wing there is an early seventeenth-century ceiling, ornamented with devices in the panels, and a chimney-piece with heraldic overmantel similar to those in the tower rooms adjoining the Green Drawing-room. Little now remains of the eighteenth-century decoration. Most of it was swept away when George Wingfield Digby renovated the house in 1859–60, employing Philip Hardwick as his architect. But the decoration of the library in the south-east wing was left unaltered. Here the walls are lined with Gothic book-cases in the Strawberry Hill taste, surmounted by a series of roundels containing bronze busts.

There is not space to describe the contents of the house, which is full of treasures—pictures, miniatures, china and furniture of many dates. Cornelius Johnson and Van Dyck, Lely and Kneller, Reynolds and Gainsborough are among the artists who

[1] There is a similar lock by Wilkes in the Victoria and Albert Museum, and other signed locks by him have been recorded, for instance on the chapel door at Arbury, Warwickshire.

146. SHERBORNE CASTLE

The Green Drawing-room with the great chimney-piece displaying the Digby arms.

147 and 148. SHERBORNE CASTLE

(*Left*) The small chimney-piece in a recess of the Green Drawing-room. (*Right*) Internal porch with carved cresting in the Oak Room.

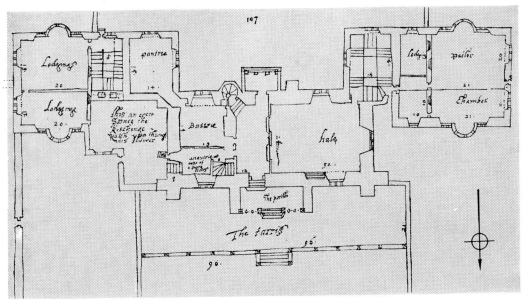

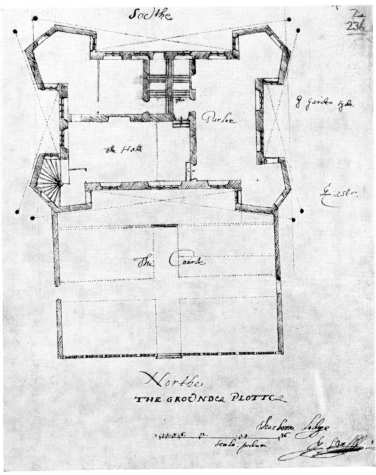

149.
**CRANBORNE
MANOR HOUSE**
Plan, preserved at
Hatfield, showing
the additions made
by Robert Cecil.
Probably the 'plott'
drawn by William
Arnold in 1609. The
east wing may have
been left uncompleted.

150.
**SHERBORNE
CASTLE**
Plan inscribed 'The
Grounde Plotte.
Sherborne Lodge. Sy:
Basill 1600'. It shows
Sir Walter Raleigh's
house before the
addition of the
wings. North and
South are indicated
incorrectly. From
a collection of
maps and plans
preserved at Hatfield.

have painted successive generations of the Digbys and their kin. The famous picture of Queen Elizabeth borne in a litter on the shoulders of gentlemen of the Court was painted to commemorate her visit to Blackfriars on the occasion of the marriage of Henry, Lord Herbert (later first Marquess of Worcester) to Anne, daughter of John Russell (June 16, 1600).[1] It is usually attributed to Marc Gheeraerdts. There is another version of this picture at Melbury. Both were noted by Walpole on his tour in July, 1762.

The park, one of the loveliest in Dorset, owes its present character to Brown, who formed the long winding lake (pl. 145) in the depression between the old castle and the lodge. When Pope visited the house, there was still a formal lay-out of terraces, groves and topiary work, with a T-shaped canal, but in a letter written to his friend, Miss Blount, he mentions that 'a line of wildernesses with winding walks' was in contemplation. The plantation on Jerusalem Hill is said to have been suggested by him. The lake and cascade were formed by the sixth Lord Digby in 1756 under Brown's direction, but in the following year he died unmarried at the age of 27. His brother, who succeeded him and later became the first Earl Digby, employed Brown for further work between 1776 and 1779,[2] and in 1790 Pinford Bridge at the end of the lake was built by him from designs by Robert Mylne. Robert Adam had made a design for a bridge in the park in 1767, and there is another, somewhat later, signed by the Hon. Capt. Digby 'architectus.' Adam also made designs for alterations to the house, but they do not seem to have been carried out. Near the house on the west side there is a late eighteenth-century Gothic dairy and, facing it, a greenhouse, for which designs, dated 1779, exist. The stables, forming three sides of a square, were built partly in 1759 and partly in the nineteenth century. Although Walpole dismissed the house as 'indifferent but pretty,' he admired the 'noble Lake' and the setting, which he compared with that of Longleat. The view from the east front over the sloping lawns along the lake to Mylne's bridge is eighteenth-century landscape at its best. Among the walks beside the lake is 'the rustic seat of stone,' which Pope mentions in his letter, and also what is traditionally known as 'Raleigh's seat.'

[1] An article by the Earl of Ilchester in the ninth volume of the Walpole Society establishes the identity of most of the principal figures.

[2] Dorothy Stroud, *Capability Brown* (1950), p. 54.

CHAPTER FOUR

Classic Houses: 1650 to 1800

SEVERAL houses in Dorset have been ascribed to Inigo Jones, among them Kingston Lacy, Forde Abbey, the west wing of Cranborne Manor House, and even Anderson Manor, Lulworth Castle and part of Wolfeton. All these attributions are without any sound foundation, but it is interesting to note that the last two were current in the seventeen-fifties when Dr Pococke made his tours through the county, though he was sufficiently knowledgeable to reject both. Nevertheless, the influence of Inigo Jones and the new type of architecture began to show itself in Dorset during the Commonwealth, which divides the last of the traditional manor houses from those in which Classic elements control the whole design. At first, porticoes, columns and pilasters, as employed on a large scale by Inigo Jones and the Renaissance architects of Italy who were his models, are not in evidence, and the inspiration comes diluted by way of Holland. The change of style is marked by the acceptance of Classic rules and proportions both for the designs of elevations and the treatment of interiors: before, it had been a matter of copying and applying a few Renaissance features to buildings designed in the traditional way. Gables disappear and are replaced by hipped roofs rising from a Classic cornice (or, later, from behind a parapet), giving a marked horizontal definition to the elevation; windows are regularly spaced, in sequences, and have the upright form observing Classic rule, and sometimes are emphasised by architraves, with or without cornice or accented keystone; plain bands take the place of string courses, and Classic profiles are used for mouldings. A comparison between the entrance front of Hanford House (pl. 98) and Roger Pratt's elevation of Kingston Lacy (pl. 151), separated by an interval of only forty years, shows the revolutionary nature of these changes. Although the fronts of such houses as Hanford or Anderson were regular in the sense that they were symmetrical, they did not conform to Classic rule. This was the meaning of the term 'regular architecture' by which the new style was known and contrasted, whether explicitly or by inference, with the 'Gothic' or barbarous, unregulated architecture of the past. Henceforth, the vertical elements so evident in early Tudor and Elizabethan houses, which in many respects perpetuated the traditional Perpendicular style, play a much less important part than the horizontal lines of plinth and cornice. We are conscious of some loss of vitality and of a new emphasis on balanced order and repose. If the Elizabethan and Jacobean houses

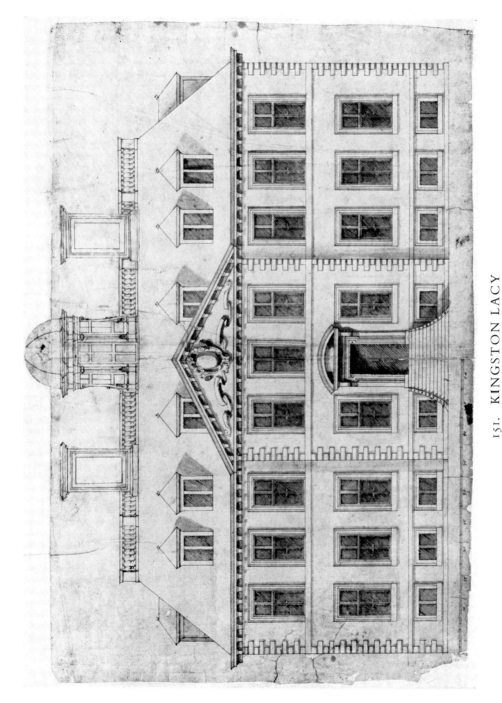

151. KINGSTON LACY

Original elevation of the north front. Built by Sir Ralph Bankes between 1663 and 1666 from designs by Sir Roger Pratt.

152. CRANBORNE MANOR HOUSE

The west wing, rebuilt in 1647 to the design of Richard Rider. An early use of the hipped roof
with cornice.

153. ST GILES'S HOUSE

An early example of a Classic house in the new manner which Inigo Jones had introduced.
Begun in 1651 by Sir Anthony Ashley Cooper, later Earl of Shaftesbury.

154. WIMBORNE ST GILES

The almshouses, built by Sir Anthony Ashley in 1624, and the tower of the church (1732).

155. CHARBOROUGH PARK

The north front. Built by Sir Walter Erle during the Commonwealth, the house was altered and enlarged at the beginning of the nineteenth century.

156. EASTBURY

An eighteenth century painting, showing the house in its entirety. Bubb Dodington entering the courtyard in his coach and six.

157. EASTBURY

Vanbrugh's elevation of the garden front. From *Vitruvius Britannicus* (Vol. III).

often seem to grow out of the earth, their successors give the impression of having been deliberately set down on it.

The new style makes its first full-dress appearance in Dorset at St Giles's House (pl. 153), the foundation-stone of which was laid in 1651[1]. But there is an earlier essay in the west wing of Cranborne Manor House, where the bounding line of cornice and the hipped roof are set on walls with mullioned windows (pl. 152). This wing, which was reconstructed in 1647 after the damage sustained in the Civil War, was designed by Richard Rider (p. 127), who appears to have been associated with Inigo Jones. The pitch is unusually steep for a roof of hipped form, but there were special reasons for this. In reporting to the Earl of Salisbury, the mason, Fort, defended it by pointing out how 'agreeable' it was to the form of the house. 'Consider the high turrets and the low turrets and looke upon Captain Rider's roofe and they doe agree. Howsoever, it agrees to look on, I am sure its better for all that end of the house for the defence of the weather, for as fast as the weather cometh up, it flyeth off every way.' At St Giles's House the hips are of more normal pitch than at Cranborne and the only archaism is the battlementing, if this is original. Charborough, in the form in which it appears in old paintings, followed hard on St Giles, and then came Pratt's design for Kingston Lacy (1663). These houses may be said to have introduced the new style into Dorset. All show the revolutionary effect of Inigo Jones's innovations, even if his veneration for Palladio, the sixteenth-century architect of Vicenza, who later on was to be the guiding light of our early Georgian designers, has not as yet become a cult of its own. Forde Abbey, where the Classic alterations were going on at the same time as the rebuilding of St Giles, reveals the new manner of decorating interiors. Both panelling and ceilings are treated on a larger scale than had been customary before the Civil War; and the Flemish exuberance of detail, though still apparent in some of the ceilings, has given place to more orthodox Italian motives. In the Classic façades of Melbury (pl. 133) we see what a provincial architect made of the new style in the reign of William and Mary. They lag far behind the contemporary work of Wren and Talman, and are farther still from what Vanbrugh was to create only twenty years later at Eastbury.

[1] Probably the earliest building of true Classic character in Dorset was at Stalbridge Park. In 1638 the first Earl of Cork paid Isaac de Caus £5 'for drawing me a plott, for contriving my new intended bwylding over the great sellar at Stalbridge' (*Lismore Papers*, ed. A. B. Grosart, 1st series, v (1886), p. 64). Isaac de Caus, a naturalised Frenchman, was associated with Inigo Jones; he designed and laid out the garden at Wilton House and in consultation with Jones was responsible for the great south front of the house erected before the fire of 1647. See H. M. Colvin, 'The South Front of Wilton House' in *The Archaeological Journal*, vol. xci (1955), pp. 181–190. The house at Stalbridge Park was pulled down in 1822, but a fine pair of seventeenth-century stone gate-piers bearing the Boyle lions remain. The first Earl of Cork left Stalbridge to his youngest son, Robert Boyle, the famous mathematician.

Eastbury (pl. 156) was among the most important examples of what is now called the Baroque phase in our Classic architecture. In England the Baroque style never secured a firm hold, and the form it took in the work of Vanbrugh and Hawksmoor was something very different from anything found on the Continent; nevertheless, Baroque ideas were implicit in Vanbrugh's bold handling of masses, in his dramatic contrasts, exaggerations and surprises, and in the liberties taken with Classic ornament. Only an office court, a great archway and some gate-piers now remain of his huge mansion, but drawings and paintings show what it looked like in its entirety. Within a few miles of Eastbury, Chettle (pl. 174) displays some of the same principles applied to a smaller house. Its architect was in all probability Thomas Archer, who had studied the work of the Baroque masters in Italy and went farther than any of his contemporaries in his attempt to introduce Baroque details. Kingston Maurward (pl. 175), altered later in the century, has also been attributed to him. It is strange that Dorset should have acquired these three examples of what was only a brief episode in English architecture and none of any importance, by a London architect, of the much more enduring Palladian style that followed. By the time Eastbury was completed by Roger Morris, the Vanbrugh period had come to be regarded as a kind of Babylonian captivity, and Lord Burlington and his architects had re-instated Palladio as supreme pontiff. Among the designs of James Gibbs there is one for a house in Dorset, which does not appear to have been built. The Palladians—Colin Campbell, William Kent, Leoni, Flitcroft and company—are represented only at secondhand in the buildings of the Blandford school of architects—John and William Bastard and Francis Cartwright—whose work often shows the lingering impress of the earlier phase. Their idiosyncrasies, in particular their use of the 'Bastard' capital, a strange Baroque survival in an age of Palladian orthodoxy, have been discussed in the Introduction (pp. 31–36), and it need only be pointed out here that on the whole they followed, with some dialect forms of their own, the Palladian language of their London contemporaries.

Most of the houses described in the latter part of this chapter are the work of these local builders; but towards the end of the eighteenth century several London architects received commissions in Dorset. Duntish Court (pl. 191), built in the seventeen-sixties, is a little-known house by Sir William Chambers, the architect of Somerset House. As we have seen, he also designed the Gothic exterior of Milton Abbey (pl. 116), but by conviction he was an orthodox Palladian, and in the neo-Classical movement of his time he remained one of the more conservative figures. His great rival, Robert Adam, did nothing in Dorset; but James Wyatt, besides designing the saloon and other interiors at Milton Abbey, rebuilt Bryanston for Henry William Portman (1778), and his manner is to be found in the fine suite

158. ST GILES'S HOUSE

Looking east up the great beech avenue from the parterre below the east front.

160. ST GILES'S HOUSE

The dining-room. Decoration by Stephen Wright (*circa* 1750).

159. ST GILES'S HOUSE

The small drawing-room—the ceiling is mid-seventeenth century.

of rooms which Humphry Sturt commissioned for Crichel (pl. 197 and 198). Lulworth Castle, before the fire, contained some notable rooms treated in the same fashion (pl. 142). The architect for this work seems to have been John Tasker[1]. Sadborow (pl. 202), close to the Devon border, is a house of some importance, having a domed staircase and retaining other original features. This was built between 1773 and 1775 for William Bragge from the designs of John Johnson, the Leicester architect, who practised in London for a time and was for thirty years the County Surveyor for Essex. In the seventeen-seventies John Crunden designed Woolcombe Hall, near Melbury (for Lawrence Cox), and Belfield near Weymouth (for Isaac Buxton). Only the latter survives (pl. 203). Another of these lesser lights of the late eighteenth century, William Tyler, was better known as a sculptor. In Dorset he was architect of the County Gaol at Dorchester (1784–5) and the Town Hall at Bridport (1785–6). Downe Hall, Bridport, standing on the hill above the town and built in 1789, has an impressive pilastered front of Portland stone, also, perhaps, of London breeding.

Among local practitioners in the later years of the century James Hamilton, of Weymouth, calls for notice. The obelisk commemorating James Frampton in the grounds of Moreton was designed and erected by him (1785–6), and he was the mason employed on the Town Hall at Bridport. His work at Weymouth overlaps into the nineteenth century. There he was responsible for the monument to George III erected in 1809 and executed in Coade stone. Mention of this artificial stone, manufactured at Lambeth by Mrs Eleanor Coade, is a reminder that that astute business woman had Dorset connections. Her husband was a native of Lyme Regis, where a property known as Castle Bunter was made over to her by his uncle, Samuel Coade, in 1784. The house, now called Belmont, has a front lavishly decorated with Coade stone ornaments of the kind which the firm supplied to London houses.

St Giles's House. Wimborne St Giles or Upwimborne, as it is called in old documents, once lay within the limits of Cranborne Chase, which for a short time, towards the end of the seventeenth century, was in the possession of the Earls of Shaftesbury. The little village with its eighteenth-century church and the long row of brick almshouses adjoining it is grouped around a broad expanse of green, at the south-east corner of which is the tree-girt approach to the great house. The earliest family known to have been established here was that of the Malmaynes, from whom it passed by an heiress to a Plecy. Towards the end of the fourteenth century the male line of the Plecys also became extinct, and their heiress married Sir John

---

[1] Among the Milton Abbey drawings in the library of the Royal Institute of British Architects is one of the east end of a Gothic chapel signed 'Jno Tasker'.

Hamely, who died in 1398. There were no children by this marriage, and the property was settled on Sir John's daughter by his second wife, who married Robert Ashley, of an old Wiltshire family. To their descendants, the Ashleys and the Ashley Coopers, St Giles has belonged ever since—an unbroken ownership of more than five and a half centuries.

Of the sixteenth-century Ashleys of St Giles two were knighted, a father and a son, and on the death of the latter the property passed to his first cousin, Sir Anthony Ashley, a man of greater note. He was Clerk of the Privy Council and held the office of 'secretary for war' in the famous expedition to Cadiz of 1596, being knighted for the part he played in it. He translated from the Dutch the first known collection of sea-charts by Lucas Waghenaer; he is also said to have been the first to introduce cabbages into England from Holland. At St. Giles he built the almshouses, which are dated 1624. In the church stands his magnificent canopied tomb, at the foot of which kneels his only child Anne, who by her marriage with Sir John Cooper of Rockbourne became the mother of Sir Anthony Ashley Cooper, afterwards first Earl of Shaftesbury. The career of this brilliant politician,

> The fiery soul, which working out its way
> Fretted the pigmy body to decay,

can only be touched on here, so far as it is concerned with his native county. He was born in 1621 and, as his father died when he was only ten, he became a king's ward and suffered a considerable diminution of his property by the mismanagement of his trustees. When the Civil War broke out he first joined the King's side and was made Governor of Weymouth. But in 1644 he went over to the Parliamentary cause and was instrumental in reducing the Royalist garrisons at Wareham and Abbotsbury. After the subjugation of the West had been completed, for some years he took part in no public event of importance outside his county, and it was during this period that he began the rebuilding of his house, which outwardly retains the character he gave it, though it has been much enlarged subsequently. At the Restoration he was created Baron Ashley and made Chancellor of the Exchequer, and from that time onwards he was ceaselessly engaged in the turmoil of public life and political intrigue. He was one of the famous Cabal, and in 1672 held the office of Lord Chancellor, being created Earl of Shaftesbury the same year. The stormy close of his career, when he fanned the anti-Catholic feeling of the nation, revealed him as the demagogue and brought out the worse qualities of his ambitious character; but it is as the champion of tolerance, the founder of the Whig party and the first politician of the modern type that he has earned a place in the nation's history. He died in

Holland in 1683, a few months after flying from the country on the failure of his plot for a rising against the King.

St Giles's House provides the earliest instance in Dorset of the new manner of architecture which was the result of the introduction by Inigo Jones of the full Renaissance style into England. Its designer is unknown, but he must have been familiar with Jones's work, although, by the retention of a courtyard plan and battlements (which before 1850 surrounded the whole building and appear to have been original), traditional features find a place. There is a note in the first Earl's diary under the date March 19, 1650/1: 'I laid the first stone of my house at St Giles's.' This seems to imply a complete rebuilding, but the new house was erected on the foundations of its predecessor and may incorporate parts of its walls. The main, quadrangular block of 1650 faces east and looks out over a sunk garden up a magnificent avenue of beeches three-quarters of a mile long (pl. 158). The original entrance was in the north front (pl. 153). It has a Doric doorcase with rusticated pilasters but this is now a window. Two long wings running westward were added in the eighteenth century. The two towers, placed at the junction of the wings with the main building, were built by the seventh Lord Shaftesbury after he succeeded in 1851. At this time the battlements were removed from the south and east fronts and the roofs were given dormers. Some alteration of windows seems to have taken place in the middle of the eighteenth century.

In the interior little remains of the first Earl's work beyond an enriched ceiling in the small drawing-room (pl. 159) and the chimney-piece in the large drawing-room, both in the style of Inigo Jones. These rooms are in the east range. The ceiling, divided into compartments and having a central oval, is a more restrained example than the contemporary ceilings at Forde Abbey. The majority of the rooms were redecorated for the fourth Earl about 1750 and are excellent examples of their period. The dining-room (pl. 160) is known to have been the work of Stephen Wright, the architect employed by the Duke of Newcastle, and he may have been responsible for all that was done at this time. Richard Pococke, who visited the house in 1754, remarks of one room that it had been 'lately finished in a very elegant manner.' The principal rooms in the north range are (from west to east) the White Hall, the dining-room, which has a high coved ceiling, and the Tapestry Room, so called from a set of Brussels tapestries in Gobelins style forming part of the suite designed by Noel Coypel illustrating the Triumphs of the Gods. The library is a long Regency room in the south range. About the end of the eighteenth century the courtyard was covered in and converted into a galleried hall lit from a dome. The fourth Earl commissioned a great deal of new furniture, of the finest quality, much of which by its likeness to the designs in the *Director* can with very little doubt be assigned to Thomas Chippendale. Indeed, the interior of the house is a compendium of mid-eighteenth-century taste. Many of the family portraits hang in richly carved frames of this date; the 'Judgment of Hercules,' a picture commissioned in Italy by the third Earl to illustrate his platonic theory of morals, has an exceptionally fine frame carved in rococo style, which is also represented in a superb series of carved and gilt mirrors. The grounds also received attention from the fourth Earl, who created a landscape garden about the serpentining river. Pococke gives a description of it. Among its principal features were an island with a castle on it, a gateway with towers, a cascade, a thatched house, a pavilion on a mount, a temple to Shakespeare, a Chinese bridge and a stone bridge. Most of these structures disappeared with the taste for them. A very elaborate grotto of shells at the end of the long avenue is stated by Pococke to have been 'finished by Mr Castles of Marybone.' In place of the fourth Earl's artificial landscape there are now the great belts of trees, the broad lake and the grand avenue of beeches.

The church at St Giles, rebuilt in 1732, redecorated by Bodley, but burnt in 1908, was restored by the present Earl and reconsecrated in 1910. Its interior is an impressive example of Sir Ninian Comper's work. The tower (pl. 154) and south wall date from the Classic rebuilding of 1732. The beautiful flint and stone masonry recalls that at Charlton Marshall, and, perhaps, both buildings were designed by one of the Bastards of Blandford. Besides the sumptuous monument to Sir Anthony Ashley, the church contains the memorials of the Earls of Shaftesbury—among them the first Earl, whose body was brought back to St Giles from Holland; his grandson the third Earl, the philosopher and author of the *Characteristics*, who died in Naples; the fourth Earl, whose monument was designed by James Stuart and carved by Thomas Scheemakers; and the seventh Earl, the great social reformer and philanthropist.

Charborough Park (5 miles W. of Wimborne Minster). The present house at Charborough, although it is disguised in an early nineteenth-century dress of stucco, incorporates the building that Sir Walter Erle erected during the Commonwealth. As the commander of the local Parliamentary force that besieged Corfe Castle at the opening of the Civil War, Sir Walter has earned a somewhat ridiculous name in history. His care not to endanger his own person, his discomfiture over the failure of those antiquated siege engines the 'Boar' and the 'Sow,' which untimely cast their farrow, and his precipitate departure on the approach of the Earl of Carnarvon have stamped him as the fool in the piece in which Lady Bankes played the rôle of heroine; but allowance has to be made for the fact that our information about him is derived from Royalist sources, which were not likely to be careful of the truth.

161. CHARBOROUGH PARK

The main staircase with decorative paintings by Sir James Thornhill (1718).

162. KINGSTON LACY

From the north-east. The house, designed by Sir Roger Pratt, was altered and cased in stone by Sir Charles Barry (1835–39).

During the months when the King's troops were masters of Dorset Sir Walter's house was burnt, so that at the conclusion of hostilities he was faced with the task of rebuilding it. Some eighteenth-century paintings show it to have been a building of the same type as Kingston Lacy, though without the cupola—a rectangular pile with hipped roof and dormer windows. In its construction stone and timber from the ruins of Corfe Castle were made use of, and at the Restoration Sir Ralph Bankes approached Sir Walter demanding restitution. Short of pulling the house down this could not be effected, and a great beam, probably from the keep of the Castle, still remains in position supporting a part of the ground floor. A description of Charborough, left by Celia Fiennes when she paid a visit about 1685, fills in some of the details. She speaks of 'a very good Hall at the entrance,' a large parlour opening on to the gardens, 'another parlour for smoakeing'—all 'good and lofty' and 'well wainscoated and painted.' None of the rooms now remain as she saw them, and the great staircase with its fine paintings by Sir James Thornhill (pl. 161) had not then been inserted. This is the most interesting feature in the house. The series of paintings was commissioned in 1718 by General Thomas Erle, who had fought in William III's campaigns in Ireland and later in Flanders and Spain. Thornhill, a Dorset man, was recognised as the leading historical and decorative painter of the day by the time General Erle employed him at Charborough. The theme of the paintings is the Triumph of Love as illustrated by the Contest of Beauty and the Rape of Helen. The ceiling shows the Courts of Heaven with the three goddesses sitting on clouds and Hermes departing with the apple. In the first of the wall scenes he gives the apple to Paris, who in a second scene makes the award to Venus. The third scene shows Paris carrying off Helen and the ship waiting to set sail for Troy. The paintings form a fine example of Thornhill's work, though they were rather too zealously restored in 1840. There is another series by Thornhill in the staircase hall of Lord Digby's School at Sherborne. There the theme is Atalanta hunting the Calydonian boar, observed from the ceiling by Diana and her celestial attendants.

As far back as records go, Charborough has never changed hands by sale, but it has repeatedly passed through heiresses. The Erles acquired the property by marriage in the time of Queen Elizabeth, and in the eighteenth century it passed to Henry Drax, the friend and secretary of Frederick, Prince of Wales. The Prince paid a visit to Charborough in 1741, his host having added a new wing on to the house to accommodate him. The house was greatly enlarged about 1810, when the walls were plastered and the pilasters and pediment added to the north front (pl. 155). There is a large picture gallery containing several old paintings of Charborough and a series of portraits of William III's generals. It has a dado formed from a re-markable assemblage of early Tudor carved panels. The tower on the height to the east of the house was built in 1790; it was struck by lightning in 1838, but rebuilt in the following year. From its summit one can see the Isle of Wight and into parts of Wiltshire and Somerset. The great deer park was extended to its present limits in the eighteen-forties by John Sawbridge Erle-Drax. It covers nearly 800 acres and is finely planted with clumps and belts of beeches. The old paintings show a forecourt in front of the house and formal gardens immediately to the west of it, but these were swept away in the wave of picturesque landscape gardening, which seems to have reached Charborough early in the nineteenth century.

The present owner, who inherited the estate through his mother, is Admiral the Honourable Sir Reginald Plunkett-Ernle-Erle-Drax, brother of the late Lord Dunsany.

Kingston Lacy. For over two and a half centuries the seat of the Bankes family, Kingston Lacy is both architecturally and historically one of the most interesting houses in Dorset. Its builder was Sir Ralph Bankes, son of Lady Mary, the heroic defender of Corfe Castle at the outbreak of the Civil War, when in the summer of 1643 she successfully withstood a six weeks' siege. Sir Ralph's father, Sir John Bankes, was Attorney-General during the latter part of Charles I's reign. He had purchased Corfe Castle in 1635 from the widow of Sir Edward Coke, and two years later added to his Dorset estates the manor of Kingston Lacy, lying west of Wimborne Minster. In the second part of its name the place commemorates its thirteenth-century owners, the de Lacys, Earls of Lincoln, from whom it afterwards passed into the Duchy of Lancaster. Sir John Bankes purchased from Mountjoy Blount, Earl of Newport, the natural son of Charles Blount, Queen Elizabeth's favourite, to whom the manor had been granted by James I.

The destruction of Corfe Castle made it necessary for Sir Ralph Bankes to provide himself with a new seat, and he chose for it a site on his Kingston Lacy property, lying below Badbury Rings. Here, according to tradition, had been a palace of the West Saxon kings and, in later times, 'a faire manor place,' in which Margaret, Countess of Beaufort, the mother of Henry VII, was born. Sir Ralph began the building of his house in April, 1663, and it was nearing completion by the autumn of 1665. Until the discovery and publication of Sir Roger Pratt's note-books[1] it had always been assumed that Kingston Lacy was built by John Webb from designs left by Inigo Jones. But the very full details that Pratt set down in his note-books prove that he was Sir Ralph's architect and that the whole course of the building operations was supervised by him. From the death of Inigo Jones in 1652 to the beginning of Wren's architectural career, Webb used to be regarded as the only

---

[1] *The Architecture of Sir Roger Pratt*, by R. T. Gunther, 1928. Pratt was born in 1620 and died in 1684.

164. KINGSTON LACY

Bronze statues of Charles I and Dame Mary Bankes, defendress of
Corfe Castle, by Baron Marochetti.

163. KINGSTON LACY

The obelisk, brought from Philae and set up in 1827, and the
south front of the house.

165.   WADDON MANOR

The surviving wing, built about 1700. Looking seawards from the hill behind the house.

important link between the two men. We can now point to Sir Roger Pratt as an architect who was fully as important as Webb, and the bulk of his work falls within this period. It was not Inigo Jones but Pratt who designed and built Coleshill, the recent destruction of which has robbed us of the finest country house of its age. He was also the architect of Clarendon House, the splendid palace that Charles II's Lord Chancellor built for himself in Piccadilly, and of Horseheath Hall in Cambridgeshire, whose quality can now be appreciated only from engravings. Finally, in 1669, after coming into Ryston, the Norfolk property of his cousin, he rebuilt the Hall there, and thenceforth gave up the practice of architecture for the pursuits and occupations of a country gentleman. In 1643, at the age of twenty-three, he set out on a grand tour of France, Italy, Flanders and Holland, which lasted six and a half years; when at Rome in 1644-5 he met John Evelyn, the diarist, who from that time became his life-long friend. How deeply he studied Classic architecture while he was in Italy is shown by his notes and observations that have been preserved. Like Wren, he was an amateur who made it his business to master the practical side of his profession. The high regard in which he was held during his life is evident from Evelyn's opinion of him, from the fact that he was knighted, and from his appointment with Wren and Hugh May as one of the three Commissioners for the rebuilding of London after the Fire.

The alterations which Sir Charles Barry carried out at Kingston Lacy between 1835 and 1839 have to a certain extent obscured the original design; but he was responsible for reinstating the roof platform and cupola, which had been removed at some time in the eighteenth century. The house, as originally built, was of red brick with stone dressings. In form it bears a general resemblance to Coleshill, which, however, was longer in proportion to the width. By the kindness of Mr Ralph Bankes, the present owner, an original drawing for the elevation of the principal (north) front is reproduced (pl. 151). It should be mentioned that the chimneys and cupola are drawn on a separate piece of paper, which has been stuck on to the sheet, showing that considerable thought was given to their size and appearance. As at Coleshill, the principal floor is raised up on what Pratt calls a *mezzano*. The main entrance is now placed in this basement storey, Barry having sunk the level of the ground on the north side of the house. Besides casing it with stone, Barry added the four chimney stacks at the angles, the present dormers and the attic feature in the centre of the south front; he also introduced the arched loggia on the east side (pl. 162). It would appear from the drawing that the central mullion of each window was not carried down below the level of the transom, in order to admit pairs of opening casements after the French manner; the stone mullions and transoms survive on the west side, where they have not given place to sashes.

It is, perhaps, worth setting down a few of the items relating to the building which Pratt recorded in his note-books. The bricklayer was a certain Thomas Fitts, of Farnham in Surrey, with whom the architect entered into articles of agreement on April 9th, 1663. His chief mason was a man called Goodfellow. Before choosing the stone for the dressings he obtained information about the prices of Portland, but eventually used stone from Chilmark. There is a memorandum: 'Masons in Chilmarke Thomas Swite, Richard Masy. In Portland Christofer Gibbs, Switzer overseer for the King there etc.' He made a note that 'the great stone shield' in the pediment 'was long $5\frac{1}{2}$ ft., broad 4 ft., thick 1 ft. 6 inches.' He estimated that on the house, stables and garden walls about two million bricks were used, costing about £1,000. In front of the house there was a great walled forecourt, entered by brick gate-piers, and, behind, a walled garden, at the end of which there was a little 'banketting house' with three arches.

The formal lay-out must have been swept away in the eighteenth century, since an engraving in Neale's *Seats* shows greensward extending right up to the walls of the house. Barry, however, reverted to formality, laying out an Italian terrace before the south front and disposing in formal fashion the urns, Venetian well-tops and bronze lions which his client had collected. William John Bankes, who embarked on these far-reaching alterations soon after inheriting the property in 1834, was a distinguished connoisseur; he was the friend of Byron and Hobhouse and had travelled extensively in the Mediterranean and the Levant; and in Barry he found an architect who shared his enthusiasm for the art of Italy during the High Renaissance. The extent to which the exterior was remodelled has already been indicated. At the same time the interior was largely transformed. A grand staircase of Carrara marble, worthy of an Italian palace, goes up from the first to the second floor and is continued downward on a modified scale to the ground floor, at which level the main entrance was now placed. At a half-landing, where through three arches a delightful vista of the park is obtained, two niches frame the bronze statues by Baron Marochetti of Charles I and Dame Mary, holding the sword and key (pl. 164). (The keys of Corfe Castle are a treasured possession still preserved in the house.) Two large works by Snyders are framed in the walls at the head of the staircase; the ceiling painting came from the Grimani Palace at Venice. The suites of rooms on the main floor were decorated with extraordinary splendour. The saloon in the centre of the north front takes up two storeys and has a segmental ceiling painted in the Adam manner and dating probably from about 1780. The pictures here include works by Titian, Rubens, Van Dyck and Lely. A 'Holy Family' by Raphael was in the collection of Charles I. In the Spanish room, which is lined with Cordova leather, hang pictures by Velazquez, Murillo and Zurbaran; the ceiling here, brought from the Contarini Palace at Venice, frames a painting by Veronese ('The Creation of the Elements') and two panels of cherubs by Pordenone. The library ceiling has let into it an allegorical composition by Guido Reni ('Dawn Parting Day and Night'), but its scale is too large for the room and for the series of Lely portraits above the bookcases. Other family portraits are in the drawing-room. Among the paintings in the panelled dining-room is an unfinished work by Giorgione ('The Judgment of Solomon'); the doors in this room, carved in box wood, have little figures of *putti* in relief after Donatello and Sansovino.

There are now few private collections in country houses as rich as that at Kingston Lacy. Some of the pictures belonged to the family before William John Bankes began to fill the house with his acquisitions: by family tradition the portraits of Charles I and Henrietta Maria, the group of their three children and the double portrait of Prince Rupert and Prince Maurice, as also the Sir John and Lady Borlase, by Van Dyck, originally hung at Corfe Castle. The series of family portraits is especially notable for the Lelys, but Cornelius Johnson, Reynolds, Romney and Lawrence are also represented. Reynolds, when on a visit to Kingston Lacy, is said to have remarked: 'I never had appreciated Sir Peter Lely till I had seen these portraits.' It was on this occasion that he was accompanied by Dr Johnson, whose uncouth gestures so much perplexed his host. Boswell records: 'The conversation turning on pictures, which he could not well see, he retired to a corner of the room, stretching out his right leg as far as he could before him, then bringing up his left leg, and stretching his right leg further on. Mr Bankes observing him, went up to him, and in a very courteous manner assured him that, though it was not a new house, the flooring was perfectly safe. The doctor started from his reverie like a person wakened out of his sleep, but spoke not a word.'

During the minority of John Bankes, son of the builder of the house, Kingston Lacy was let to the Duke of Ormonde, who died here in 1688. The great obelisk of Egyptian granite opposite the south front of the house (pl. 163) came from the island of Philae and was set up in 1827; the foundation-stone of the plinth was laid by the Duke of Wellington. The inscriptions on it proved of great importance in the early stages of deciphering the hieroglyphic characters. The park with its noble limes, elms and beeches forms a perfect setting for the house, whose white mass nearer at hand is foiled by the stately forms of cedars and the great expanses of lawn.

Waddon Manor (1 miles E. of Portisham). Although only a wing and a little office court remain of a building that was once considerably larger, Waddon Manor is still a house of much charm. It is to be found, tucked against the hills, on the north side of the winding lane that goes from Portisham to Upwey, a lane that in its manner of hugging the slopes of the downs, which here shut off the Weymouth triangle from the hinterland, reminds one a little of the Pilgrim's Way in Surrey. A group of fine old walnut trees (pl. 166) shelters the homestead of East or Gerard's Waddon, to give it its alternative names. The second prefix came from the family that owned the manor in the sixteenth century and which also acquired Trent on the Somerset border. Thomas Gerard of Trent, the author of *The Survey of Dorset*, left as his heirs three daughters, the eldest of whom brought Waddon to her husband, Colonel Bullen Reymes, the friend of Pepys. In the Civil War Reymes took up arms for the King and was obliged to compound for his estates, but at the Restoration he was made Vice-Admiral of Dorset and was sent on a mission to Tangier. He was a man of business-like habits and was fond of plays—two qualities that endeared him to Pepys. 'Sat by Col. Reames, who understands and loves a play as well as I, and I love him for it' is one of the entries in the *Diary*. The Colonel made Waddon his home— he was M.P. for Melcombe Regis—and he seems to have rebuilt the old house. But the main building, which appears in an old painting of about 1700, was burnt down in 1704, only a few years after the tall wing that survives (pl. 165) had been added to it. The outline of the main building can be seen on the west side of the wing, which is a characteristic example of William III or Queen Anne domestic work, built of fine grey ashlar with a good cornice, tall sashed windows and a stone-slated roof. Charming features of the house are its massive stone gate-piers (pl. 167 and 168). Within, there are two finely panelled rooms and an oak staircase with a dog-gate. The handrail of the staircase ends, according to the usual Dorset method, in a fat scroll supported on a plain newel post (pl. 200). In 1695 Bullen Reymes's son died, and his widow married Harry Chafin of Zeals, near Mere, who built the wing that survives to-day. After his death Waddon became a farmhouse for nearly two centuries, until in 1928 Mr B. O. Corbett took a lease of it, repaired it and made it his home.

Dewlish House. Dewlish, or Develish, as it is sometimes written in old documents, takes its name from the brook that comes down from the heights above Bingham's Melcombe to join the Piddle close to Athelhampton. The valley which the stream has carved out has the smooth, rounded contours one always finds in a chalk country, and in this soft cradle lies Dewlish House, some distance to the south of the village. It is a long Queen Anne building with green lawns spreading down to the stream, which passes to the east of it and beyond which a long line of hanging beechwood clothes the farther side of the valley. According to Hutchins the house was built in 1702, a date which agrees well with its architecture. It is probable, how-

166. WADDON MANOR
Old walnut trees in the lane beside the house.

167 and 168. WADDON MANOR
The stone gate-piers are notable features of the house.

169. DEWLISH HOUSE

Built by Thomas Skinner in 1702. The south front, of mellow red brick.

170. DEWLISH HOUSE

The north front, cased in stone.

171. EASTBURY

The surviving fragment of Bubb Dodington's gigantic mansion (W on the plan, page 151).

172. EASTBURY

Gate-piers at one of the park entrances.

173. EASTBURY

Vanburgh's monumental archway to the office court, producing with its fantastic outcrop an
effect reminiscent of a Piranesi engraving.

ever, that some walls of an earlier building were retained and influenced its planning. In its present state three different kinds of material are to be seen on the exterior—on the south front brick (pl. 169), on the north grey Purbeck or Portisham limestone (pl. 170), at the east end yellow Ham Hill stone. The south front, with its run of eleven windows, is the least altered. The north front appears to have been faced in stone at a later date; but the original entrance doorway, with a finely carved shield over it, remains. On this side the two ends of the elevation are treated as rudimentary wings, and there is a shaped gable in the centre given a cornice smaller in scale and more richly treated than the simple modillion cornice elsewhere. The finest feature inside the house is the grand oak staircase, behind the entrance hall, with its carved brackets and twisted and fluted balusters. The room at the east end of the north front has rich Georgian panelling and a good ceiling (*circa* 1740). About that time the central feature of the south front appears to have been re-designed and, perhaps, heightened.

Dewlish House has never been the manor house of the village: the estate was a sub-manor for which its possessors paid a quit-rent. From the time of Henry VIII until the Restoration it was owned by the Basketts. In 1663 John Baskett sold to Nicholas Skinner, a London merchant, whose son, Thomas, built the present house, setting up his family's arms over the entrance. After the death of Thomas II in 1756, the estate was bought by David Robert Michel of Kingston Russell. His son, General John Michel, and his grandson, Field-Marshal Sir John Michel, both had distinguished careers in the Army. The late owner, Lady Frankfort de Montmorency, who died in 1936, was a daughter of the Field-Marshal.

Eastbury (5 miles N.E. of Blandford). In spite of the fact that it is now only a fragment, Eastbury must claim a prominent place among the Georgian houses of Dorset, both on account of its former magnificence and of the influence it exerted on contemporary buildings in the neighbourhood. Its construction, which went on for more than twenty years, must have caused a great stir in the county and have been received among the local gentry with mingled feelings of curiosity, ridicule and envy. About the year 1709 a farm at Tarrant Gunville, on the edge of Cranborne Chase, was bought by George Dodington, a Lord of the Admiralty. By 1717 he had commissioned Sir John Vanbrugh to prepare designs for a vast mansion, which, with its balancing outbuildings, was to embrace five courts having a total width of 570 ft. Eastbury came third in size among Vanbrugh's great houses, being only exceeded by Blenheim and Castle Howard. When was it completed, in 1738, it is said to have cost more than £140,000.

George Dodington died in 1720, leaving Eastbury to his nephew, George Bubb, as owner for life, and earmarking £30,000 out of his large estate for the completion of the building. Bubb, who took his uncle's surname, was the son of a Weymouth apothecary, and spent a lifetime in the servile intrigues of back-stair politics to gain a position commensurate with his fortune. The apotheosis of pomposity and unctuous virtue, he courted in turn, and sometimes simultaneously, all the leading political figures of his day—Walpole, Frederick Prince of Wales, Argyll, the Pelhams, Bute—recording his complicated dealings in the curious diary which was published after his death. In the last year of his life success attended his costly efforts when George III granted him a peerage: he became Baron Melcombe of Melcombe Regis. It was not until four years after his uncle's death that Bubb Dodington went on with the great building project, which Vanbrugh himself did not live to see completed. What the whole building looked like we can see from two oil-paintings still preserved at Eastbury, one of which shows the great man driving up in his magnificent coach, drawn by six black horses. In its main dispositions it foreshadowed Seaton Delaval, in Northumberland—a massive central block, prefaced by a wide forecourt, with balancing wings on either side connected to the main building by long arcades. The main block, coming as the climax at the end of this elaborate overture, had four towers at the angles and a colossal portico of six ringed Tuscan columns. It is part of the north wing, which contained the stables, with its arcade and the court behind, that constitutes the present house (pl. 171). The most impressive surviving feature is the tremendous Roman archway giving entrance to this stable court (pl. 173). It recalls the archway to the hospice buildings at Castle Howard, where the same 'Gothic' corbel table appears, but there the flanking Baroque consoles are omitted. Two pine saplings have been allowed to take root on it, producing a truly Piranesian effect.

Vanbrugh's plan and elevations for Eastbury were published in the third volume of *Vitruvius Britannicus* (1725). A preliminary design ('for a Person of Quality in Dorset') had been included in the second volume, published in 1717, and in the Victoria and Albert Museum there is a sequence of drawings for the house which makes it possible to trace and analyse, as Mr Laurence Whistler has done,[1] the development of the whole scheme in the architect's mind. The crowning feature of the main block, and one essential to Vanbrugh's monumental conception, was an attic storey rising above the portico (pl. 151). This was never executed. Instead, the portico on the entrance front was finished with a pediment, as the painting shows (pl. 155). Vanbrugh died in 1726, when the building was unfinished, and its completion was entrusted to Roger Morris, a protégé of the Duke of Argyll and the Earl of Pembroke. Morris also built Dodington's house by the river at Hammersmith. The state rooms at Eastbury comprised a great hall, set athwart the axis, with

[1] *Country Life*, Dec. 31, 1948, pp. 1386–9, and *The Imagination of Vanbrugh* (1954), pp. 156–77.

twin staircases behind it separated by a lobby to admit a continuous vista through the middle of the house; a grand salon faced over the gardens; on the south side there were 'a great eating room' and a drawing-room; on the north, a suite of three apartments, which were gorgeously hung with velvet and silk. Bishop Pococke, who visited Eastbury in October, 1754, has left a long description of the magnificent interior. An extensive garden lay-out was designed by Bridgeman,[1] doubtless in

A. Great Hall. G. Great Eating Room.
B. Salon. H. Chapel.
C. Antiroom. I. Eating Room.
D. Drawing Room. KK. Stable.
E. Bedchamber. Courts.
F. Drawing Room. L. Great Court.

M. Kitchen Court. R. Laundry.
N. Brewhouse Court.
O. Servants Common Hall.
P. Kitchen. S. Brewhouse.
Q. Wash-house. T.T. Dairy.
V. Store Room. W. Arcade.

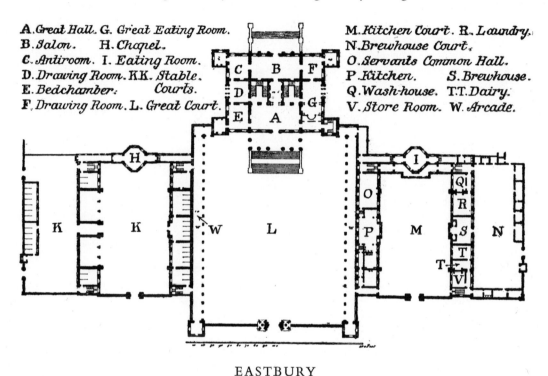

EASTBURY

Plan of the complete house taken from *Vitruvius Britannicus* (Vol. III) (1725).

consultation with the architect. The scheme was in the old, rigid formal style of the beginning of the century, with a parterre, oblong pool and vista terminated by a terraced amphitheatre and portico; on either side groves of trees were planted, with miles of intersecting grass walks. The beech groves remain, now grown to a great size, and most of Bridgeman's lay-out can still be traced. Two of the entrance gates to the park also remain, their stone piers seen against a dark background of yews (pl. 172).

---

[1] Three large coloured plans of the gardens and park are in the Bodleian Library (MS. Gough Drawings, a. 3, ff. 9, 10; a. 4, f. 21).

Bubb Dodington delighted in playing the rôle of Maecenas. James Thomson, Henry Fielding and Dr Young of *Night Thoughts* were among the more distinguished poets and writers he entertained at Eastbury. Cumberland, who with his patron, Lord Halifax, stayed at Eastbury in the summer of 1756, gives an amusing portrait of Dodington in his *Memoirs*.

'Our splendid host was excelled by no man in doing the honours of his house and table; to the ladies he had all the courtly and profound devotion of a Spaniard, with the ease and gaiety of a Frenchman towards the men. The interior of his mansion was as proud and splendid as the exterior was bold and imposing. . . . He was not to be approached but through a suite of apartments and was rarely seated but under painted ceilings and gilt entablatures.'

His dress was equally remarkable.

'He had a wardrobe loaded with rich and flaring suits . . . many were coeval with his embassy [to Spain in 1717–19] and every birthday added to the stock. In doing this he so contrived as never to put the old dresses out of countenance by any variations in the fashion of the new; in the meantime his bulk and corpulency gave full display to a vast expanse and profusion of brocade and embroidery, and this, when set off with an enormous tye-periwig and deep laced ruffles, gave the picture of an ancient courtier in his gala habit or Quin in his stage dress.'

There is also an engaging picture of him entertaining that other eighteenth-century *parvenu*, 'Alderman' Beckford, whose cousin, Julines, had recently purchased Stepleton.

'It was an interlude truly comic and amusing: Beckford loud, voluble, self-sufficient. Dodington, lolling in his chair, in perfect apathy and self-command, dozing, and even snoring at intervals, in his lethargic way, broke out every now and then into such gleams and flashes of wit and irony as by the contrast, set the table in a roar.'

On his death in 1762 Lord Melcombe left to his friend, Sir Francis Dashwood, with whom he had been a fellow 'brother' in the notorious Medmenham Abbey 'Fraternity,' a legacy to erect a mausoleum in his memory at West Wycombe in Buckinghamshire on the hill in front of the church. That remains, while the greater part of his house at Eastbury has gone. Under his uncle's will it passed to Earl Temple, who, after vainly offering it for sale and even promising an annuity of £200 a year to anyone who would live in it, finally resorted to the expedient of pulling it down.[1] Gunpowder had to be used to demolish some of the walls. The remaining wing was

[1] John Byng noted on his return from Weymouth in 1782 that Eastbury was then being demolished (*Torrington Diaries*, vol. i, p. 105.).

174. CHETTLE HOUSE

Built early in the eighteenth century by George Chafin, probably from designs by Thomas Archer.
The south front.

175. KINGSTON MAURWARD

Originally a red brick house, built by George Pitt 1717–1720, and cased in Portland stone in 1794. The south front.

176. ENCOMBE

The south front of the wide-spreading house. Built in or soon after 1735 by John Pitt.

for a time inhabited by the second Josiah Wedgwood, and in 1806 the estate was bought by the famous sportsman, James John Farquharson, ancestor of the present owner.

Chettle House (about 7 miles N.E. of Blandford). Chettle, the home of the Chafins in the eighteenth century, is an unusually interesting Classic house of the age of Vanbrugh. It was built by George Chafin, according to Hutchins in 1710, though the architectural evidence might suggest a date ten or fifteen years later. Thomas Chafin, the father of George, commanded a troop of horse against Monmouth in 1685, and George sat as Member of Parliament for the county from 1713 to 1747, but it was as rangers of Cranborne Chase that the family earned its redoubtable reputation. George Chafin's jealous guardianship of the rights and privileges of the Chase on one occasion brought him into collision with his neighbour, Bubb Dodington, who had dared to set up a private gamekeeper within the boundaries. On meeting the keeper and his dogs beating for game, after having previously warned his master of the offence, Chafin shot the dogs dead, whereupon Dodington challenged him to a duel. When, however, the challenge was accepted and Chafin's second 'waited on Mr Dodington to fix time and place for meeting, he found him peaceably inclined,' and the incident ended in a jovial evening at Eastbury. The story is told by the Rev. William Chafin, George's youngest son, who shared to the full his father's passion for sport and celebrated its glories in *Anecdotes of Cranbourne Chase*, a book that certainly deserves reprinting. But it was only at the end of his life, 'being struck by lightning at the age of eighty-five,' that the Reverend William abandoned field sports and took to literature. After reading his pious wish that the Chase might 'remain in a flourishing state until the general dissolution of all things,' it is satisfactory to know that the old gentleman did not live to see the Disafforestation Act of 1830. He died in 1818, and with him the family came to an end.

The intriguing question of the authorship of this house has been discussed in the Introduction (p. 32), where the evidence is given for attributing the design to Vanbrugh's contemporary, Thomas Archer,[1] another exponent of those Baroque ideas which make a fleeting appearance in England during the years immediately preceding Lord Burlington's ascendancy. In a house of the size of Chettle there could be no great scope for dramatic contrast or theatrical effect. None the less, Baroque principles can be detected in the grand scale adopted in the treatment of the elevations,

[1] The late Major E. W. F. Castleman of Chettle was told by his mother that although the architect was always said to be Vanbrugh, she had heard from his grandmother that 'a pupil of his called Archer had most to do with it.' In a letter to the author setting this on record Major Castleman commented: 'Archer meant no more to her than Jones or Smith, so I am sure she could not have imagined it!'

in the bold and individual handling of detail, and in the rounding off of angles to give variety of plan (pl. 174). The two ends of the house were originally square and only one storey high, but the rounded additions, echoing the curves on the entrance front (pl. 19), and the raising of the walls, effected in 1912, whilst altering the appearance of the house, were managed with sympathetic regard to its character. In the centre, behind the balustrade, there was an attic storey with a cupola. These were removed in the middle of last century. Internally, the original treatment is preserved in the fine entrance hall with its Doric entablatures and rounded angles and in the staircase hall on the east front with its converging flights and its galleries (pl. 182). The large drawing-room at the south end was formed about 1846–50, when Edward Castleman came to live at Chettle, which his father, a partner in the old Wimborne Bank, had purchased at auction in 1826. In the decoration of the drawing-room, which was designed by a Mr Blake of Wareham, the father of Alfred Stevens was employed as decorator. Alfred Stevens himself is said to have assisted in the work and it is known that he executed the reliefs over the doors in the staircase hall. The late Major E. W. F. Castleman quoted his father's former agent as having said that he remembered watching Stevens at work on them. Since the death of Major Castleman in 1946, Chettle has been divided into flats. The present owner is Mrs E. M. Bourke.

Kingston Maurward. *The Eighteenth-Century House.* The 'elegant and stately pile,' as Hutchins describes it, still 'makes a grand figure' at the end of a long vista which suddenly opens about half-way along the high road from Puddletown to Dorchester; and from the south (pl. 175) it is equally impressive when seen from beyond the Frome crowning the low ridge that rises from the water meadows. This new seat was built between 1717 and 1720 by George Pitt of Stratfieldsaye to replace the old manor house of the Greys described on p. 91. By marrying Lora Grey, the last of the old family, 'he made ample Provision for a numerous Issue and rendred the Figure of his Relict not unworthy of his Ancestors'—so runs the epitaph on his monument, erected by his appreciative widow, in Stinsford church.[1] As originally built, the house was of brick with stone dressings. So it appears in the engraving of it in the first edition of Hutchins' *History* (1774). The design of the house, as seen in this plate, has suggested an attribution to Thomas Archer (see p. 33), but as good a claim can be made for John James of Greenwich. In 1711, when applying for one of the surveyorships to the Commissioners for Building Fifty New Churches, James mentioned among his patrons and sponsors 'Mr Geo: Pitt of Hampshire', i.e.

---

[1] Grey's Bridge over the Frome was built at her expense. There is a bell on the stable range at Kingston inscribed 'The Ladey Pitt's bell 1739.'

of Stratfieldsaye, and there is John Bastard's statement in his letter to Sir Peter Thompson (see p. 37) that James was often in Dorset.[1]

In 1794 George Pitt's building was completely cased in Portland stone by his grandson, William Morton Pitt, and about the same time much new decoration was done in the interior. The casing of the house is said to have been suggested by George III. On one of the King's visits from Weymouth the proud owner was expatiating on the beauty of his house, hoping that it would receive the royal commendation. 'The King, however, with his well-known iteration, did nothing but utter the words, "Brick, Mr Pitt, brick." The impression that they made upon his host may be judged of from the fact that before King George made his appearance again in the neighbourhood of Dorchester the quarrymen and masons had made theirs; and Mr Pitt, at a vast expense, had contrived, between the visits, to effect the wished-for alteration.' The landscaping of the park and the formation of the great lake south of the house had been effected by his father, John Pitt of Encombe, who succeeded to Kingston in 1774 on the death of his elder brother. The charming temple by the lake (pl. 193) probably dates from his time. The north front of the house has had a *porte-cochère* added to it. This opens into a square two-storey hall of the kind found in so many early Georgian houses and retaining its original plaster decoration. All the other early Georgian work has disappeared. Between the First and Second World Wars much was done to the house by the late Sir Cecil Hanbury. He added the fine Portland stone chimneys, modelled on those at Coleshill, and in the interior he was responsible for the oak staircase, marble fireplaces and other decoration; he also laid out the formal gardens west of the house. Kingston Maurward is now the headquarters of the Dorset Farm Institute.

Encombe (2½ miles S. of Corfe Castle). A deep valley cut back into the limestone ridge of Purbeck between St Alban's Head and the Kimmeridge Ledges shelters Encombe, which is reached by a drive descending steeply from the high-placed village of Kingston. The house, built of the local stone, spreads almost from slope to slope of the narrow combe and looks seaward over a long lake formed in the bed of the valley by the damming of the stream (pl. 176). The sea, however, is nearly a mile away.

Until the Dissolution, Encombe, as part of Kingston, belonged to Shaftesbury Abbey. In 1552 it was acquired by Robert Culliford and remained with his family until 1734, when William Culliford obtained an Act of Parliament to sell the estate in order to pay his debts. It was bought by George Pitt, of Stratfieldsaye and Kingston Maurward, shortly before his death and settled on his second son, John,

---

[1] James was the son of a Hampshire parson, who was vicar of Basingstoke from 1697 to 1717, when he became rector of Stratfield Turgis, the next parish to Stratfieldsaye.

who soon afterwards built the present house. Only two storeys high, it has a recessed centre, balancing blocks coming forward at right angles, and wings projecting from them to east and west, but the east wing is incomplete. The main building is in three sections with Doric colonnades flanking the central block, which in common with the inward-facing blocks has in the middle a narrow pedimented bay breaking forward and carried up above the parapet. The various units in the composition were given independent hipped roofs, but a bold cornice and solid parapet, extending from end to end of the building at the same height, bind together the loosely-knit components and establish a marked horizontality. The architect was clearly indebted to Vanbrugh, who in some of his houses—his remodelling of Claremont, for instance—used this low, wide-spreading type of composition, but there is none of Vanbrugh's boldness of handling, the units are small in scale, and, though kept plain to severity, they are not unorthodox in their detail. The work of Roger Morris has something of this character, and as he was completing Eastbury (p. 150) at the time when Encombe was built, it is not unlikely that John Pitt engaged him to design the house. Such a spread-out building, so emphatically horizontal, seems a strangely unsuitable choice for the site, but it was probably intended to be seen against a background of trees, as it appears in the engraving in Hutchins' *Dorset* (1774), with the lake to mirror its wide extent.

In 1774 John Pitt succeeded his elder brother at Kingston Maurward. He died in 1787, and twenty years later his son, William Morton Pitt, sold Encombe to Lord Eldon, the Lord Chancellor, in whose family it has since remained. In the eighteen-seventies the third Earl of Eldon commissioned Anthony Salvin to make alterations, one of which was to move the entrance from the south to the north. The original entrance court between the wings is now a lawn and the colonnades are glazed with plate glass. The present owner, Lieutenant-Colonel Harold Scott, inherited Encombe in 1953.

Kingston Russell House (7 miles E. of Bridport). A family from which the Dukes of Bedford are probably descended gave their name to Kingston Russell, in the parish of Long Bredy, which as early as the time of King John they held 'by the service of being marshals of the King's buttery on Christmas Day and at Whitsun.' The story of John Russell's rise to fortune has been told under Wolfeton (p. 61); his father had an estate at Berwick, near Swyre, a few miles to the west. Before his time the male line at Kingston Russell had died out, but his son, Francis, the second Earl of Bedford, bought the property back early in Queen Elizabeth's reign. The manor of Kingston Russell remained in Bedford ownership until the present century, and the farm at Berwick still does.

177. KINGSTON RUSSELL HOUSE

The entrance front, added about 1730 to an older house.

178. KINGSTON RUSSELL HOUSE

The east front (late seventeenth century) from the yew garden. The two ends were added in 1913.

179. KINGSTON RUSSELL HOUSE

The formal garden, with walls and bastions of yew, designed by Philip Tilden.

180.   CAME HOUSE
Built by John Damer and dated 1754. His architect was probably Francis Cartwright of
Blandford St Mary.

181.   CAME HOUSE
The saloon.

182. CHETTLE HOUSE
The staircase hall.

183. STEPLETON HOUSE
From the north-west. The main block is of late seventeenth-century date ; the wings
are dated 1758. In George III's reign Stepleton was the home of Peter Beckford,
author of *Thoughts on Hunting*.

There is some doubt whether Kingston Russell House can be considered the representative of the mediaeval home of the Russells, for although purchased by the Duke of Bedford about 1862, it had previously belonged to the Michels, who had acquired land in the parish of Long Bredy early in the seventeenth century. They were responsible for building the present house, to which the fourth John Michel (died 1739) gave its Palladian stone front, but his son, David Robert Michel, migrated to Dewlish (p. 148), and for long periods the house was let. It lies below the hills in the secluded valley of the Bride, a little south-east of the village of Long Bredy, and its white stone façade, with a bodyguard of yews posted like sentries in front of it, and a few old trees framing it, not too closely, faces the setting sun. This early Georgian front (pl. 177) has as its central feature a wide pediment and four Ionic pilasters. The treatment of the windows reflects the influence of Vanbrugh, and it is possible that the designer was Francis Cartwright (see Introduction, p. 34), who will have known Eastbury and may have been one of the mason contractors who worked on that house. The beautiful Portland stone masonry, the sharp outlines and the fine reserve with which this front is treated give it great distinction. It is something of a surprise, on walking round to the back, to find a quite different and older elevation of Charles II's reign with tall mullioned and transomed windows (pl. 178), but only the front of the house was rebuilt in the eighteenth century. There used to be a still earlier survival, a relic of the original house, in the form of a low wing which ran out eastward from the north end of the garden front. This was removed by Mr George Gribble after he had bought the property from the Duke of Bedford in 1913.

For many years the house had stood alone in the fields, derelict and overgrown with ivy. With the late Philip Tilden as his architect, Mr Gribble undertook its restoration, and in a short time effected a remarkable transformation. He laid out lawns and approaches, set up the entrance gates, and at the back of the house planted an extensive formal garden, with walls and bastions of cut yew, designed by Mr Tilden and now well established (pl. 179). The house was lengthened by a three-storey bay at either end, and the old wing was pulled down to give the garden front a greater degree of symmetry. The panelling in the sitting-room, on the right of the entrance hall, which had been removed by the Duke of Bedford, was re-covered and reinstated. Some alterations to the interior were effected when Mr and Mrs William Vestey bought the house in 1939. The entrance hall was redecorated and the early eighteenth-century stone fireplace removed. A fine early nineteenth-century scenic wallpaper, with views of Chinese architecture and landscape, formerly at Felix Hall, Essex, was installed in the dining-room.

Kingston Russell has two interesting historic associations. Thomas Masterman Hardy, Nelson's flag captain at Trafalgar, whose monument stands on the summit of Blackdown, was born in the house in 1769, when his parents were tenants of the Michels; and J. L. Motley, the American ambassador and historian of the Dutch Republic, died here on a visit in 1877.

Came House (1½ miles S.E. of Dorchester). This is one of the best examples in the county of a Palladian country house of moderate size. It was built in 1754 by John Damer, a younger brother of the Joseph Damer who purchased Milton Abbey and was afterwards created Lord Milton and eventually Earl of Dorchester. The house has been attributed to Francis Cartwright of Blandford St Mary (see Introduction, p. 34), and this was probably his most important work. It is well placed on rising ground, looking northwards over the valley of the Winterborne, which has left Herringston only a mile to the west. Although the main entrance was originally on the south side, the north front was made the more imposing of the two, an engaged portico of the Composite order forming the central feature, in the pediment of which are carved the Damer arms and the date 1754 (pl. 180). The central feature of the south front is in two stages: below there is an Ionic doorcase, the entablature of which is extended on either side to frame with flanking pilasters the adjoining windows; above comes a Palladian window with pilasters having the peculiar 'Bastard' capitals with outward-curving volutes. The interior contains a finely decorated saloon with a white marble fireplace and a rococo ceiling, in the centre of which the eagle of Jove is represented against a cloud from which issue lightnings and thunderbolts (pl. 181). There is another fine fireplace in the dining-room, which also has a ceiling of rococo character. These two rooms were probably decorated by London craftsmen. In the saloon, above the doors, there are grisaille paintings of classical subjects, after Cipriani, which were added later. The staircase is similar to those at Whatcombe and Stepleton. About a hundred and twenty years ago a conservatory was built on to the west end of the house, and a new entrance formed at the side of the north front. The park, which is well wooded with beeches, covers both sides of the valley and embraces the little church of Winterborne Came and what remains of the village. The second part of the name is a corruption of Caen, and commemorates the early ownership of the manor, which was granted by the Conqueror to the abbey of S. Etienne at Caen, and belonged to its dependent priory at Frampton. The post-Reformation owners were the Mellors, from whom Joseph Damer, father of the man who built the house, purchased the property early in the eighteenth century. From the Damers it descended to the late owner, Lady Christian Martin, who died in 1959. William Barnes, the Dorset poet, was rector of Came for many years. He died in the beautiful old thatch-roofed rectory, which stands away from the church by the Dorchester road.

Stepleton House (4 miles N.W. of Blandford). Peter Beckford, the noted sportsman and author of *Thoughts on Hunting*, lived at Stepleton for the greater part of his life. Although his famous book was not written here, but at Bristol Hot Wells, where he went to recover from an accident, it was in Dorset, over the wide acres of Cranborne Chase, that he gained his unrivalled experience of fox-hunting, and it was at Stepleton that he kept his celebrated pack of hounds. Beckford's pre-eminence as a sportsman has overshadowed every other aspect of his personality; but he was also a scholar, a dilettante and even a Member of Parliament. 'Never,' it was said, 'had fox or hare the honour of being chased to death by so accomplished a hunter. . . . He would bag a fox in Greek, find a hare in Latin, inspect his kennels in Italian, and direct the economy of his stables in exquisite French.' So fine a connoisseur might have been expected to have left his impress on the house; but Stepleton to-day bears practically no traces of his handiwork, unless, as tradition tells, he was responsible for the series of exacting corners by which the road from Blandford to Shaftesbury is carried round the park. It is said that when the Highway Commissioners visited Stepleton to obtain wayleaves for the new road, which would have cut straight across the park, Beckford entertained them with his customary hospitality, and after plying them energetically with drink placed a paper before them containing 'a few trifling alterations,' to which they signed their agreement. Only next morning did they discover what a circuitous route they had accepted.

Stepleton is the southernmost of the Iwerne villages, which take their name from the rivulet that runs under the western edge of Cranborne Chase, cutting off from the main ridge the two fortified heights of Hod Hill and Hambledon Hill. As it flows through the park the stream has been dammed to form a lake, on the east side of which the house stands. At first sight the building appears to be all of one date, since the two wings harmonise well enough with the main block (pl. 183). Actually, the wings are mid-eighteenth-century additions and the main block is a late Stuart building, with hipped roofs and dormer windows, incorporating portions of an earlier, possibly Elizabethan, house. On a window appears the date 1673, which probably marks the time of the rebuilding. From de Stepletons and Daccombs the manor passed in James I's reign to Sir William Pitt of Stratfieldsaye. In 1654 it was bought by Thomas Fownes, and in 1745 another Thomas Fownes sold it to Julines Beckford, cousin of 'Alderman' Beckford and father of Peter. This Thomas Fownes was himself a noted sportsman and a pioneer in the scientific breeding of foxhounds; his pack was one of the first to be kept exclusively for fox-hunting, and after he had been compelled to sell Stepleton in order to pay his creditors, the hounds were bought by a Mr Bowes of Yorkshire. Although the house is of seventeenth-century type, a miniature of the Kingston Lacy model, alterations were made to it by Fownes not long before he sold it, as is shown by the dining-room ceiling, in the centre of which are the shields of Fownes (quartering Armstrong) and Fitch: Thomas Fownes married one of the daughters of William Fitch of High Hall, Wimborne, who had previously been married to Henry Seymour Portman, builder of the fine house in Sherborne that contains the staircase painted by Thornhill. It is possible that Fownes did not complete the alterations he began. Some of the work looks later than 1745, and when Gibbon was entertained by Julines Beckford at Stepleton in 1762, he found the place 'unmeaning, expensive and unfinished.' Beckford certainly built the balancing wings, which are dated 1758 on their rain-water heads. These modest Georgian blocks with parapets and hipped roofs, recalling the detached stable building at Came, may have been the work of Francis Cartwright. The south front and east side of the main block owe their pedimented central features to Fownes or Julines Beckford. The one on the south or entrance front is an attractive piece of provincial designing, into which is worked a clever adaptation of the *motif Palladio*: the place of the central arched opening is taken by a deep niche, round which the main cornice deftly pirouettes. Inside the house there are several interesting chimney-pieces and ceilings showing the mannerisms of the Blandford joiners and plasterers; the fine staircase (pl. 187) has a wrought-iron balustrade similar to those at Whatcombe, Moreton and Came.

There used to hang at Stepleton a painting by Francis Sartorius of Peter Beckford and his hounds with the house in the background. This is now in the Bearsted collection at Upton House, Warwickshire. The stables (pl. 184), where Peter Beckford kept his hunters, were probably built by Thomas Fownes. They are of brick, in contrast to the house and its wings, which are stone-faced and stone-slated. Beckford's kennels, a plan of which he gives in his book, survive as gardeners' cottages; they stand opposite the garden gate near the turn of the road. Near the stables is the little Norman church, in which the great Peter lies buried. The brief epitaph is characteristic of him:

'To the Memory of Peter Beckford Esqre who
departed this Life A.D. 1811. Aged 71 years.

We die and are forgotten: 'tis Heaven's decree.
Thus the Fate of others will be the Fate of me.'

Peter Beckford's son took the name of Pitt-Rivers in 1828, on succeeding to the Rivers barony in right of his mother, and his descendants owned Stepleton until 1880. The estate was bought by Sir Ronald Lindsay in 1923 and was left by him to

184.   STEPLETON HOUSE
The stables, where Peter Beckford kept his hunters.

185.   RANSTON
The west front, added to an earlier building in 1758 by Thomas Ryves.

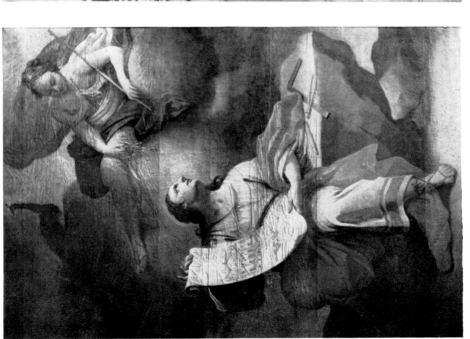

186 and 187. RANSTON

(*Left*) 'Architecture', one of a series of paintings by Andrea Casali on the walls of the staircase. On the scroll is a drawing of the west front of the house. (*Right*) The wrought-iron balustrade of the staircase (1758).

his nephew, the Earl of Crawford and Balcarres. Stepleton is now the home of Mrs Stanley Robinson.

Ranston (5 miles N.W. of Blandford). Half a mile beyond Stepleton the road from Blandford to Shaftesbury passes another finely timbered park, lying in the hollow between Hambledon Hill and the western slopes of Cranborne Chase. The house stands below the road, on the left-hand side, with east and west views up the hills which close in on either hand. Ranston now consists of little more than the house; it is a tithing of Shroton, a village also known as Iwerne Courtenay, a little distance to the north. The name is a contraction of Randolfston, an intermediate form, Randleston, occurring in the sixteenth century. Anciently held by the de Bruyns, the manor was acquired in 1545 by Robert Ryves of Blandford, and it remained with his descendants until 1781. It was then bought by Peter William Baker, the agent of Mr Portman of Bryanston, whom he assisted in the development of the Portman estate in Marylebone, giving his name to Baker Street. On his death in 1814 he was succeeded by a cousin, Sir Edward Littlehales, who took the Baker name. Sir Randolf Baker, the present owner, is his grandson.

The building now only shows features of the eighteenth and early nineteenth centuries, but probably incorporates walls of a house which the author of the early seventeenth-century *Survey of Dorset* mentions as having been built in his time. (There is a weathervane dated 1673 on one of the chimneys.) It is a square block, three gables deep, with a neat Georgian front facing the garden on the west (pl. 185). This façade, which has an order of Corinthian pilasters, triangular pediment and parapet adorned with vases, was added by Thomas Ryves in 1758. William Watts published an engraving of the house in his *Views of Seats* (1779), where he states that Ryves designed the new front himself. No doubt, the building and decoration were entrusted to the Bastards of Blandford. A large saloon and drawing-room were formed in the Georgian addition, and to this time belongs the most interesting feature of the house, a fine staircase with wrought-iron balustrade (pl. 187) and walls and ceiling elaborately decorated in stucco. On the walls, set in frames surrounded by stucco ornament, are four paintings by Casali[1], representing painting, sculpture, music and architecture, the last showing a seated figure holding a roll on which is drawn the elevation of the west front of the house (pl. 186). A screen of pillars at the

---

[1] Andrea Casali, a native of Civitavecchia, born *c.* 1700, came to England in 1741, was much employed by the aristocracy as a painter of historical and allegorical subjects, left England in 1766. At Ranston there are also by him a copy of Titian's 'Cupid Blinded' at the Villa Borghese and a 'St. Cecilia' in the drawing-room ceiling. Casali also worked at Fonthill. A ceiling painting by him, 'The Council of the Gods,' originally at Fonthill, is now in the Manor House, Beaminster.

head of the staircase has the curious 'Bastard' capitals with inward-curving volutes, like those on the Red Lion at Blandford (pl. 23). The east front of the house was altered and cased in stone in 1808, when one-storey wings were added, the north one containing a library. The park contains some magnificent trees; a gigantic cedar of Lebanon stands just north of the house.

Smedmore (4 miles S.W. of Corfe Castle). The limestone ridge which runs sickle-wise across the south-west side of Purbeck encloses a narrow segment of land sloping down to the sea, in which lie Kimmeridge and its little bay. Half a mile south-east of the village, above the Kimmeridge Ledges, Smedmore stands ensconced in trees, planted as a protection from the storms which once gave the rum-runner and the wrecker their chances on this lonely stretch of coast. From the house the sea is only visible through a 'window' cut in the screen of foliage and revealing a little vista of Kimmeridge Bay. But north-westwards the view is open, and, as you approach, the white front of Smedmore is seen flanked by the belts on either hand. Outwardly the house shows only eighteenth-century features, but the prim Georgian front with its portly bows conceals behind it an earlier house, the front of which is round the corner facing seawards. The nucleus of the present building is 'the little Newe House,' mentioned in *The Survey of Dorset*, which Sir William Clavell built in the time of James I. He moved to Smedmore from Barnston, the family's earlier home (p. 48), in order to be near the alum works which he opened on his property at Kimmeridge; this was one of a number of attempts that have been made to wrest mineral wealth from the Kimmeridge beds. Sir William ruined himself over the undertaking, since a monopoly for the making of alum had already been granted, and he was compelled to abandon the enterprise. He afterwards turned to glass-making and salt manufacture, using as fuel the local bituminous shale. In the bay can still be seen the ruins of the little quay or cobb which he built 'in Imitation of that at Lime' for exporting the alum. Sir William's Jacobean house was given its present garden front, facing south-west, by Edward Clavell about 1700; it is a charming example of vernacular Classic work of the time of Wren. The north-west front (pl. 188) was added by George Clavell, the last of the family in the male line. An estimate for this addition, dated 1761, has been preserved in the house, but unfortunately the name of the architect does not appear on it. The dining-room has a pretty wall treatment of plaster decoration, probably the work of the Blandford school. There are some good marble fireplaces and an early eighteenth-century oak staircase.

Smedmore has one of the longest continuous descents in Dorset, not having changed hands by sale since the time of Richard II. Over a century ago it came by

188. SMEDMORE

From the west. The entrance front with its twin bows was added by George Clavell in or soon after 1761.

189. WHATCOMBE HOUSE

Built in 1750 and enlarged in 1802. From the south-east.

190. MERLY HOUSE

Built by Ralph Willett between 1751 and 1760 from his own designs. The south front.

marriage into the Mansel family, but the present owner, Major Rhys Mansel, can trace his descent back through the Clavells to the Norman Walter de Clavile, who held lands in Purbeck at the time of Domesday. Until recently Sir Arthur Bryant, the historian, held a tenancy of Smedmore.

Whatcombe House (5 miles S.W. of Blandford). In writing of Winterborne Clenston we showed how that manor descended from the de la Lyndes to the Mortons of Milborne St Andrew and from them to the Pleydells (p. 55). Between 1750 and 1752 Edmund Morton Pleydell removed from Milborne to Whatcombe, which had come down in the same descent as Clenston from the de la Lyndes. Here he built himself a new seat on the west side of the Winterborne valley and planted the beautiful park which clothes its slopes. The house was originally a square block, built of red brick with stone dressings, its architect probably being one of the Blandford school. In 1802 it was altered and considerably enlarged by the addition of two wings to the north; at the same time the main fronts were covered with stucco and the entrance moved from the south to the east side (pl. 189). Although in the process the house lost much of its original character, it retains some Georgian features, including a rococo ceiling and chimney-piece in the drawing-room and a staircase with ironwork balustrade similar to that at Came House. A large oil-painting of Milborne St Andrew is preserved in the house; this fine Jacobean building was pulled down in 1802, the year in which Whatcombe was enlarged, and only the office buildings now remain. The finely carved trophies of arms and armour, which adorned the stone gate-piers at the old entrance to Milborne, have been moved to Whatcombe and set up at the lodge gates. Whatcombe has since descended by marriage through the Mansel family of Smedmore to Mrs Pleydell-Railston, the present owner, who lives at Clenston.

Merly House (1 mile S. of Wimborne Minster). A contemporary of Came House and Whatcombe, Merly is the product of an eighteenth-century connoisseur, who had 'ideas' about architecture and claimed to have designed the house himself. It stands on the high ground south of Wimborne, and commands a fine view of the Stour valley with the red roofs of the town and the towers of its Minster prominent in the middle distance. Ralph Willett, the son of a wealthy West India sugar planter, bought the estate in 1751, and proceeded to build the present house on a site half a mile away from its predecessor. On its rain-water pipes appears the date 1756, but the building was not completed until four years later. A cube of red brick with Portland stone dressings, the building is probably the result of a collaboration between the owner and a local architect. The central feature of the main front, all in stone, has an Ionic order of engaged columns, raised above the ground floor, as became the fashion in the later Georgian houses (pl. 190). The south front is more simply treated, but here the red brick has been covered with stucco. In 1772 the house was enlarged by the addition of two balancing wings on either side of the main block, the east wing being fitted up as a large room to take the owner's valuable library. The details of its ambitious scheme of decoration were planned by Willett himself and afterwards published in a folio volume of engravings. Its chief feature was a great coved ceiling, ornamented with a series of stucco reliefs intended to trace nothing less than the rise and progress of civilisation. In the four corners he introduced as a new motive the sugar-cane, which as 'the foundation of all the compliment the designer has attempted to pay it, may,' he says, 'be allowed a place which it really fills with some beauty.' The execution of all the plasterwork was entrusted to William Collins. The building and its companion block were pulled down not long after the sale of the library in 1813. Willett's liking for florid ornament is to be seen in the elaborate ceilings of the interior, which show the rococo taste at its zenith. The staircase is a remarkably fine example of eighteenth-century joinery, the balusters and handrail being of *lignum vitae*. Among more recent owners and occupants of Merly have been the Duke of Hamilton, Lady Rodney, Lady Wimborne and Captain Angus Hambro. Unfortunately, most of the original fireplaces were sold about 1928, and since the Second World War the house has been divided into flats. The stables were designed by John Nash.

Duntish Court (about 7 miles S.E. of Sherborne). The architect of this house was Sir William Chambers, who a few years later was responsible for the rebuilding of Milton Abbey. Chambers' designs for it are given in the fifth volume of *Vitruvius Britannicus* (1771), where it is called Castle Hill (pl. 191). The old Duntish Court stood on a lower site, to the south of the present house, which has a fine position looking out eastwards over the Blackmore Vale; to the north rises a hill crowned with an earthwork after which the house was named. It is a plain rectangular block of stuccoed brick with stone dressings, supported by two detached wings for stables and outhouses (pl. 192). On the west front there is a charming octagonal entrance porch, evidently an afterthought, since it is not shown in the plan given in *Vitruvius Britannicus*. The principal rooms, raised up on a *piano nobile*, have an eastward aspect; a square hall occupies the centre of the front, flanked by drawing-room and dining-room, in each of which are good marble chimney-pieces and ceilings with the thyrsus design, which was also much favoured by Adam in his early period. The house was built about 1760 by Fitzwalter Foy, whose grandfather had bought the estate from the first Duke of Marlborough. Alterations to the roof were made in the

191. DUNTISH COURT

Formerly called CASTLE HILL. East elevation from *Vitruvius Britannicus* (vol. v).
Architect: Sir William Chambers.

192. DUNTISH COURT

The east front as it appeared in 1934.

193. KINGSTON MAURWARD

An eighteenth-century garden house and a figure of Mercury.

194. CRICHEL

The old manor house, which was burnt in the fire of 1742. An early eighteenth-century painting.

195. CRICHEL

The south front with its portico. Between 1765 and 1775 Humphry Sturt greatly enlarged
the house built by Sir William Napier after the fire.

196. CRICHEL

Looking out from the portico on the south front towards the lake.

197. CRICHEL

The drawing-room. One of the rooms added by Humphry Sturt and decorated about 1775, perhaps from designs by James Wyatt.

199. CRICHEL

The main staircase. As the balustrade is of an early Georgian pattern, it was probably reconstructed in the 1770s.

198. CRICHEL

The dining-room. One of the suite of rooms on the east front, decorated in the Wyatt manner about 1775.

nineteenth century, and the lanterns on the wings were given Gothic terminations. At the time of writing the future of the building is uncertain.

Crichel is perhaps the best example in Dorset of a great eighteenth-century seat. It was not built all at one time; in fact, its erection covered some thirty or forty years, in the course of which the original plan was greatly enlarged; but if it lacks the grandeur of a single conception, it is an apt illustration of the English genius for compromise, and the decoration of its interior summarises both the earlier and the later phases of Georgian taste. The setting of the house also displays in vivid fashion the eighteenth-century ideal. Here, as at Milton, there were no half-measures; the entire village was removed to what is still called New Town, in order to leave an uninterrupted field for the landscape designer. Only the church (rebuilt in 1850) was thought sufficiently ornamental to take its place in the carefully contrived picture of woods and lawns and serpentining lake.

There are three Crichels—Long, Little and More—which lie in the borderland north of Wimborne Minster between the Stour valley and Cranborne Chase. It is a tributary of the Stour, the little Allen, which on its way down from the Chase forms a narrow strip of land that must always have contrasted in its gentle fertility with the forest country to the north. At More Crichel a family of the name of Cyfrewast was in possession in the sixteenth century, but in the time of James I the manor was acquired by the Napiers or Nappers, whose ancestor had first settled at Swyre near Bridport (see p. 83). Sir Nathaniel Napier, son of Sir Robert, the judge, whose seat was at Middlemarsh, Minterne Magna, used part of his inheritance to purchase Crichel and build for himself a substantial house. Its appearance has been preserved by a painting (pl. 194), which shows a neat four-gabled front with mullioned windows and a central projecting porch; the block to the right will have been a late Stuart addition made by the builder's grandson. But in 1742 the whole house was burnt down. The owner was then Sir William, the fourth baronet, and great-great-grandson of the builder; his mother was the sister and heiress of the second Lord Alington of Horseheath Hall in Cambridgeshire, so that he had ample resources for setting about the task of rebuilding. After a younger brother and his son had in turn succeeded and died, the male line of the Napiers became extinct, and in 1765 Crichel went to Humphry Sturt of Horton, a nephew of Sir William. At Horton, a few miles to the east, near the Hampshire border, his grandfather, Sir Anthony Sturt, about 1718, had built a new house close to the church; his father, Humphry senior, had enlarged it and also formed a great artificial lake, and, on the hill above, built the gaunt observatory tower, which was never completed. The younger Humphry, on inheriting Crichel, lost interest in Horton, where the mansion became a farmhouse and the lake reverted to meadow. Having increased his considerable fortune by marrying an heiress, he embarked on great alterations and additions to the Napiers' house, more than doubling its size.

In the plan reproduced from Hutchins (the 1774 edition) Sir William Napier's building is represented by the rectangular block in the centre. It was a brick house with stone dressings, probably not unlike Whatcombe (p. 163) before its enlargement, and from its surviving features may be ascribed to one of the Blandford architects. It must have been altogether too small for a man of Humphry Sturt's great wealth and grand ideas. By him, as the second edition of the *History* records, the building

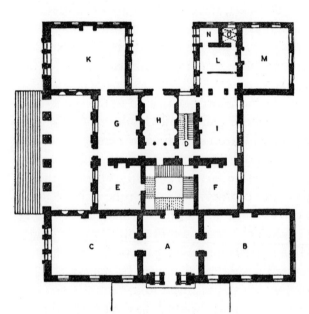

CRICHEL

Ground-floor plan as given in the first edition of Hutchins' *History of Dorset* (1774). The central block represents the house built by Sir William Napier after the fire of 1742. The wings and portico were added by Humphry Sturt. North point is to the right. A, Hall; B, Dining-room; C, Drawing-room; D, Principal staircase; E and F, Bedrooms; G, Dressing-room; H, Vestibule; I, Breakfast room; K, Library; L, Mr Sturt's writing-closet; M, Eating-parlour; N, W.C.; O, Fire closet.

was 'so immensely enlarged that it has the appearance of a mansion of a prince more than that of a country gentleman.' Sturt added two blocks at the north-west and south-west angles, the latter containing a library (K); across the east front he built an entirely new range 120 ft. long, consisting of a hall (A), dining-room (B) and drawing-room (C); finally, at the south end, he filled the gap between the library and drawing-room with a loggia or portico (pl. 196) carrying an upper floor so as to form an unbroken south façade (pl. 195). The large scale of the new ground-floor rooms can be appreciated when it is realised that their height is equivalent to the height of two of Sir William Napier's storeys; it is due to this fact that the proportions of the exterior are not altogether happy. As red brick was no longer a fashionable material, the walls were covered with plaster, but what is remarkable about the

201. STEPLETON HOUSE

An example of the later type of staircase, with wrought-iron balustrade, adopted by the Blandford architects in the latter part of George II's reign.

200. WADDON MANOR

A typical early eighteenth-century Dorset staircase, with tapering balusters and the hand-rail ending in a fist-like scroll.

203. BELFIELD

A house near Weymouth, built about 1775. Architect: John Crunden.

202. SADBOROW

Worm's-eye view of the staircase. The house was built between 1773 and 1775 from designs by John Johnson.

façades is that they are essentially early Georgian in character. It is not known whom Sturt employed as his architect; whoever he was, he ignored the new fashions that Robert Adam was introducing during the 1760s. Adam's exteriors are severe and sparingly ornamented, but here we find not only moulded architraves and cornices to all the smaller windows but a series of Venetian windows such as one of Lord Burlington's architects would have designed thirty or forty years earlier. The great Venetian window in the centre of the east front resembles the work of the later Palladians, Henry Flitcroft or Stephen Wright. Indeed, there are several features in the elevations that are reminiscent of Wright's work at Clumber and in the front of the old University Library (now the Schools) at Cambridge, and as he was employed at St Giles's House, only a few miles away (p. 141), he seems the likeliest architect for Sturt to have engaged.

The entrance hall of Sir William Napier's house was in the middle of the east front where the main staircase (D) now is. His staircase lay behind, occupying the position of the vestibule (H), which Sturt formed with an entrance doorway to the west. The panelled room (F) on the north side retains its original woodwork and chimney-piece, characteristic of the Blandford school. Sturt's staircase (pl. 199) also shows a local idiosyncrasy in the stout newel-post and scroll which terminate the balustrade. This is a very late example of the early Georgian type of staircase with twisted balusters and carved brackets, and it is possible that when it was made the joiners utilised Sir William Napier's stair, adapting and copying where necessary. Of Sturt's new rooms the library (K) was the first to be fitted up. It has a fine marble chimney-piece with carved overmantel and a huge architectural bookcase, both in the style that William Kent was using thirty years before. The overmantel frames a copy (believed to have been made by Sir Joshua Reynolds) of Van Dyck's painting of Lord Strafford and his secretary. A gilded sunburst occupies the centre of the ceiling, round which are panels painted with the Signs of the Zodiac and the Four Seasons. Although Hutchins shows two rooms (E and G) adjoining the loggia, they are now one, and it is probable that the alteration was made by Sturt. This long drawing-room has a rococo ceiling, but the chimney-piece with its caryatids is of later date. Among the notable pieces of furniture acquired by Sturt were a series of splendid gilt rococo mirrors, which can be assigned to Chippendale, since they correspond to designs in his *Director*.

When the eastern suite of rooms is reached (A, B and C on the plan), the style of decoration completely changes. Here the neo-Classical manner of the Adam and Wyatt brothers makes its appearance. Evidently Sturt had come to realise that Wright's work (if Wright was his architect) was no longer fashionable, and he turned to someone else. Mr H. A. Tipping has given good reasons for attributing the decoration of these rooms to James Wyatt,[1] who, in the late 1770s, made designs for the interior of Milton Abbey and was employed to rebuild Bryanston. From a letter describing a visit to Crichel in 1773 it is known that the east rooms were then still unfinished. In default of documentary evidence, Wyatt, rather than any of the other imitators of Adam, seems the likeliest name to cite in view of analogies with other interiors of his and the highly accomplished nature of the work. In the hall (A) it is only in the design of the painted ceiling that the new manner is clearly discernible; the doorcases are Palladian, and the wall treatment might be called intermediate or transitional between the earlier and later phases. But the dining-room and drawing-room are entirely in the neo-Classical style of decoration, which extends also to the coved ceiling of the main staircase, the boudoir and the treatment of the corridor on the first floor. Like the saloon at Milton, the Crichel drawing-room has a barrel ceiling of segmental form (pl. 197), and it combines delicate stucco ornamentation with painted panels in classical taste. The walls are divided by pilasters decorated with arabesques and supporting a delicately enriched frieze; but the designer found difficulty in accommodating his predecessor's large Venetian window at the south end; the arch of this cuts awkwardly across the frieze and into the lunette above. The painted panels in the ceiling are ascribed to Biagio Rebecca; the medallions in the hall ceiling and the grisaille paintings on the walls of the dining-room are believed to be by Zucchi and Angelica Kauffmann. The dining-room (B) is undoubtedly the finest room in the house (pl. 198). Its coved ceiling is a masterly example of neo-Classical refinement, and it is all the more effective in being seen above wall surfaces kept relatively plain. Both on walls and ceiling there are medallions painted in imitation of bas-reliefs: those in the ceiling are again traditionally ascribed to Rebecca. Perfect in all its details, the room also preserves its original colour scheme—white ornament on a blue-green ground for the ceiling, with a lilac background for the cameo-like figures, pale buff for the walls.

Humphry Sturt lived until 1786 and was succeeded at Crichel by his younger son, Charles. He, however, did not take kindly to it, and was happier at Brownsea Castle, in Poole Harbour. The old blockhouse on the island had been acquired by his father and adapted as a summer residence, and the son, always passionately fond of yachting, found it entirely to his liking. His grandson, created Lord Alington in 1876, made some further additions to the house and rebuilt the church. The formal garden before the south front, with its little domed temple, was laid out by Mr Harold Peto about 1905, after the second Lord Alington had succeeded. It introduces

[1] *English Homes, Period VI*, vol. i (1926), pp. 58–60. The Adam brothers may be ruled out. There are no drawings for Crichel in the comprehensive collection of Adam designs in Sir John Soane's Museum, Lincoln's Inn Fields.

a transitional interval between the house and the park without shutting off from the portico the lovely view of the lake and its woods winding away down the valley.

Crichel in recent years has been occupied by Cranborne Chase School. The fine collection of family portraits, in which Gainsborough, Hoppner, Romney and Lawrence are all represented, remains in the house. The late Lord Alington died in 1940, and his daughter and her husband, Lieutenant-Commander G. G. Marten, are the present owners. They intend shortly to take up residence.

Sadborow (about 5 miles S.E. of Chard). The parish of Thorncombe, to which Sadborow and Forde Abbey both belong, was transferred from Devon to Dorset in 1842. The present house, of three storeys, with a wide bow in the middle of the south front, was built for John Bragge between 1773 and 1775 in place of an earlier one. Its architect was John Johnson (1732–1814), a native of Leicester, but for thirty years the County Surveyor for Essex, where his work included the Shire Hall, Chelmsford. In addition to Sadborow, he designed Killerton House in Devon, between Exeter and Cullompton. The accounts for the building of the house are preserved at Dorchester in the Dorset County Museum, and a number of drawings exist, some showing variants of the plan and elevations. Ham Hill stone was used for the ashlar facing; Robert Scriven and John Templeman are named as masons. The total cost of the work was £2,589 2s. 4½d.

Alterations to the north and east fronts were made in the first half of the nine-teenth century, perhaps in 1843, when a wing was added to the west, and there have been recent changes in the outline of the roofs. The severity of the exterior conforms with a tendency found in much of the architecture of the last thirty years of the eighteenth century, when also the bow as a feature was exploited largely for the sake of the variety of room-shapes it admitted. An entrance hall on the east opens through an elliptical arch, carried on a fluted entablature with columns and pilasters, into a domed staircase hall in the middle of the house. The staircase, going up round a semi-circular apse, is beautifully contrived; it has an elegant balustrade with wrought-iron scrolls and is lit by a sky-light in the dome (pl. 202). Neo-Classical decoration was used with restrained effect, and certain Greek motives, notably in the entrance hall, show Johnson's indebtedness to Stuart and Revett. It is unfor-tunate that in some of the rooms the original treatment has been subjected to nineteenth-century alterations.

The builder of the house was a descendant of Matthew Bragge, who purchased Sadborow from the Crown in the reign of Queen Elizabeth and also the manor of Thorncombe, formerly a possession of Forde Abbey. Sadborow remained in the

Bragges' possession until after the First World War, when the property was sold. In 1934 it was bought by the present owner, Commander W. J. Eyre, and his father, the Rev. G. F. Eyre, of Lyme Regis. The house was then empty and derelict, but since 1947 it has been put into repair and is now the home of Commander and the Hon. Mrs Eyre.

Belfield (1 mile S.W. of Weymouth). This house, nearly contemporary with Sadborow, was built about 1775 by Isaac Buxton between Weymouth and what was then the little village of Wyke Regis. The architect was John Crunden, whose best-known building is Boodle's Club in St James's Street, designed in the style of Robert Adam and often mistaken for his work. Adam's influence is equally apparent at Belfield, which has a front with a projecting Ionic portico raised above a rusticated basement (pl. 203). On either side of the portico there is a Palladian window framed under a semi-circular arch, recalling the more elaborate version of the same motive on the front of Boodle's. The interior contains some contemporary decoration and fireplaces.

In the third edition of the *Weymouth Guide* (1790) Belfield is described as having been 'designed and executed by Mr Crunden, in a style of elegance which does credit to the taste and abilities of the artist.' An account of the house and its owners is given in *Belfield and the Buxtons*, by G. D. Squibb, privately printed at Dorchester in 1954.

Frome House. This late eighteenth-century house stands in the village of Frome St Quintin, three miles north of Maiden Newton. On the porch (pl. 208) appears the name of its builder, George Baker, with the date 1782. This is a small, symmetrical, brick-built house with parapet and hipped roof, rather similar in type to Racedown, but distinguished by its charming porch supporting a three-sided bay. The porch is in stone and nicely detailed in the Adam manner. The front door has a semicircular head and fanlight, and is flanked by tall niches. Frome St Quintin derives the second part of its name from the family which held it of the de Clares, Earls of Gloucester, during the twelfth and thirteenth centuries.

Bettiscombe and Racedown. These two houses lie on the extreme western border of the county in that tumbled country of steep hills and deep combes which is already a half-way land to Devon. Both were built by members of the Pinney family, which has long been established in this part of Dorset, as well as over the Somerset border, and in whose ownership both, until 1958, remained. Racedown is of note for its association with Wordsworth.

204. BETTISCOMBE

A farmhouse in the west of the county, built by John Pinney towards the end of the
seventeenth century and completed by his son and grandson. From the north.

205. BETTISCOMBE
The north doorway with shell hood.

206. BETTISCOMBE
The early eighteenth-century staircase.

207. RACEDOWN
Built by John Frederick
Pinney in 1758 and
given a third storey
about 1790. William
and Dorothy Words-
worth stayed here from
1795 to 1797.

208. FROME
HOUSE
The three-sided porch
of the entrance front
dated 1782.

John Pinney, who followed Thomas Fuller (of *The Worthies*) as rector of Broad-windsor, had a farm at Bettiscombe in the time of Charles II. He died in 1705, when he was succeeded by his son, Nathaniel. There is evidence that the present house was built in 1694. It stands north-east of the church, under the flank of Pilsdon Hill, and looks out across the Marshwood Vale to the line of hills that run down to Lyme. It consists of a main block and two balancing wings running back northward, is built of brick with stone quoins at the angles, and has roofs of moderate pitch that finish with gables and chimney-stacks (pl. 204). The north doorway between the wings has a hood shaped as a shell resting on carved brackets (pl. 205). This may be contemporary with the building, but the hood to the south doorway is of later date and takes the form of a pediment with Doric entablature supported by carved consoles, which, having proved unequal to their task, have needed reinforcement from two slender iron stanchions. The windows in the south front are late eighteenth-century insertions. Dividing the hall there is a triple-arched screen, a memory perhaps of the traditional screen of mediaeval and Tudor halls. The staircase in the east wing is elegantly designed with ramped handrail and slender fluted balusters. Some of the original fireplaces, woodwork, doors and door furniture remain, but the staircase (pl. 206) and some of the panelling appear to be later and may date from after 1724, when Nathaniel Pinney was succeeded by his son, Azariah. Though of small architectural pretensions, this farmhouse is as good an example as one could find of country building of its period, and it remains completely unspoiled. Mr Michael Pinney is the present owner.

Nathaniel Pinney had a brother who was sentenced to transportation for having taken part in Monmouth's rebellion. But he prospered in the West Indies and his grandson, John Frederick, was wealthy enough to retire. Returning to Dorset, he joined his cousin, Azariah, and became M.P. for Bridport. At Bettiscombe there is a skull, believed to be that of a faithful negro which he brought back with him; it has the reputation of screaming at night. In order to have a home of his own, he built a small house, to which he gave the name Pylemarsh Lodge, subsequently changed to Racedown. Azariah died in 1760, John Frederick in 1762. The one a childless widower, the other a bachelor, they had looked about for a suitable heir, and their choice had fallen on John Frederick's second cousin, John Pretor, who was required to assume the surname of Pinney on succeeding. Having served as High Sheriff of Dorset when only twenty-four, he spent some years in the West Indies looking after his estates there, and in the late seventeen-eighties returned to England and settled at Bristol, where he built for himself a house in Great George Street (now the Georgian Museum). He decided, however, to keep the little house in Dorset that John Frederick had built, so as to have, in his own phrase, 'a lee-port in a storm.'

Racedown stands more than 500 feet up, about a mile north of Bettiscombe, where the road from Lyme to Crewkerne climbs up over to Blackdown. From the road its prim Georgian front is seen framed by tall beeches (pl. 207); westward, where the ground falls steeply, there is a fine view over the valley. As built in 1758 by John Frederick, the house had only two storeys. The third storey was added about 1790, when John Pretor Pinney installed his father-in-law and the name was changed to Racedown. John Pretor's disappointment over the way in which the alterations turned out ('You have put my chinies where I wanted my pleasance,' he complained) led him to give up the idea of using the house himself and to hand over the place to his son, John Frederick, who lent Racedown to the Wordsworths from 1795 to 1797.[1] The inventory of what was in the house, with Wordsworth's notes in the margin, was until recently at Racedown; so, too, was the 'perambulator' or way-wiser (now lent to the County Museum) which Dorothy once trundled all the way to Crewkerne and back to measure the mileage. While he was at Racedown Wordsworth wrote *The Borderers*. In the summer of 1797 Coleridge came over from Nether Stowey and persuaded the Wordsworths to join him in the Quantocks: they went on a visit of ten days and then decided not to return. The original house is a square Georgian 'box,' built of variegated bricks, which were made in a neighbouring field. It was extended by the late Major-General Sir Reginald Pinney, whose widow, Lady Pinney, continued to live at Racedown until her death in 1958.

[1] See *Racedown and the Wordsworths*, by Bergen Evans and Hester Pinney (1934), reprinted from *The Review of English Studies*, vol. viii, No. 29.

CHAPTER FIVE

After 1800

A FEW notes are given here on some of the more important country houses in Dorset built since 1800. When the new century opened, the neo-Classic style of Adam, Wyatt and their followers still continued, changing almost imperceptibly into the simplified version of it associated with the Regency, and soon there came the short-lived Greek Revival. This phase of the expiring Classic tradition is not well represented in Dorset, although the architecture of the Regency is to be seen in the terraces of Weymouth and many stucco-faced villas at Bridport, Charmouth and Lyme Regis. The most important house of the period before Queen Victoria's accession was Langton, near Blandford, one of the few country houses by C. R. Cockerell, built for James John Farquharson (1827–33). It was demolished after the Second World War, and only the stable court and kitchen block now remain.

Meanwhile, the Gothic Revival, which had grown out of the cult of the romantic and the picturesque, had come to be generally accepted. The proximity and associations of an abbey had dictated a Gothic style for the exterior of Lord Dorchester's house at Milton, but, as we have seen, Sir William Chambers' façades are really Classic compositions in a Gothic dress, and Wyatt's interiors were all designed in his neo-Classic manner. A library at Sherborne Castle fitted up in the Gothic style, probably not later than 1770, is another early instance of the vogue.

In the first decade of the nineteenth century Leverton attempted a Gothic design for the new front of Herringston and Nash used a Tudor type of Gothic for the alterations and additions at Parnham. Bride Head, a sixteenth-century house taking its name from the river which rises close to it in Little Bredy, was enlarged and altered by P. F. Robinson in 1831–2 and received further attentions from Benjamin Ferrey somewhat later. Both used a brand of Gothic. By 1840 the revival was acquiring a more scholarly and antiquarian character. The contemporary interest in Tudor and Elizabethan houses is reflected in Joseph Nash's *Mansions of England in the Olden Time*, which began to appear in 1839 and includes five manor houses in Dorset. The new front given to Creech Grange in 1846 shows a much more sensitive appreciation of the native Tudor style than does Nash's work at Parnham. There was now a vogue for what came to be called 'the Manorial Style,' inspired by Tudor and Elizabethan buildings. This is seen in Blore's rebuilding of

Canford and Ferrey's Clyffe House, Tincleton, and, later in the century, in George Devey's additions to Melbury and Sir Ernest George's Motcombe House. Midway between came Alfred Waterhouse's Iwerne Minster House (1877), typical of its architect's forceful personality. Anthony Salvin, in his work at Encombe (1871–4), respected the Georgian character of that house; at Melbury he was responsible for the great library added in 1872. Near the end of the century at Bryanston, entirely rebuilt by Norman Shaw, the big guns of Classic went into action again.

Among twentieth-century houses Minterne, by Leonard Stokes, and Ashley Chase, by Sir Guy Dawber, deserve particular mention. In the latter the traditional Dorset materials are used with a sensitive regard for the landscape that is characteristic of Dawber's work. Ernest Newton was responsible for the Abbotsbury Castle, on the edge of Chesil Beach, which was built in 1913 after a fire had destroyed its predecessor, but the new house was never occupied and was pulled down in 1934.

CANFORD MANOR. Only the kitchens (pl. 34) remain of the ancient manor house which in Plantagenet times was a possession of the Earls of Salisbury and, later, of Beauforts, Courtenays and Blounts. The traditional name, 'John of Gaunt's Kitchen,' is misleading, for Canford did not become part of the Duchy of Lancaster until after Gaunt's death. The greater part of the mediaeval house was pulled down in 1765. A new house was built by Lord de Mauley in 1826. His architect was Edward Blore, whose work is seen in the south front (pl. 210). In 1848, after Sir John Guest had bought the estate, large additions were made by Sir Charles Barry; these include the great hall with its grand staircase, the gallery and the tower. Further additions were made in 1887. In its studied mediaevalism and asymmetrical grouping Canford is an embodiment of the Gothic Revivalist's ideal of a stately home. Since 1923 it has been a public school.

CLYFFE HOUSE, TINCLETON. Built in 1842 for Charles Porcher 'in pure Tudor style.' Unfortunately, an older house of great interest was pulled down to make way for it; it is said to have been very similar to Anderson, and there was a tradition that the two houses were built at the same time and by the same architect. Benjamin Ferrey, who designed the nineteenth-century house, was responsible for a good deal of work in Dorset in his earlier years. He was born at Christchurch, Hampshire, went to school at Wimborne, and was concerned with the early development of Bournemouth.

BROWNSEA CASTLE. William Benson, Wren's successor as Surveyor-General, built a house on Brownsea Island, on the site of the fort erected by Henry VIII for

209. BROWNSEA CASTLE

A house that has experienced many vicissitudes since it grew out of the Tudor blockhouse defending Poole Harbour.

210. CANFORD MANOR
Begun in 1826 from designs by Blore and enlarged twenty years later by Sir Charles Barry.

211. MOTCOMBE HOUSE
A characteristic work of Sir Ernest George (1893–5)

212. BRYANSTON
Built in the eighteen-nineties for the second Viscount Portman to supersede a house by
James Wyatt. Architect: Norman Shaw.

the defence of Poole. This house was enlarged and Gothicised by Humphry Sturt of Crichel. Both he and his son used it as a summer residence. Further extensions in a Tudor Gothic style were carried out in the middle of the nineteenth century by a Colonel Waugh, who ruined himself in trying to exploit the china-clay deposits on the island. When the castle was rebuilt between 1897 and 1901, after a disastrous fire, the main lines of the old building were followed and the greater part of the walls preserved. Seen across the water, the whole group of castellated buildings (pl. 209), backed by the pine woods of the island, makes a beautiful and romantic picture.

MOTCOMBE HOUSE. A large and characteristic work of Sir Ernest George, who built it for Lord Stalbridge in 1893–5. The house is in the Elizabethan style, of red brick with Ham Hill dressings, and planned in the form of an E with a large office court attached to one side. The south front with its five gables (pl. 211) is a composition of considerable merit. The house is now occupied by a boys' preparatory school.

BRYANSTON HOUSE. The old manor house of Bryanston lay down by the river. In 1778 a new house was built on a different site by Henry William Portman to the designs of James Wyatt. His kitchen block survives, and so does his entrance gateway with flanking lodges near the south end of Blandford Bridge. The present house, which in 1927 became Bryanston School, was erected in the 'nineties by the second Viscount Portman. Norman Shaw, its architect, had a similar opportunity to Vanbrugh's at Eastbury, and a finer site, to create a monumental building, but, although imposing in its bulk and conceived on an ambitious scale, the result is not very successful in its attempt to combine something of Vanbrugh's *bravura* with the milder character of Wren's domestic work (pl. 212). The walls are of an intensely bright red brick with sharply contrasting dressings of Portland stone. From its position on the hill above Blandford the house dominates the town in the seigniorial fashion of earlier times.

MINTERNE HOUSE. Built by the late Lord Digby in 1903–6 in place of a Victorian house of no merit. It is an interesting example of Leonard Stokes's individual style, which was one of the offshoots of the Arts and Crafts movement. The house stands at the head of the Cerne valley, where a wild garden devoted to rhododendrons, azaleas and flowering shrubs flourishes under the shelter of magnificent trees planted during the latter part of the eighteenth century.

HOUSES AND GARDENS OPEN AT CERTAIN TIMES
TO VISITORS

It should be understood that most of the houses illustrated in this book are not ordinarily accessible to the public. Although permission to visit is sometimes granted by the kindness of owners, it can be obtained only by written application except where there are regular hours of opening, and these are advertised locally and can be found in *Country Houses Open to the Public*, published annually by *Country Life*.

In 1959 the following houses were open to visitors at certain times.

ATHELHAMPTON	Mr R. V. Cooke, F.R.C.S.
CHETTLE HOUSE	Mrs E. M. Bourke
CREECH GRANGE	Lt.-Col. A. R. Bond
FORDE ABBEY	Mr G. D. Roper
KINGSTON LACY	Mr H. J. R. Bankes
ST GILES'S HOUSE	The Earl of Shaftesbury
WADDON MANOR	Mr and Mrs B. O. Corbett
WINTERBORNE CLENSTON MANOR	Mrs Pleydell-Railston
WOLFETON HOUSE	Countess Zamoyska.

In addition to the above, the gardens of certain houses are opened on advertised days during the summer in aid of the Queen's Institute of District Nursing. A county list is published each year.

BOOKS OF REFERENCE

The Survey of Dorset. Written in the time of Charles I, but not published until 1732. It was for long attributed to John Coker of Mappowder, but its real author was Thomas Gerard of Trent.

The History and Antiquities of the County of Dorset, by John Hutchins. First published in two volumes in 1774. Second edition in 4 vols., edited by R. Gough and J. B. Nichols, 1796–1815. Third edition in 4 vols., edited by William Shipp and James Whitworth Hodson, 1861–73.

Dorsetshire Photographically Illustrated, by John Pouncy (1857). Contains views and accounts of some fifty Dorset houses.

Some Dorset Manor Houses, by Sidney Heath and W. de C. Prideaux (1907). Descriptions of twenty houses dealing more particularly with the histories of their owners.

Companion into Dorset, by Dorothy Gardiner (1937).

An Inventory of the Historical Monuments in Dorset: Volume I—West (1952). Published by the Royal Commission on Historical Monuments, England. Volumes covering the remainder of the county are in preparation.

Watts' *Seats of the Nobility and Gentry* (1779–86). The Dorset houses described and illustrated by engravings are Ranston, Milton Abbey, Lulworth Castle and Bryanston.

Neale's *Views of Seats*. Volume I (1818) contains views and short accounts of five Dorset houses; five more are included in Volume IV of the second series (1828).

Nash's *Mansions of England in the Olden Time* (1839–49). Lithographs of Athelhampton, Bingham's Melcombe, Cranborne Manor House, Milton Abbey and Waterston.

The Domestic Architecture of England during the Tudor Period, by Thomas Garner and Arthur Stratton. Second edition, revised and enlarged, 1929. Many of the Tudor houses are described and illustrated.

Accounts of a number of the houses described and illustrated have appeared in *Country Life*, and there are shorter accounts of many in the *Proceedings of the Dorset Field Club* and in *Notes and Queries for Somerset and Dorset*.

Of the numerous books which deal with Thomas Hardy's Wessex, identifying the names of places and houses that figure in the novels, the best are:

The Wessex of Thomas Hardy, by B. C. A. Windle, with drawings by E. H. New (1902).

The Hardy Country, by C. G. Harper (1904).

Thomas Hardy's Wessex, by Hermann Lea (1913).

Index

Houses described individually are given in capitals. A number in heavy type indicates the page on which the description of the house appears.